The Concise Guide to Mergers, Acquisitions and Divestitures

The Concise Guide to Mergers, Acquisitions and Divestitures

Business, Legal, Finance, Accounting, Tax and Process Aspects

Robert L. Brown

With a Tax Chapter by Richard Westin

palgrave
macmillan

THE CONCISE GUIDE TO MERGERS, ACQUISITIONS AND DIVESTITURES

Copyright © Robert L. Brown, 2007.

First published in 2007 by
PALGRAVE MACMILLAN™
175 Fifth Avenue, New York, NY 10010 and
Houndmills, Basingstoke, Hampshire, England RG21 6XS.
Companies and representatives throughout the world.

PALGRAVE MACMILLAN is the global academic imprint of the Palgrave Macmillan division of St. Martin's Press, LLC and of Palgrave Macmillan Ltd. Macmillan© is a registered trademark in the United States, United Kingdom and other countries. Palgrave is a registered trademark in the European Union and other countries.

ISBN-13: 978-0-230-60078-2
ISBN-10: 0-230-60078-6

Library of Congress Cataloging-in-Publication Data

Brown, Robert L., JD
Concise guide to mergers, acquisitions, and divestitures : business, legal, finance, accounting, tax, and process aspects / Robert Brown ; with a tax chapter by Richard Westin.
    p. cm.
 Includes bibliographical references and index.
 ISBN 0-230-60078-6 (alk. paper)
 1. Consolidation and merger of corporations—Handbooks, manuals, etc. 2. Corporate divestiture—Handbooks, manuals, etc. 3. Corporations—Finance—Handbooks, manuals, etc. 4. Corporations—Accounting—Handbooks, manuals, etc. 5. Corporations—Taxation—Handbooks, manuals, etc. I. Westin, Richard A., 1945– II. Title.
 HD2746.5.B765 2007
 658.1'6—dc22   2007010135

A catalogue record of the book is available from the British Library.

Design by Scribe Inc.

First edition: November 2007

10 9 8 7 6 5 4 3 2 1

Printed in the United States of America.

Contents

List of Tables

Introduction

I recently took a European executive to his first U.S. basketball game. Although I had received two tickets in the first row, for the first half of the game I took him to seats up much higher that I had also received tickets for. I wanted him to get an overview of the game before getting close to see the details. My concern was that if we started by being in the front row, he would get lost in the specifics without understanding the overall process.

In the business context of this book, over the past several decades, I have been involved in many major mergers and acquisitions—some of them worth over $1 billion. In other cases, clients have moved in the opposite direction by selling off or closing subsidiaries, divisions, branches, and offices. During that time I have often had clients ask for a standard reference book that they could use to understand the process before undertaking a merger, acquisition, or divestiture.

Unfortunately, I have had to refer them to multi-volume studies, each on a different aspect of such transactions. Most of the books have been so intense that clients have become lost looking not just at the trees but also at the leaves, without being able to see the forest. Using my basketball analogy, they became lost in different parts of the game and could not see the integrated whole picture—the passing, set-up, plays, and strategy.

This book is an attempt to show you the dynamics of mergers, acquisitions, and divestitures without drowning you in so many details that you lose sight of the underlying game.

You will learn about the key business trends driving the increase in mergers, acquisitions, and divestitures. You will also learn about the stages in any deal, including the investigation, negotiation, and underappreciated postclosing integration. You will also learn how to set up your team—both internal and external members—as well as handling issues of concern to shareholders and directors. You will also learn about the key forms of mergers and acquisitions—asset, stock, merger, and others.

From a legal standpoint, you will learn about the major issues affecting successors, employers, creditors, shareholder, boards of directors, as well as various third parties such as managers, bankers, and ESOPS. You will also learn about securities, antitakeover, and antitrust rules and how they affect mergers and acquisitions. Special cases of regulated industries and rules for foreign investors will also be covered.

In finance, you will learn about the types of equity and debt financing, including rights and funding sources of each. There are also special sections on junk bonds, leveraged and management buyouts, and valuation.

From an accounting perspective, I describe the purchase method, as well as the prior alternative of pooling of interests method. You will also learn about accounting for divestitures and spin offs.

In the tax area you will learn about the key tax issues behind any merger or acquisition. This will include the main forms of tax-free reorganization under the tax laws—Type A, B, C, D, and G. You will also learn about taxable reorganizations as well as key topics such as nonqualified preferred stock, management buyout, use of debt, net operating losses, elections, pre-acquisition redemption, golden parachutes, greenmail, and poison pills.

You will learn about the process involved in a merger or acquisition, including preparation of a confidentiality agreement, letter of intent, due diligence list, and purchase and sale agreement. You will also learn about the various consents that must be obtained.

In a separate chapter on divestiture, you will learn about recent trends that have increased the number of divestitures in the United States. Finally, you will learn about the difference between workout and reorganization.

And all of this is in a form that is easy to read and can serve as a desktop reference book for your next merger, acquisition, or divestiture.

1

Business

Trends

The twenty-first century opened with two trends still firmly in place—the importance of the Internet and mergers. During the 1990s, many Internet-related stocks rose by thousands of percent. Most of those that survived the subsequent dot.bomb collapse have recovered and seen their stock prices return to higher levels than at the beginning of the dot-com era.

The astronomical technology and stock market numbers hid an important fact. While overall market averages rose in the 1990s, many stocks actually declined. The highflyers hid the slower growth of nontechnology company stocks. While hi-tech stocks reflected market demand—some of it from new online traders for their personal accounts—other stocks reflected earnings. In the future, analysts might value technology-related stocks like traditional stocks—that is, on the basis of profits and losses.

Despite such careful valuation, the growth of mergers was equally dramatic.

- In the 1980s, billion dollar mergers or acquisitions were infrequent. By the 1990s, they were common with many of them reaching two digits—in billions.
- In 1998, the value of two mergers alone reached three digits (or $100 billion)—NationsBank Corp.—BankAmerica Corp merger was valued at $61.6 billion, and WorldCom Inc.'s acquisition of MCI Communications cost $41.9 billion.
- In 1998, the value of the largest 976 deals (out of 2,323 completed transactions) was $357.9 billion. By 2000, the aggregate value of mergers reached $1.78 trillion.[1]
- The new century shows no sign of slowing. It started with a bang—a triple-digit billion dollar merger. The AOL/Time-Warner deal weighed in at $160 billion.

- In 2005 and 2006, AT&T was behind some of the biggest deals. It acquired SBC in 2005, and paid $66.67 billion for BellSouth in 2006. The biggest technology mergers over the past several years appear in Table 1.1.
- Overall, 2006 saw another record year for technology acquisitions. The value of technology and telecommunication deals alone, excluding debt, increased nearly 5 percent to over $600 billion.[2] On the private equity side, 2006 was also a record year. Facilitated by cheap credit and supplemented by leverage, private-equity firms accumulated sufficient funds to make $738 billion in buyouts.[3] Some of the leading buyouts of 2006 appear in Table 1.2.

One significant change over the past ten years is that, globally, buyouts make up more than 20 percent of the $3.5 billion in mergers and acquisitions, compared to 3 percent a decade ago.[5]

Will the trends continue? According to most business forecasts at the beginning of the decade, century and millennium, the consensus was yes but in a different way. The numbers, tables and excerpts above confirm the predictions. While I will address driving factors behind acquisitions in more detail later, at this point I can emphasize several factors supporting these trends—baby boomers fueling stock market, the Internet and technology, international competition, economies of scale, government attitude toward mergers, and businesses becoming accustomed to billion dollar deals.

One interesting perspective is that of Harry Dent. He has argued in a number of books that stock market growth does not reflect employment, money supply or many of the other factors traditionally perceived as indicators. For Dent, there are two major determinants—baby boomers (supplemented by immigration) and disposable income.[6]

- The United States is presently enjoying its greatest population growth—bar none. It is a result of the post–World War II baby boomers and a tremendous increase in the number of legitimate (and yes, of course, illegal) immigrants.
- Disposable income is greatest between the ages of 45 and 50.

Combining these two factors, if you move the baby boomers and immigrants forward to the 45–50 age group, you can plot a steeply rising line. This line over

Table 1.1 Largest Technology Mergers over Past Five Years

Year	Buyer	Target	Value (billions)
2006	AT&T	BellSouth	$66.87
2005	Telefonica	Britain O2	$31.53
2004	Cingular	AT&T Wireless	$40.77
2003	Olivetti	60% of Telecom Italia	$24.39
2002	Buyout	Global Crossing	$11.90

Table 1.2 Largest Private-Equity Buyouts of 2006

Mon.	Buyer	Target	Value (billions)
July	Bain Capital Kohlberg Kravis Roberts (KKR) Merrill Lynch Global	HCA	$21.2
Nov	Bain Capital Thomas H. Lee Partners	Clear Channel Communications	$18.8
Sept	Texas Pacific Group Blackstone Group Permira Beteiligungsberatung Carlyle Group	Freescale Semiconductor	$17.7
Oct	Apollo Management Texas Pacific Group	Harrah's Entertainment	$17.1
May	GS Capital Partners Carlyle Group Riverstone Holdings	Kinder Morgan	$14.6
June	Saban Capital Group Madison Dearborn Capital Providence Equity Partners Texas Pacific Group Thomas H. Lee	Univision Communications	$12.1
Jan	SuperValu CVS Cerberus Capital Management	Albertsons	$11.0
Dec	Blackstone Group GS Capital Partners KKR Texas Pacific Group	Biomet	$10.8
Jan	KKR Contracted Services Group Thomas H. Lee Partners Carlyle Group AlpInvest Partners Hellman & Friedman	VNU	$9.6

the past several decades is virtually identical to the stock market averages during the same period.

Based on this symmetry, Dent argues that stock markets will continue to rise as long as there are more baby boomers reaching the 45–50 plateau than leaving it. According to Dent, that transition will not occur for several more years. If so, the first part of what I call the "Oh-oh decade"—the first ten years of the new century—will continue to see rising stock prices. The price increases might not be as great as in the past decade, but they will still show strong growth.[7] Such rising stock prices mean companies are good acquisitions today since their stock value is likely to increase.

Another reason driving mergers and acquisitions is technology, particularly the Internet. Companies need technology to compete and are willing to acquire companies with such technology. This can best be seen by looking at the evolution of corporate use of technology in purchases and sales. Initially, electronic commerce was confined to "electronic data interchange" or "EDI", which involved the exchange of information in standardized forms between computers. Unlike today's Internet, EDI networks involved large businesses, were structured and used forms and formats standardized not for everyone but just between contracting parties

The most common use of EDI was by large businesses wishing to cut purchasing costs. Many adopted computerized purchasing systems. Seller and buyer would sign a formal trading partner agreement (to be discussed later) setting out how orders were to be placed, accepted and filled. The message format was also agreed upon. Unlike the Internet that relies on conventions and standards applicable to all users, EDI ordering and message format was usually specific to the parties.[8]

Under more sophisticated systems, human interaction was eliminated. When a buyer's computer recognized that the inventory of particular goods was low, it was programmed to automatically draft and send an electronic purchase order to a predetermined supplier. The purchase order contained a description of the good, price and delivery date. The supplier's computer would send an electronic confirmation verifying the information in the order. Upon receipt of buyer's return confirmation, supplier's computer would send an electronic acceptance of the order to buyer and processing instructions to appropriate departments within supplier's organization.

As the 1990s moved on, electronic commerce became defined by the mass media acceptance of the Internet. Large and small businesses, both established and new, began trading in traditional goods and services as well as in new forms of property like software. Advertisers and direct marketers increased their use of the Web to advertise and facilitate business transactions.

Businesses and consumers found that online transactions could be faster, less expensive and more convenient than transactions conducted via human interaction. Surveys indicate that over 20 percent of U.S. Internet users have made a purchase over the Web. Among lower value purchases on the Internet, nearly half tend to be for personal and private use.[9]

The Internet has a variety of features that are attractive to businesses, including:

- cost reduction by eliminating intermediaries and reducing inventory costs;
- improved delivery time;
- establishing dialogues and one-to-one relationships with potential customers;
- receiving direct feedback and adapting products in response to such feedback;
- reaching broad, global audiences, since Web sites can be accessed from anywhere in the world;

- targeting online advertising to populations within specific regions or countries, users with desirable demographic characteristics and people with specific interests;
- measuring the number of times a particular site has been viewed, responses to the site and certain demographic characteristics of the viewers.

For these reasons the Internet is increasingly used by business. And the more that consumers and business are using the Internet, the more that business must be internationally competitive.

Another driving force behind mergers is international competition. As a result of technology developments, businesses are more likely to recognize that their market is international—not national, regional or local. A competitor located anywhere in the world is now more of a threat since Internet shoppers find buying online just as easy as driving to a local supplier. It is no longer sufficient to watch and beat local competitors—you must beat them around the world. Acquiring international competitors is one way of beating them.

In addition, to compete on the international level businesses need more resources. This ability requires assets and money. Sales and income are not enough to fund the competitive battle. Sales require assets to produce products and services being sold. And assets require money. In the early stages of companies, investors and lenders can meet this need. As the necessity for assets and money increases, however, mergers and acquisitions become more likely sources.

For other companies, the driving force behind mergers and acquisitions is an economic principle—economies of scale. For instance, two companies with similar products being distributed through similar sales channels might find that they can significantly reduce their merged sales force by having the same staff selling both sets of products. Similar savings in headcount may be achieved in other departments as well.

Another, unspoken reason for the merger trend is more pragmatic. In the United States the government has not interfered with the trend. Consider these examples:

- At the beginning of the twentieth century, the U.S. government split up Rockefeller's oil conglomerate. In 1999, two of them, Mobil and Exxon, merged.
- Thirty years ago, when Federated Department Stores attempted to acquire Bullock's, it was forced to sign a consent decree with the federal government agreeing not to proceed with the acquisition. A few years ago, it acquired Bullock's and a number of other companies.

Many senior executives realize that now is their opportunity and that the window of opportunity is wider than it has ever been.

It is also likely that deals will continue to grow in size. To some extent this reflects senior executives becoming accustomed to $1 billion, $10 billion and

$100 billion deals. Having seen others do them, they are more willing to under-take them for their own company. Similarly, bankers and investors are becoming more accustomed to, if not jaded by, large deals, and are more willing to finance them. In confirmation of this observation, the acquisitions described above are examples.

Recent Studies

In the previous section, we saw that mergers and acquisitions will continue to be important in the new century. Not all of them will be successful. As can be seen in various studies, the success of mergers ranged from successful to little change to not necessarily successful. The results depended on the measurement and the period studied.

First, the good news. When measured as the number of merged companies that subsequently went into bankruptcy or were liquidated, few mergers in the 1980s or 1990s were unsuccessful. More specifically, studies found:

- Merged firms improve asset productivity and cash flow well above industry averages, particularly where merged firms have overlapping business.[10]
- Substantial gains exist in friendly transactions involving firms with overlap-ping businesses. However, the best that hostile takeovers could expect, par-ticularly between firms with unrelated businesses, was to break even.[11]
- A total of 60 percent of acquirers produced net income that was signifi-cantly greater than nonacquirers' net income.[12]
- Shareholder returns in 37 percent of the 1980s deal exceeded industry aver-ages, while in the 1990s 52 percent exceeded industry averages.[13]

Second, the average news. On a short-term basis (usually three months or less) stock prices of acquiring companies stay about the same, while stock prices of target companies go up. At a minimum, target company stocks benefit from the premium that must be paid to encourage existing shareholders to sell their shares. Additionally, one company's offer for the target will attract other bidders, with exiting shareholders reaping the benefit of the competition. The average, however, is skewed, with those leaving the deal benefiting and those staying not benefiting.[14] If you consider the benefit only of those still involved in the merged or acquired company, there is little gain.

Third, the not-so-good news. On a long-term basis (usually three years or more), studies show mixed results.

- Of companies that had grown through mergers in 1979, 44 percent had return on equity (ROE) below that of companies listed on the New York Stock Exchange (NYSE) and return on assets (ROA) well below NYSE listed companies.[15]

- Of acquisitions in 1987, 61 percent did not earn back the equity invested in them within three years.[16]
- Acquiring firms did not increase profitability or productivity through use of the target's assets that they acquired.[17]
- Over the long run, 80 percent of acquisitions negatively impact acquirer's share prices. In 5 years, their prices fell behind by 61 percent.[18] Similarly, returns decline over time, dropping to 20 percent by year four.[19]
- While 58 percent of the acquirers had returns above industry averages, this was well below the 69 percent of nonacquirers who exceeded industry averages.[20]
- A total of 70 percent of the mergers fail to achieve expectations. (The actual breakdown was 30 percent found them successful; 53 percent found them satisfactory; 11 percent found them unsatisfactory; and 5 percent found them disastrous.)[21]
- Only 17 percent of mergers result in substantial returns for the acquiring companies; 33 percent showed marginal returns; 20 percent reduced returns; and 30 percent substantially reduced returns for shareholders.[22]
- Stock mergers had significantly lower returns than cash mergers, since acquirers using stock may be more likely to do so if their stock is overvalued, while companies using cash will do so if they believe their stock is undervalued. Following the acquisition, the true value is more likely to be discovered.[23]

While the above results are not particularly encouraging, it is unlikely that the quest for mergers and acquisitions will abate. The threat of international competition, whether perceived or real and whether next door or over the Internet, will continue to be a driving force along with the desire to achieve economies of scale. The above studies did offer one lesson to me. This book should cover not only mergers and acquisitions but also divestitures.

Stages—Investigation, Negotiation and Integration

There are three stages to acquisitions and mergers—investigation, negotiation and integration.

Investigation and Negotiation

In the investigation stage, buyer or seller forms its teams, considers the driving factors and targets, and addresses the structural questions. I will discuss each of these in the following sections.

In the negotiation stage, letters of intent usually establish an estimated (or, in some case a fixed) closing date, possibly with one or more extensions. The letter, however, should do more. It should fix a date for turning over due diligence documents, for seller's executives meeting with buyer's executives, for buyer obtaining financing, for buyer completing due diligence, and (if other agreements will be involved) for establishing a deadline for completing them.

The timing of these dates is open to negotiation. Normally, buyer and seller prefer to have closings as soon as possible.

The buyer, for instance, wants to close before someone else can step in and close the deal. Even if the letter of intent contains statements prohibiting seller negotiating with other parties and penalties for doing so, in some cases, seller or his or her agents might do so. Under fiduciary rules applicable to seller's board of directors, it may even be required to do so.

The buyer also wants to close before news of the proposed acquisition reaches the marketplace. Such knowledge could cause the value of seller's assets to drop. For instance, I was recently involved in a transaction where one of seller's representatives, as a courtesy, advised a long-term customer that seller was going to be selling its business. Between receiving the news and closing, the customer made arrangements with a different long-term supplier. The loss of this customer amounted to about 10 percent of seller's total sales. This meant the value of seller's business declined by 10 percent, and the sales price had to be renegotiated. Fortunately, for buyer, it became aware of the leak before the closing and had more leverage to negotiate a lower sales price. On a $100 million deal, that is a lot of money. Without such a price adjustment, the deal would not have closed. Loose lips not only can sink ships in acquisitions but also can be very expensive.

There may be other incentives for buyer to close, such as:

- lack of a binding letter of intent allowing seller to shop the deal for higher prices;
- taking advantage of a pressing opportunity;
- stopping deterioration of seller's business as soon as possible;
- capturing earnings as soon as possible.

Similar reasons apply to seller. If it is getting a premium for its assets, seller has strong incentive to close before adverse changes affect its business, market or economy. With the premium, such changes are more likely to bring bad news than good news. Additionally, if the transaction has become public knowledge and does not close, it could discourage other buyers from bidding and drive the price down. From a practical standpoint, seller will also be concerned that the longer the deal is pending, the longer that buyer has to conduct due diligence and the longer that buyer has to uncover issues that it can use to back out or negotiate a lower price.

On the other hand, there may be reasons for a lengthy period before closing. This is more likely a preference for buyer. For instance, it might want a lengthy period to conduct due diligence, particularly if the business is new to it or if seller has troubled assets. This might not be such a bad thing for seller, since the longer the due diligence period the better position it is in to reduce its representations and warranties by arguing that seller has had ample time to investigate.

Pending government approvals might also be an incentive for buyer to postpone. As I will discuss, the deal might not be able to close until federal government approval is obtained under the Hart-Scott-Rodino Act. Buyer might also want to await a favorable tax ruling. In addition, seller may be awaiting a license or approval for a new product or service, and buyer might not want to close until it is received.

Integration

Integration is a lengthy process, beginning well before the closing and continuing long afterwards. Unfortunately, most mergers fail for lack of efficient and effective integration.

The main reason for failure is lack of advance planning, since there are many tasks and most of them must be accomplished in a very short period. The public announcement is an example, and must be prepared well in advance. For the buyer, it is an introduction to buyer's company, employees, suppliers and customers, and it should give them a good sense of who and what buyer is. It is, and should be treated as, the basis for buyer's future with them.

When dealing with important customers and suppliers, buyer should not limit itself to the announcement. Send them a personal letter, possibly with a packet of materials. It can be sent by courier and timed to coincide with the announcement. A telephone call at the closing, possibly by seller and buyer, is another personal touch for particularly important relations.

The announcement must be also addressed to seller and buyer's employees. Seller's employees will be particularly concerned about the impact the merger will have on their jobs, which for many equates with their livelihood and self-identity. Buyer cannot stop their worries, but buyer can help employees adapt to the change and make it as painless as possible.

One way to help is that if buyer knows something, whether good or bad, tell them as soon as possible. Until buyer does, much of everything else it tells them will be lost in background clutter. It is much better on morale to tell some bad news and give them a year to plan versus letting them worry for a year before giving notice. In addition, uncertainty can drive away many of the people you might otherwise have kept.

Another way to help is that if layoffs will happen let employees know the range, even if buyer has not identified whom. Whatever number buyer announces will be much lower that what rumors will be projecting. At the same time, if buyer knows what benefits are going to be made available, let employees know with the first public announcement.

For buyer's employees, they will also want to know what impact the merger or acquisition will have on them. Particularly when the two companies are of equivalent size, buyer's staff will wonder who will be kept when there are duplicative departments between the two.

At a minimum, if seller or target's employees will become new employees of the buyer or acquirer (meaning acquirer will not assume target's employment contracts and obligations), acquirer will probably want to give transferred employees credit for any benefits they accrued with target. This will include seniority, unused vacation and sick leave. If this is not possible, at closing, target should reimburse its employees for the accrued value of their benefits that they will lose. Acquirer might also want to maintain target employee benefits at least at the preclosing level.

Many buyers have found that the lowest point in the integration process occurs at the time of the announcement. It seems the announcement crystallizes all the worries about whether the merger can be effectively implemented. It is often the nadir for:

- new employees worrying how the merger will affect them;
- customers', suppliers' and the stock market's evaluation of the merger;
- managers' ability to cope with the enormous tasks ahead of them.

With time employees who are being retained understand they still have to do their work—hopefully with more help and more efficiently. Customers and suppliers become accustomed to the new letterhead and business cards, see they still get purchase orders or deliveries, and are satisfied if not pleasantly surprised. And managers see that each day the monolith of integration facing them shrinks.

At least by the date of the merger announcement, many acquirers start weekly meetings of key employees from both companies. The meetings identify integration issues, problems and opportunities. Ways of addressing them are identified, with appropriate individuals assigned the responsibility. Coordination is also assigned.

It is best to start with basic issues. Where products are related or complementary, this could mean making certain sales people have materials and training on both companies' products, centralizing order processing, and providing after-sales service. However, for antitrust purposes, pricing data must not be disclosed until the merger occurs.

In a later stage, more time and labor-intensive tasks can be addressed for complementary and related products. Initially, this means coordination of ad campaigns and packaging. Ultimately, to maximize efficiency gains, reallocation of production will be addressed.

As noted, integration is a difficult and seldom achieved process. I have dealt with executives in American and foreign companies who, 20 years after a merger, still refer to themselves as coming from one side or another of a merger. Integration has to reach down to the individual level. If operations have been combined, the integration will never fully succeed if former members of one company go to lunch with each other and members of the other former company go their separate way. Managers must encourage cross-fraternization if the origins are ever going to be lost.

Another way to make acquired company employees feel like a part of the same team is to look for positive things they do. If some processes they use are effective, adopt them for the entire company. That can send a powerful message.

There should also be an impartial ombudsman office to resolve issues. Members of only the acquiring company should not staff it nor should it predominantly rule in favor of the acquiring company's employees. If it does, it will be ignored. If perceived as a true means of resolving issues and increasing integration, it can be valuable.

Similarly, future assignments, growth and business development must be handled impartially. If the good tasks are assigned to the acquiring company and its former employees, if the hot new products are given to its manufacturing facilities, or if the most challenging research is sent to its scientists, full integration will never occur. The acquired company's employees will consider themselves as being treated like a colony and will never accept integration.

After six months and yearly thereafter, buyer should double-check himself or herself to see how the acquisition is going. Start with employees of the acquired company. By confidential questionnaire, ask them how they were treated and how they felt. Ask them if they feel like a part of the new company. Buyer can learn a great deal on what it did right and what it did wrong. The lessons can be invaluable for its next acquisition. By monitoring responses from period to period, it can also see if it is continuing to make progress. If not, more action may be necessary.

The questionnaire should also be sent to suppliers and customers. Rather than anonymously, however, key employees should sit down with them and get their thoughts. It will make them feel like a part of the team and that their input is important. It also makes them more involved and thus more committed to buyer's success. Most importantly, buyer can get some valuable insights and suggestions on how to improve its relationship with them.

From buyer's standpoint, every six months, if not sooner, it should evaluate the performance of the combined company against projections. Where is it ahead and where is it behind? Why did it succeed with the positive results? What can be done to address the deficiencies? What learned lessons can be applied to other areas? The information can be used in two ways—to correct problems and to apply to the next acquisition.

Team—Internal and External

The success of an acquisition starts with the individuals involved. Many companies active in making acquisitions believe the process begins with selecting a small core group of individuals to handle the identification and implementation of acquisitions. Such a team should bring together necessary skills but should not be so large that discipline and confidentiality is lost. The team is composed of two parts—the internal and external members.

The first members to be brought together are the internal members. They are drawn from the functional areas that must evaluate acquisition candidates. This usually means legal, product group, engineering and finance. As the acquisition proceeds, members can be added from other groups, such as human resources and tax. The internal members are also important in helping to conduct, understand and analyze the target during the due diligence period.

The external members are just as important. Depending on the company, they may be brought in very early in the process—even before targets are identified— or may be brought in as late as after identification of targets.

Where a business **broker** is involved, it is usually the first outsider. It might have an existing target that it represents and brings to the acquiring company, or it may be hired by the acquiring company to identify targets. Brokers usually— and hopefully—have expertise within the particular industry. If so, they can be important players during the negotiations to close the deal.

When retaining a broker, many questions beyond qualification have to be considered:

- Exclusivity: will the seller or buyer have the right to identify its own partners or retain other brokers? A related question is whether the broker can represent both parties.
- Compensation: how and when will the broker be compensated? What percentage of the acquisition price will the broker receive—fixed or declining percentage for each million/billion? Will the compensation be in cash, stock or a combination? Will some or all of the payment be made when the letter of intent is signed, at the closing, or postclosing when certain milestones are reached?
- Registration: is the broker registered or licensed? This is important since unregistered securities broker-dealers cannot sue for compensation. Finders, on the other hand, who introduce the parties and do not participate in the negotiations, are exempt from broker registration requirements.

Investment bankers are usually the next outsiders to be brought in. At times, they may be the first because they originate the transaction by acting as brokers. At other times, they have a critical initial role since they have to advise how much money will be available and, therefore, what targets are possible. The appropriate investment bankers can offer capital advice in two ways. First, they will have considerable market experience and can evaluate the market in general and specific companies in particular. They can advise on appropriate price ranges, how the capital markets will perceive the acquisition, and whether a particular target is worth pursuing. Second, they can help raise the money needed to make the deal go forward. In this role, they can be crucial players in highly leveraged deals, usually by arranging the investors and lenders.

Investment bankers might also provide a "fairness opinion" to the board of directors. Many boards require independent analysis of acquisitions before approval. Such analysis considers whether a fair price is being paid and whether the other terms are fair and reasonable to the company's shareholders.

In the postclosing period, investment bankers can be of valuable assistance in locating managers for the acquired or merged entity.

The third external member usually brought into a transaction is **outside lawyers**. Frequently, they are brought in after the investment bankers have recommended a particular deal and structure and are asked to review the proposal. This can be by considering a letter of intent, term sheet or memorandum of agreement. At this stage they can make recommendations on the structure and the enforceability of the documents.

As negotiations progress, the attorneys are at center stage. They bear the brunt work of meeting with clients, meeting with the other side, and then drafting documents that reflect the parties' intent. They have an ongoing burden of explaining the transaction to their clients and protecting their interests. Their responsiveness is critical in keeping the transaction moving along at the appropriate pace.

The approach or attitude of the attorneys at this point is critical. Personally, I have been influenced by the comment of J. P. Morgan at the turn of the century to his lawyer. Morgan commented that other attorneys tell him why he can't do a deal, while his attorney told him how. For me, that is the creativity and thrill of practicing law. When two parties want to close a deal but are blocked by an issue, one of the great satisfactions is finding a solution. When putting together a legal team, I look for creators and solvers, not objectors. Clients seek and benefit most from these advisors.

It is also important, for attorneys to describe risks and attempt to quantify them for their clients. Does the problem have a high or remote risk of being realized? Doing the best to identify risks is the easiest part of the job. Attorneys let down their clients when they stop there. They should also analyze the risk. With such information, clients are better able to evaluate the risk.

While negotiations are proceeding, attorneys will also be asked to take part in the due diligence investigation. From the target's side, they will want to make certain the seller is suitable. Can it make the acquisition from a legal, regulatory and financial standpoint? From the acquiring company's side, the target will be asked to turn over many documents about its business. Acquirer's attorneys must review, analyze and study the documents in detail.

The parties' attorneys will also be asked to file and obtain necessary governmental approvals and opinions. Depending on the size of the transaction and industry, this could be a filing with the Department of Justice and Federal Trade Commission or an industry-regulatory body.

In addition to the in-house staff, **accountants** are also key external team members. They assist transactions in several ways:

- In early stages, they might evaluate the proposed structure. They might also assist in pricing the transaction and allocating purchase price.
- In due diligence, they evaluate the financial condition of the other party. This could be a basic review or a more detailed independent audit.
- For the closing, they may be asked to provide a "cold comfort" opinion attesting to acquirer's financial stability. This is done by testing and sampling acquirer's financial data, looking for inconsistencies, checking whether internal financial controls are adequate, testing underlying assumptions, and evaluating sufficiency of working capital.
- When the target has a relatively brief operating history, buyer's accountants might undertake a "business review." This will include an evaluation and valuation of the company's financial condition and business.
- In the postclosing period, they might determine the appropriateness of price adjustments and calculate them accordingly.

In recent years, accountants have expanded their services to include preparing strategic business plans, acting as brokers, structuring deals, consulting on management searches, and advising on information systems.

Driving Factors and Targets

As an acquirer, having selected the acquisition team, it must next analyze the candidate. In this stage, buyer must understand the business factors behind the transaction and how they apply to the candidate.

The basic question to be addressed is what is driving the acquisition? What is buyer seeking to accomplish by the transaction? Earlier I described several factors supporting the trend of increasing mergers and acquisitions:

- Baby boomers fueling stock market
- Internet and technology
- International competition
- Economies of scale
- Government attitude toward mergers
- Business becoming accustomed to billion dollar deals.

Additionally, in interviews with business leaders active in mergers, some of the most commonly cited drivers for buyers were:

- acquisition of technology;
- acquisition of key personnel;
- acquisition of raw material sources;
- acquisition of production facilities;
- supplement internal product development and shorten time to market new products;
- acquisition of products—often to increase product offering and permit one-stop shopping;
- acquisition of brand name;
- improve marketing efforts;
- acquisition of distribution system;
- globalization—be everywhere and anywhere;
- achieve critical mass and economies of scale;
- consolidation—which may be the same as critical mass and economies of scale;
- acquisition of key customer;
- vertical integration from production to after-sale service—which may be same as acquisition of raw materials, distribution system and key customer;
- increase market share;
- maximization of shareholder value—although this could be used to justify most actions;
- increase earnings growth by expanding business to faster-growing sectors;
- acquire tax loss carryforwards to offset taxable income.

Some writers have summarized the above factors as having two basic goals—survival and growth.

For sellers some of the most commonly cited drivers were:

- concentrate on core business;
- increase flexibility;
- respond to regulatory pressures and laws;
- pending or threatened litigation;
- maximize shareholder value—although this can be used to justify nearly any action.

Having selected which of the above goals apply and their relative importance, the goals must be applied to the candidate. If a target has not been identified, many companies have sales and other staff in the applicable industry identify the best targets and then rank them according to how good they are in general or how well they fit the above factors. To do so, they often rely on their own dealings or contacts in the industry. In this regard, vendors and customers of targets are often valuable sources of information.

Structural Questions

Now that buyer has clarified the factors driving the acquisition and identified possible targets, the next step is answering some basic questions on the structure of the transaction. In the early acquisition stages, many points will have to be discussed and coordinated with the other party.

The most important structural questions are:

- Timing of closing: when the closing of the deal will take place depends on a number of factors, primarily driven by the parties' needs. Is the seller in a distressed situation and needs the money quickly? Is the end of the tax year approaching, and is it to the parties' benefit to close before then? Is seller conducting an auction with several buyers competing with each other and the winner is the first to close? From a customer's standpoint, is it important to close before rumors of the deal leak to outsiders and deteriorate the value of the target? An example would be customers reducing purchases as they worry whether the company will remain in existence. On the other hand, is buyer looking at a number of possible acquisitions, and is it to seller's advantage to close as soon as possible?

- Up front or deferred payment: buyer and seller must have a clear understanding about when they want to pay or be paid. Does seller want cash at the closing to take away and use elsewhere? Is seller willing to receive stock in the acquired company or the acquirer, and thus invest in its future? Or is it willing to take a note for deferred payment of some or all of the sales price? Seller may be able to get a higher price for accepting the higher risk of installment payments in a "bootstrap" transaction, since payments will be dependent on future earnings.

- Does buyer want to cash out and get rid of seller? Or does it want to keep seller around by giving it stock and a vested interest in how well target does? Can it afford to pay cash, or must it give seller some equity or debt to finance the deal?

- Form of deferred payment: if payment is deferred, what form will it be in? As noted, it could be equity or debt. As equity, there are two basic questions. First, is it retained equity in the target or new shares in the acquiring company? Second, is it fixed or an "earn-out" dependent on meeting certain thresholds? Seller may be able to obtain a higher price under an earn-out arrangement where the amount to be paid is dependent on target's performance. The disadvantage is that seller's revenue is dependent on buyer's performance and management of the acquired company. Where earn-out applies, seller might want some input or control over the operation of what is being sold to make certain maximum returns are achieved. Seller might also ask for an escrow of certain payments or preferential shareholder treatment over other shareholders.

- As debt, there are many possible types and three basic questions. First, is it unsecured, such as a promissory note, or secured, such as a debenture? Second, can the holder transfer the debt—is it negotiable? A negotiable instrument transferred to a third party has the disadvantage of virtually eliminating the possibility of buyer offsetting against it for claims against seller. Buyer's only recourse for breaches of representations and warranties will be against seller's remaining assets, which may be insufficient. Third, will the debt be subordinated to other debt or have some priority? The more subordinated it is, the more likely that seller will demand equity incentives. The answers to these questions will usually depend on the demands of third parties financing the transaction.
- Seller: who is selling, the company or its shareholders? Will the buyer be buying target's shares held by its stockholders, or will it be acquiring target's assets?
- Assets: if only target's assets are being purchased, is it all assets or only some of them? In other words, can buyer pick and chose the assets it wants?
- Liabilities: when assets instead of stock are being purchased, is buyer also assuming target company's liabilities? If yes, will all liabilities be assumed or only certain ones?
- Taxable: will the transaction be structured as a tax-free exchange or a taxable transaction? Frequently, tax considerations determine the form of the transaction.

Protections for Shareholders and Directors

There are several methods available to a corporation to prevent (or reduce the likelihood of) unwanted takeovers. The most common involve two approaches—blocking takeovers by restrictions on shareholders and board of directors.

Shareholders

Many emerging companies issue stock under restrictive agreements. At the time an investor purchases shares it agrees to be bound by certain restrictions. They include:

- Convertible note: in the most severe case, the investors are not even shareholders. Instead, they provide money to the company as a debt under a note that is convertible into equity under certain conditions. These notes could be called (that is the lender can convert the debt into equity) upon the company going public or at some distant date in the future.

- Nontransferability: shareholders are not allowed to transfer the shares to another person.
- Put: shareholders have the right to put their shares to the company—that is, make the company buy their shares—but not to sell to someone else.
- Right of first refusal: Before selling its shares to another person, the investor must first offer the shares to the company, controlling shareholders or existing shareholders.

The effect of these restrictions is that outsiders are not able to acquire the company's shares. It blocks them from accumulating shares in the first place.

Board of Directors

The second approach looks to the board of directors, who under corporate statutes must give approval for statutory mergers or asset sales. This approach strives to prevent the board from giving such approval.

Boards can adopt a number of structural impediments. They can be applied to stock acquisitions to begin with, or proxy solicitations intended to change board membership and get necessary board approval.

Courts and states are divided over what boards can do to restrict their ability to approve stock acquisitions and proxy solicitations. Some see it as a matter of contract or corporate approval. Others see it as denying board members their ability to exercise their fiduciary responsibilities to the company.

The defenses fall into three categories depending on who must approve them and are designed to limit the ability of someone who has recently acquired voting shares from taking immediate control.

Specific Shareholder Approval or Shark Repellent

There are several examples of this approach:

- Staggered boards: board members are elected on a rotating or staggered basis, for instance, one third each year. This means a controlling shareholder must take two years to get control (and three years for total control) of the board.
- Mandatory shareholder meetings: this prevents the holding of shareholder meetings by written consent, thus requiring the more cumbersome actual holding of a meeting, which in turn would require a minimum number of attendees (or quorum).
- Limitation on ability of shareholders to call special meetings: without this right, shareholders must wait until the next scheduled annual meeting.

- Limitation on ability of shareholders to remove a director, except for cause: this prevents new shareholders from replacing a director with one of their own.
- Limitation on ability to create new director positions.
- Giving directors (rather than shareholders) the ability to replace a withdrawing director.

The effectiveness of defenses in this category is limited. Once a new shareholder gains voting control of the stock, directors owe the new owner fiduciary duties. When faced with threatened litigation, most comply with its requests or resign. As an example, recently, the board of directors of a client voted to sell the company, even though the company had sufficient cash from a divestiture that the client could have made the acquisition, particularly since the acquirer was of similar size. The reasons for the decision was that the board was simply tired of complying with the Sarbanes-Oxley Act—to be discussed later—and there was a possibility of litigation by a vocal minority shareholder.

Charter Power or Blank Check: Directors might rely on their general authority under the company's charter document. Such power might have been recently approved by shareholders as a charter amendment.

When lawyers and corporations find the first type of defense described above ineffective, they might rely on a second, stronger defense line. Some examples are:

- Supermajority votes to approve all combinations between a controlling shareholder and the company, unless the board has granted its approval or certain fair price criteria have been met.
- Cap on voting power of any one shareholder, regardless of the number of shares held.
- Restricted voting power for a certain period after acquisition. For instance, during the three-year period following purchase, the acquirer cannot vote more than a fixed percentage. This number could increase each year.
- Right of nontendering shareholders to put their stock to the company within a specified period of time at a very generous price. This discourages shareholders from selling their shares in takeovers, since they can get a higher price by putting their shares to the company after the acquisition. It also discourages takeovers since the acquirer will have to buy out the nontendering shareholders at a more expensive price.
- Reduced voting rights of acquirers unless the acquisition is approved by nonselling shareholders or meets certain fair price criteria.
- Two-tier voting stock: one class held by insiders has more than its pro rata share of voting power and dilution rights. The class held by third parties has less than its pro rata share of voting power. Where the two-tier did not exist on formation, the company must persuade outside shareholders to trade in

their shares by offering a higher return in exchange for lower voting and dilution rights. This concentrates power with insiders.

There are several disadvantages to this second type of defenses. They are slow, inflexible and must be described in detailed disclosure documents under federal proxy solicitation regulations. Due to these weaknesses, a third defense level has emerged.

General Powers are defenses based on the board's general powers under state law, which the board uses to make the company less valuable and thus less interesting to potential acquirers. No shareholder approval is required, thus requiring less time to implement and less disclosure under securities laws. There are many types of defenses under this category. The most common are:

- **Crown Jewel**: the board agrees to sell the firm's key asset to a third party.
- **Lock-Up Option**: rather than a direct sale, in this case, the board grants an option to a third party who can buy the key asset in case of an unwanted bid.
- **Greenmail**: the board agrees to buy back the shares bought by the acquirer, usually at a premium.
- **Golden Parachutes**: the board grants senior managers lucrative severance payments that become effective if a takeover occurs. They will presumably be less willing to remain with the company following such a takeover.
- **White Squire**: the company issues stock to a friendly party who agrees to hold them and not resell under a standstill agreement.
- **ESOP**: the company establishes an employee stock ownership plan (ESOP), and has the ESOP purchase or receive contributions of shares in the company. The block held by the ESOP is presumably less likely to be sold to an acquirer.
- **Pentagon Play**: the company acquires companies that will raise national defense or antitrust problems for the bidder, thus making it less likely the bidder can obtain government approval.
- **Pac-Man Defense**: the company tries to acquire control of the bidder.
- **Leveraged Recap or One-Time Stock Dividend**: the company releverages itself by selling debt and distributing the proceeds to shareholders. This exhausts the company's debt capacity and cash reserves, so a bidder cannot use them to pay the acquisition cost.
- **Poison Pill**: if a certain percentage of the company's stock ("trigger") is acquired, and the acquisition has not been approved by the board (or possibly nontendering shareholders), shareholders can exercise special conversion options or buy at a discount. These securities can be stock, stock rights, or notes with special redemption or conversion rules. Shareholders can also put their stock back to the company for new stock under a two-tier voting system. The two-tier concentrates voting power and dilution with insiders. Often, boards are only allowed to delete a poison pill if the directors elected

before any takeover agree. This is known as a **dead hand poison pill**. In a **no hand poison pill**, newly elected board members are prohibited for a certain period from redeeming or canceling the pill to facilitate a combination with someone who supported their election.

The disadvantage of these defenses is that the company must spend money (or give up a valuable asset). They are, therefore, very expensive.

Even when the board has acted without shareholder approval, possibly in the second line of defense, or in any case in the third, shareholders have certain remedies. For instance, under Rule 14a8 of the Securities and Exchange Commission (SEC), they can pass a resolution recommending that the board withdraw particular defenses. The SEC has also issued Rule 19c4, which bars national securities exchanges and associations from listing stock of a company that nullified, restricted or disparately reduced per share voting rights of existing shareholders. Additionally, some national securities exchanges have adopted rules prohibiting certain defenses in the first category.

Empirical evidence on these defenses is not good. For the most part, when takeover defenses are announced, the firm's stock declines. The more stringent the defense, the greater the decline. More specifically:

- fair price amendments tend to have no significant effect on stock prices, while classified board and supermajority clauses might have significant negative impact on target shareholder value;
- supermajority amendments lower institutional stockholding and raise insider stockholding;
- two-tier voting has a negative effect on stock prices;
- even where shareholder approval is required, stock prices are affected negatively, particularly with the more restrictive poison pill plans;
- poison pills tend to be adopted by less profitable firms (based on industry averages) that are run by managers with less ownership control (again based on industry averages);
- severe corporate restructuring also negatively affects stock prices;
- if the acquisition is successful, the combined value of the acquired and target company rises. Unfortunately, most of this increase is captured by the departing shareholders of the acquired company.

Methods

In this book, I will study three basic acquisition methods—stock acquisition, asset acquisition and mergers. The rest are variations. This applies whether the acquired company is owned by another company or by individuals and whether the acquirer pays in cash, property, common or preferred stock, debentures, notes, bonds, convertible debt, warrants or options. The agreements—including representations, warranties, covenants, conditions, and indemnities—in all these possible approaches will be similar.

Stock Acquisition

This is the simplest acquisition method. Acquirer (A) purchases the stock of target (T) from target's shareholders (T-S).

The main agreement is the stock purchase agreement between acquirer and target's shareholders. It could be a single agreement signed by all shareholders or separate ones signed by each shareholder. The agreement could give A all of the shares in T, or some lesser percentage. Any consideration paid will go directly to the shareholders. Following the stock acquisition, T will become a subsidiary of A.

Asset Acquisition

Rather than purchasing T's stock, A might purchase T's assets and possibly its liabilities.

The main agreement is the asset purchase agreement between A and T. Any consideration paid goes directly to T. Following the asset acquisition, T remains in existence owned by its shareholders. With no assets, however, T will presumably distribute the consideration it receives to its shareholders and dissolve soon afterwards.

The main reason for an asset acquisition rather than a stock acquisition is the acquirer being wary of the target's liabilities and only willing to take its assets. There may also be some tax reasons, which I will discuss in Chapter 6.

If the acquirer is only interested in certain assets of the target, it might contract to buy just those assets. Alternatively, it could have those assets transferred into a new subsidiary of target and purchase that subsidiary under a stock purchase acquisition.

Merger

The third basic acquisition is a merger of target into acquirer. The two companies become a single entity. While the previous approaches are regulated by contract, this method is governed by statute.

The main agreement is an acquisition agreement and is signed by both companies. For acquirer, it resembles an asset acquisition, with the acquirer taking over target's assets. There is a difference, however. Target ceases to exist in a merger; it remains in existence after an asset purchase and is still owned by its shareholders.

For target's shareholders, the transaction might resemble a stock acquisition. Unless they refuse to participate and are cashed out, they will receive shares in the acquisition.

I now turn to variations of the three basic methods.

Three-party or Triangular Mergers

The first variation is the three-party merger. It arose as a result of changes in statutory merger rules, allowing securities in acquirer's parent to be used as consideration, and changes in tax laws that allow tax-free exchanges in certain circumstances. The two most common three-party mergers are the forward subsidiary merger and the reverse subsidiary merger.

The **forward subsidiary merger** is similar to the basic merger. Instead of merging target into the acquirer as with the basic merger, target merges into a subsidiary (S) of acquirer. As with the basic merger, S takes over the assets of target with target soon afterwards ceasing to exist. The main agreement is the acquisition agreement.

There are two steps in a **reverse subsidiary merger**. First, S mergers into T rather than the other way, with T succeeding to all of S's assets and liabilities. Since S is usually a newly created shell company with no assets or liabilities, T will be little affected by the merger. Second, outstanding shares of S are converted into shares of T. Enough shares will be converted into shares of T and held by acquirer so as to make T a subsidiary of acquirer.

Share Exchanges

Another variation is the binding share exchange. It is a stock purchase binding on all of target's stockholders if the required number of stockholders have approved the exchange. While not approved by all states, a large number recognize it. It combines the advantages of a stock purchase and a reverse subsidiary merger. Under this approach, target's shares are exchanged for cash or acquirer's stock, and acquirer purchases all of target's outstanding shares.

The main agreement is the stock purchase agreement, which requires approval of the boards of target and acquirer and the consent of the shareholders of target.

While this approach resembles a reverse subsidiary merger of the target with a subsidiary of the acquirer, it has the advantage of not constituting a merger under any contracts prohibiting target from being a party to a merger.

Short-form Mergers

Under this variation, acquirer purchases at least 80 percent of target's shares, making it a subsidiary. Target is then merged into its new parent company. Any minority shareholders are eliminated, with their shares in target converted into cash or shares in acquirer.

To effect a short-form merger, many state corporate statutes require approval of target's board and shareholders, acquirer's board, and, in certain cases, acquirer's shareholders.

In a pure short-form merger, there are no minority shareholders. In such cases, many state statutes do not require approval of target's board or shareholders. In most cases, approval of acquirer's shareholders is not required.

Short-form mergers can also be combined with forward subsidiary mergers or reverse subsidiary mergers. Under these combinations, acquirer transfers its stock in target to a newly created wholly owned subsidiary of acquirer. Or, acquirer can have the subsidiary purchase target's stock. As a result, the subsidiary is target's parent and either causes target to merge into it (short form forward subsidiary merger) or mergers into target (short-form reverse subsidiary merger).

Reverse

In some cases, the parties reverse their roles, with target purchasing acquirer or its assets, even when target is much smaller. There are several reasons for such a reversal:

- Avoid having to get numerous shareholder consents
- Avoid holdout shareholder's demands
- Avoid appraisal rights that exist in target's jurisdiction but not in acquirer's
- Avoid contractual limitations

In this transaction, shares of acquirer (and nominal target) are converted into a majority of the shares of target (and nominal acquirer).

Asset acquisitions can similarly be reversed. Instead of target selling its assets (and possibility its liabilities) to acquirer in exchange for acquirer's stock, acquirer sells its assets (and possibly liabilities) to target in exchange for stock in target. On liquidation, acquirer distributes target's stock to its shareholders. The net result is the same—one entity owns all the assets and liabilities of the two former companies.

Target Repurchase

In some cases, the merger may be accomplished by acquirer purchasing shares of target, either existing or new, followed by target repurchasing its remaining outstanding shares. If it is a publicly traded company, the repurchase must be accomplished by a tender offer.

If not all of the shares are repurchased, the transaction may be more similar to a recapitalization than an acquisition.

Consolidation

A consolidation occurs when a parent treats one or more of its subsidiaries as a part of its business for tax purposes. It can also refer to instances where a parent company combines two or more subsidiaries into a single entity.

Management Buyout

In a management buyout, existing managers of a company agree to purchase the company's shares from its shareholders—usually a parent company that has decided to sell its subsidiary. (If managers are not involved, the transaction is a leveraged buyout.) Rather than waiting for a new owner to step forward, the managers have decided they want to run the company themselves. There may be several reasons for their desire to do so. They might simply believe that they can run the company better on their own, or they might feel that the company is undervalued and with a little effort can be made more profitable, with them reaping the benefits of the resulting increase in value. They may also be worried about their jobs and be concerned that a new owner may replace them.

To finance the acquisition, managers may contribute some equity of their own but are more likely to raise money in the public markets. While there may be some equity involved, most of the financing will be in the form of debt offering high returns. A decade or more ago, with the availability of cheap money called junk bonds, it was easier to raise such funds. It is harder today, and as a result management buyouts are more difficult.

Recently, the preferred method of management buyout is the back-end statutory merger. The management group forms a shell business entity—corporation, partnership or limited liability company. The shell makes a tender offer for any and all shares that holders are willing to tender, possibly with a minimum number that must be offered. If the minimum is reached and the tender offer completed, the shell merges into the target. All nontendering minority shareholders are then cashed out.

Reorganization and Bankruptcy

Reorganizations are another approach to merger. In this method, a company will restructure itself without necessarily forming a new entity. For instance, in my first billion-dollar transaction, two corporate shareholders of a Fortune 500 company decided to rearrange their holdings. With both holding 50 percent of the shares, neither could consolidate the company for tax purposes. Since one was getting out of the market and wanted cash for other purposes, it agreed to sell 30 percent of its shares. It retained the possibility of an upswing in the market, while getting cash for its other activities.

Another form of reorganization occurs when a company restructures (changes) the rights of shareholders. For instance, distribution, liquidation or voting rights of one class could be strengthened to the detriment of another. Or a new class of shares could be created, thereby diluting existing shares.

Bankruptcies often involve reorganizations, as discussed in Chapter 8. The final plan for the bankrupt company might involve debtors agreeing to take less than the amount owed, with shareholders also giving up some percent of their holdings. The amount they give up may be granted to existing or new creditors. The net result is a restructuring of the company.

I now move from variations of mergers to alternatives to mergers.

Exclusive Appointment

At the time of writing this book, I was advising a start-up company on how to raise money to develop its sales network. Since family and friends had contributed all that they could, another source was necessary. The most obvious was outside investors, but the founder discovered that to raise the money needed, he was going to have to give up majority control of his company.

The alternative the founder chose was to locate companies with existing sales forces handling related but noncompetitive products. The founder then appointed them as his company's exclusive distributor in their region. The result was that he held on to 100 percent of the company and still got his sales force.

This is only one example of how an exclusive appointment can achieve the same result as a merger or acquisition.

Vendor Financing

Another approach to raise money without bringing in outside investors is vendor financing. For instance, if suppliers are willing to accept payment on a net-30 day basis, it takes less than 20 days to produce and sell goods, and if sales are on a net-10 day basis, a company might not need to raise additional funds.

Joint Venture

The third alternative to a merger is a joint venture. One of the best examples is Toyota. When it decided to enter the U.S. market, it could have established its own plant immediately. Instead, it decided that it first wanted to learn how to deal with the U.S. market, especially American labor.

With this in mind, it could have acquired an auto company in the United States, but antitrust rules would have probably prevented it from doing so. Its choice was to enter into a joint venture with General Motors (GM) to jointly run the former GM plant in Fremont, California.

Similarly, many large construction or research projects are handled as joint ventures. The parties can reap the benefits of joint efforts, while maintaining their separate identities. Because of the costs and risks involved in building new airplane models, Boeing similarly uses joint ventures.

Choice of Method

The choice among the above methods will depend on a number of factors:

- Majority of target shareholders opposing the acquisition means that approval of controlling shares cannot be obtained. The transaction will have to be structured as an asset acquisition.
- Target being publicly traded or having numerous shareholders usually means consent of all shareholders cannot be obtained. This will require that the acquisition be structured as a merger (especially a reverse subsidiary merger), asset sale or binding share exchange.
- Substantial number of creditors and application of bulk sale laws—to be discussed in Chapter 2—might prevent asset acquisition.
- Difficulty of valuation of various assets and allocation of purchase price among them might make asset acquisition difficult to implement.
- Significant liability might push the transaction toward an asset purchase excluding the liability.
- Reducing the number of consents from other parties may mean that stock purchase or reverse subsidiary merger is the easiest approach.

This completes the overview of the business aspects of mergers and acquisitions. I now turn to the legal aspects.

2

Legal: Part 1

In this chapter and Chapter 3, I turn to the legal aspects of mergers and acquisitions. I will cover rights and responsibilities of successors, creditors, shareholders, boards, controlling parties and employees. I will also look at particular statutory regulatory schemes, as well as employee, antitakeover, securities, antitrust and industry-specific rules.

Successors—General, Environment and Sales Taxes

Under English common law, claims against and by a company disappeared on dissolution. Any assets had to be given over to the King. In the United States, the rule was changed. On dissolution, the company's assets became a trust fund for claims by creditors and shareholders. If the assets had been distributed, creditors could bring claims against former directors and shareholders on the ground that the assets were subject to a lien by creditors. Such claims were subject to the statute of limitations, which required that claims be brought within a fixed time period.

Most present state statutes are based on the 1979 Model Business Corporation Act,[1] which provides that the dissolution of a company does not cancel claims against the company or its directors, officers and shareholders that existed prior to dissolution. Such actions must be brought within two years of dissolution.

Since the 1979 Act only addresses predissolution claims, there is considerable confusion about what remedies should be available for claims arising after dissolution. Courts will apply the same two-year limitation, unless they find some reason that would cause it to be unfair. An example is self-dealing by target's directors before dissolution.

This provision was clarified in the 1985 Revised Model Business Corporation Act,[2] which established a longer period of five years and created different rules for claims known at dissolution and for those not known. However, many state statutes remain based on the 1979 Act.

General Liability

Acquirer's responsibility for target's debts and liabilities depends on the structure of the deal and the agreements. If acquirer merges or combines with target, it becomes liable for target's debts and responsibilities. By law, the rights and obligations of target pass to acquirer "as a matter of law." For instance, under California Corporations Code, the surviving corporation will be liable for the debts of the disappearing corporation in a merger, and all liens on property of either company will continue.[3] Similarly, any action or proceeding pending against the disappearing corporation can be prosecuted against the surviving company.[4] Punitive damages can even be recovered against the surviving corporation.

If acquirer purchases target's stock, it does not become directly liable for target's liabilities. Target survives and remains liable for its own debts. Indirectly, acquirer does become liable since it is the owner of target, and the value of that ownership is reduced by target's liabilities. Those liabilities have presumably been reflected in the purchase price.

If acquirer only purchases target's assets, it is not responsible for target's liabilities and debts. If it contracted to assume only certain liabilities, it is not responsible for other liabilities and debts of target. There are certain exceptions to this principle of being only subject to what is agreed in asset acquisitions, which I will discuss below.

Perfected Security Interests
The first exception is if the assets are taken subject to recorded or perfected security interests.[5] Even if acquirer did not agree, it takes subject to any perfected interests that have been properly recorded.

Assumption
The second exception is if acquirer impliedly agreed to assume the liabilities. The implication could arise from conduct or statements. It is important, therefore, that asset purchase agreements expressly exclude any liabilities other than those specifically listed.[6]

Consolidation, Merger, Continuation or Alter Ego
The third exception is if the net effect of the transaction is a consolidation, merger or acquirer continuing target's business.

The courts have found a **de facto consolidation** if acquirer purchases all of target's assets without adequate consideration to pay off target's debts, and soon afterwards target ceases to do business.[7]

Similarly, courts have found a **de facto merger** if the consideration paid is solely in acquirer's or a subsidiary's stock, all of target's shareholders become shareholders of acquirer, acquirer assumes only liabilities necessary to carry on target's business, and target liquidates after the acquisition.[8]

Courts are more likely to find a **continuation** if there is a common identity of directors, officers or stockholders, the same or similar name, location or employees are used, inadequate consideration is paid, and only one company survives.[9] Courts feel that if acquirer has reaped the benefits of target's business, it should be responsible for its liabilities. Since cases in this area involve two corporations having the same or similar shareholders and directors, the mere continuation theory may be avoided if there is no common identity of shareholders or management.[10]

Target might own a subsidiary that is not being acquired because it has significant claims or risks. Even though the subsidiary was a separate company and was not acquired by acquirer, acquirer may be liable. This could occur if the subsidiary's business was closely controlled by target. In such a case, creditors may be able to argue that the subsidiary was operated as a mere tool of target and was its **alter ego**. If successful in their argument, target—and therefore acquirer—would be liable for the subsidiary's liabilities.

Fraud

The fourth exception is if the assets were **fraudulently transferred**. If target sells its assets in an attempt to defraud or deprive its creditors of payment, buyer will be liable for target's liabilities.[11] In applying this test, courts usually look at the consideration paid to see if it was adequate, reasonable or fictitious.

Product Line

At least one state has created another exception for manufacturers. Under California law, manufacturers of defective products are strictly liable, and their liability passes to any acquirer of its assets. The theory is that the "risk of injury can be insured by the manufacturer and distributed among the public as a cost of doing business."[12] This is called **product line theory**.

California will apply product line liability to acquirer in these instances:

- Its acquisition of target's business had, in effect, eliminated any remedy that an injured plaintiff might have had. This has been interpreted to mean that acquirer actually played some role in the destruction of plaintiff's remedies. This means that all, or substantially all, of target's assets must have been acquired.
- Acquirer has the ability to assume and spread the risk. The courts have interpreted this to mean that acquirer purchased the physical plant, equipment, inventories and technology; and has continued to use target's production personnel and managers. The individuals could be retained as employees or consultants.
- It is fair to impose the burden on acquirer as being necessarily attached to target's goodwill that acquirer purchased and enjoys. Fairness will be found if acquirer purchased target's trade name, goodwill and product

line; continued to produce the same products; and held itself out as the same enterprise.[13]

Most federal and state courts have rejected this theory at least in principle. A few states, including the highest courts in New York and Delaware, however, have not ruled on this exception. In reality, however, when plaintiff's have no other remedy and acquirer has assumed target's reputation and goodwill, other courts have found means similar to the product line theory to impose liability on acquirer.

Duty to Warn
A related theory is that acquirer should be liable if it was aware of a potential claim, such as a product defect, or should have discovered the claim or defect during its due diligence but failed to warn customers.[14] This rule only applies if there is a continuing relationship between acquirer and target's customers. Taking over target's customer contracts is clearly an example.

Avoiding and Protecting Against Liability
There are a number of strategies that acquirers can adopt to reduce their chances of being found liable for target's liabilities. To recap:

- Check for secured claims on all assets being purchased.
- Avoid any express or implied assumption of liabilities.
- Avoid any express or implied agreement to dissolve target after the acquisition. If target survives, the mere continuation theory cannot be applied.
- Have a subsidiary, newly created if necessary, buy the assets. This will isolate the liabilities to one business.
- Buy assets, not stock. This eliminates the chance of a de facto merger or consolidation.
- Do not buy all the assets. This will probably eliminate being treated as continuing target's business, since it keeps target as an ongoing business after the acquisition.
- Do not reference buying goodwill in acquisition documents. Underlying most court decisions in continuity cases is the belief that if acquirer has taken the goodwill, it should take the bad will (liabilities). This may not be possible, however, if the acquisition includes a trademark or a covenant not to compete, both of which require that some goodwill be acquired. This approach will also mean that the purchase price is only allocated to non-goodwill assets, which will raise their capitalized cost and result in higher depreciation expense.
- Give notices to customers, suppliers and employees that acquirer has purchased the business and that it is a separate business from target.

- Pay adequate consideration. This reduces the chance of a mere continuation theory.
- Pay consideration in cash, not acquirer's stock. This reduces the chance of the de facto merger doctrine being applied. It might also reduce the chance of the mere continuation theory being applied.
- Pay consideration to target, not its shareholders. This accomplishes two things. It means target continues. It also means that acquirer can argue target had sufficient assets. It was the distribution of the consideration to shareholders that deprived creditors of any recourse—not the purchase. In such cases, shareholders, not acquirer, should be liable.
- Change product lines after the acquisition.
- Warn customers of product defects.

Even where liability cannot be avoided, acquirer can protect itself by certain actions:

- Reduce the purchase price to reflect any risks.
- Insure against risks. Make certain target's product liability policy is in place. Increase coverage if necessary. If target will not continue to exist, have the policy transferred to acquirer.
- Get an indemnity from target, but make certain there will be assets to back it up. If target will be dissolved, get the indemnity from its principals, parent or major shareholders.
- Set aside some of the purchase price to cover potential claims. An independent escrow agent can hold the amount set aside if target wants more assurance that the set-aside money will ultimately be available to it.

Environment

Environmental liabilities raise special considerations. Unfortunately, the rules are not clear. Most environmental laws do not clearly address the responsibility of acquirers for target's environmental liabilities.

The Comprehensive Environmental Response, Compensation and Liability Act[15] (CERCLA) was passed in 1980 and requires companies to clean up hazardous substances they generated, transported or disposed. The Environmental Protection Agency (EPA) or any injured person can sue. CERCLA also created a Superfund for cleaning up hazardous substances where the polluter cannot afford to or cannot be found.

Since CERCLA liability can be significant, it is important for acquirers in their due diligence to look carefully for environmental risks. For instance, a landowner can be liable for hazardous materials found on its land unless it was caused by an unrelated third party. In due diligence, acquirer must look for hazardous materials found not only on property owned by target but also on nearby and adjacent land.

The EPA has taken a very aggressive position on successor liability. Its position on the liability of successors under Superfund appears in a 1984 memorandum.[16] In a merger or consolidation, the EPA stated that the surviving company assumes the Superfund liabilities of both companies. In a stock purchase it recognized that the company remains in existence, with only its owners changing. Therefore, there should be no change in CERCLA underlying liability. In an asset purchase, the EPA will apply the traditional approach described above as modified by the continuity of business exception. In some instances, the EPA has argued that the product line theory should apply.

Some states have not been willing to go as far as the EPA in assessing environmental liabilities, and limited themselves to the traditional approach without applying the continuity of business exception. Of course, if acquirer continues target's practices that gave rise to environmental liabilities, it will be liable.

Sales Taxes

There are several reasons why sales of assets in a merger or acquisition should be exempt from state sales taxes:

- Exempt: most states exempt from sales taxation transfers of property pursuant to a merger or consolidation.
- Intangibles: states that impose sales taxes on property sales generally exclude the sale of intangibles such as stock, bonds, notes and intellectual property. This means that stock for stock acquisitions will generally be exempt even from the sales taxes in states taxing property transfers. Harder questions arise for sales of assets embodying intellectual property, such as sale of computer software stored on a disc.
- Not in ordinary course of business: many states exempt transfers outside the ordinary course of business, which should include the sale of assets as part of a merger or acquisition.
- Resale: most states also exempt sales of property that the buyer intends to resell. Purchases of inventory, for instance, in such states should be exempt.
- Manufacturing: many states exempt transfers of property used or consumed in manufacturing. This should include raw materials and equipment used by a target manufacturer.
- Transaction: other states exempt property sold as part of particular transactions, including incorporations, liquidations and reorganizations.

Employers

As a general rule, acquirers are not liable for target's obligations to its employees in a sale of assets transaction. In stock purchases, target, as in previous cases, remains liable, since only its shareholders have changed, while its obligations have not changed. In mergers and consolidations, the surviving company may be liable in certain circumstances for the dissolved company's obligations to its employees.

Discrimination Claims

What effect does the acquisition have on target's liability for discrimination claims? As with general liability, a stock acquisition will have no effect—as long as target continues in existence. More difficult are cases where target is the subject of a merger or asset sale and ceases to exist. The basic principle of general liability is that, having ceased to exist, it can no longer be liable for claims, including discriminatory ones. This can impose a hardship on employees who have been discriminated against. They may be deprived of assets to recover against, since they have been transferred to a new owner, with value paid to the former shareholders. The courts are willing to impose general liability in certain instances to prevent such injustice.

Will they do the same in discriminatory claims? Courts have looked at two previously discussed factors before imposing such liability—substantial continuity and notice to acquirer of the potential liability.[17]

Collective Bargaining Agreements

There are two issues under collective bargaining agreements that acquirers must consider. First, can target's employees block the proposed sale? Target's collective bargaining agreements may be silent or specifically address the issue. When silent, most cases have not implied a right of unions to object.[18]

Express language will usually state whether the union's approval must be obtained for asset sales, mergers or consolidations. The approval may be blanket—that is, covering all such transactions—or may be limited to instances where a certain number of employees will be laid off as a result of the transaction. Although federal law controls questions concerning union rights, state law governs interpretations of whether there has been an assumption.[19]

In some cases, employees are awarded a **tin parachute** if control of the company occurs without board of directors' approval. The parachute is usually worth several month's of salary. While this provision does not mean acquirer must obtain consent of target's employees, it does mean that the acquisition will be considerably more expensive.

Second, can acquirer avoid responsibility for target's collective bargaining agreements? A buyer of assets is generally not bound by target's existing collective bargaining agreements.[20] There are two exceptions:

- Acquirer expressly or impliedly agrees to assume the contract.
- Acquirer hires a majority of target's employees.[21]

Often, these are described in the terms discussed above as a continuity of target's business by acquirer. Therefore, if acquirer is not assuming target's employment contracts, at the time of the closing it should announce this fact to the employees.

State Protections

Many states have passed legislation protecting employees in acquisitions. Delaware, for instance, allows employees to sue for unpaid wages. The state department of labor is also given the right to sue on behalf of employees injured by the acquisition.[22] Under California law, accrued but unused vacation time is the seller's retained employment obligation.[23]

Worker Adjustment and Retraining Notification (WARN) Act

The WARN Act[24] is a federal plant closing statute. It applies to employers with 100 or more employees that intend to close a plant, have a mass layoff, or have an employment loss. **Plant closing** is a permanent or temporary shutdown of a single employment site if it results in an employment loss for 50 or more employees. It also applies to **mass layoffs**, which means a reduction in force of 33 percent of the employees and at least 500 employees. **Employment loss** is a layoff for more than 6 months or a 50 percent reduction in work.

Under WARN Act, employers must give 60-day notice before a plant closing or mass layoff.[25] Exception is granted to companies actively seeking capital during that period, if the notice would eliminate any chance of raising the money.

Employers who order plant closings or mass layoffs in violation of the law are liable to injured employees for one day of back pay for each day of violation, plus benefits under employee benefit plans. Back pay is calculated at the higher of the average wage during the last three years or the final wage. Employers are also liable for a civil penalty of up to $500 for each day of violation.[26]

In cases of acquisitions, target is responsible for giving notice of any plant closing or mass layoff but only up to the closing. Thereafter, acquirer is responsible. Employees of target on the sale date are considered employees of acquirer.

Pension Plans

The Employee Retirement Income Security Act of 1974 (ERISA)[27] contains detailed rules on successor liability for pension plans. ERISA covers defined benefit pension plans and defined contribution plans.

Defined benefit pension plans reflect promises to pay retiring employees a stated accrued sum. The amount is usually an annuity paid monthly and calculated in accordance with a formula. Contributions are based on actuarial calculations reflecting salary levels, estimated investment return, mortality and turnover. Any investment risk remains with employer.

Defined contribution plans reflect promises to pay workers at either retirement or earlier termination of employment the amounts accumulated. Any investment risk is borne by participants.

If the defined benefit pension or contribution plan meets certain requirements under Internal Revenue Code (IRC),[28] it is tax-qualified. This means employees do not have to recognize taxable income until benefits are distributed, including investment income on their contributions. Employers, on the other hand, can deduct when they made any contributions to the plan—up to certain maximum levels. These rules enable employers and employees to enjoy the tax advantages.

Acquirers must evaluate target's pension plans before completing the transaction. Defined benefit pension plans are liabilities of target and can be significant, if not fully, funded at closing. Target may also be liable for tax penalties if it has not adequately funded its pension plan, since the plan would not have been qualified and its deductions for contributions would not have been eligible.

To protect employees of terminated plans, the Pension Benefit Guaranty Corporation (PBGC), a federal agency, guarantees vested benefits. If the plan has not been adequately funded to pay the amounts due, the PBGC has the right to sue employers to recover any shortfall that it funded.[29]

Unless target's collective bargaining agreement provides otherwise, acquirers have a choice on whether to assume target's plan or not. If acquirer decides not to assume the plan, what it must do depends on the type of acquisition. In a merger or stock acquisition, target terminates the plan prior to the closing. In an asset acquisition, target terminates its plan after the acquisition.

For the most part, acquirers not assuming target's pension plan are not liable. There are exceptions. In statutory mergers and stock purchases, if the pension plan was underfunded and terminated prior to the acquisition, acquirers are liable for both the underfunding and tax liabilities for the underfunding. In asset purchases, acquirer is liable if the primary purpose of the acquisition was to avoid ERISA or IRS liability, or the transaction is a fraudulent conveyance, bulk sale, or de facto merger[30]

To avoid these risks, as noted above, most acquirers in asset sales have target terminate its pension plan after the closing.

On the other hand, acquirer might assume target's assets and liabilities, which includes its pension plan, and then terminate the plan. In such cases, acquirer is liable for the plan. Target's liability in such cases depends on the type of transaction if the plan is underfunded. In a statutory merger or stock plan, target and its former shareholders are not secondarily liable. In an asset sale, target may be secondarily liable to the PGBC, and under state law it may also be liable as a fraudulent conveyance.

In multi-employer plans—as the name implies, plans to which two or more unaffiliated companies contribute under collective bargaining agreements[31]—an asset sale is deemed to be a termination by target unless acquirer elects to continue the plan for five years and posts a bond. In the acquisition agreement, target must agree to be secondarily liable during this period and also post a bond. The PGBC can grant waivers of these requirements if there is little chance of underfunding during the five-year period.[32]

There is one more scenario to consider. Suppose the pension plan is overfunded and acquirer purchases target's assets and liabilities, including the plan. After closing, can acquirer terminate the plan and keep the excess funding? Under ERISA, it can do so if the plan expressly permits it to do so. Since 1987, before an acquirer can terminate a pension plan and keep the excess funding, it must wait five years after amending the plan to insert such expressed permission.

Unemployment Insurance and Taxes

Acquirer is liable for any contribution, interest or penalties owed by target to the state unemployment fund.[33] It is also liable for federal income and social security taxes owed by target during the year in which the transaction takes place. It is important to obtain not only a representation that all such amounts have been paid, but also, when possible, confirmation from the state government.

Creditors

The interests of creditors are protected by the agreement they have with the borrower. Those rights are supplemented by statute.

An example of the interplay of these two types of protections occurred in the 1980s. Some creditors argued that highly leveraged acquisitions, primarily LBOs, drastically increased their risks by relying mostly on debt to finance the LBO and thus reducing the equity cushion. In addition, they argued that the LBO misappropriated target's assets in order to finance the LBO and distributed any excess to selling shareholders. In their view, this breached the company's written covenants and fiduciary duty to lenders. The most famous case involved bondholders of RJR Nabisco, Inc. The courts rejected their claims. They found no breach of a covenant in the bonds and did not believe the company owed the sophisticated lenders any duties other than what was set forth in the bonds.[34]

Failing to find relief in the courts, lenders turned back to their loan documents and inserted **poison put covenants**. These covenants grant investors the right to sell the bonds back to the issuer—possibly at a premium—if a triggering event, such as a merger or acquisition, occurs. Another approach was to increase the interest on the occurrence of a triggering event.

In response to the problem, many states also adopted **constituency statutes** that permit directors to consider the interests of target's constituencies other than shareholders. Directors are not required to do so, however.[35] Constituencies include creditors as well as others such as employees, suppliers, customers and communities. Some states require directors to treat all constituencies equal and without preference.

Greater statutory protection for creditors can be found in dividend restrictions, fraudulent conveyance rules, bulk sale laws and lease terms.

Dividend Restrictions and Redemption

The earliest statutory protections for creditors were dividend restriction and redemption of stock. These protections attempted to balance conflicting viewpoints. On the one hand, while debt is outstanding, it is reasonable for companies to make distributions to shareholders or redeem stock under certain conditions. It would be unreasonable to make shareholders wait until all debt is paid off, since companies usually have some debt outstanding. On the other hand, it would not be reasonable to allow excessive dividends that impair a company's value.

The solution is that most state corporate statutes prohibit distributions if the company is or would be rendered insolvent. These are called legal capital statutes.[36] Insolvency is tested in two ways: (1) can debtor pay its creditors on time, or (2) are its assets greater than its liabilities. This two-part test traces its history back to the dual structure of equity and law that existed in English courts at one time. In equity courts, insolvency was tested by whether the debtor was able to meet its obligations as they became due. This is the equity insolvency test and focuses on liquidity or cash on hand. In the law courts, the test was whether the aggregate amount of the debtor's assets was less that than its liabilities. This is the balance sheet test. The Model Act contains both tests.[37]

Fraudulent Conveyance

Most states have adopted fraudulent conveyance laws. They are based on the Uniform Fraudulent Conveyance Act[38] or the more recent Uniform Fraudulent Transfer Act (UFTA)[39]. The laws are aimed at preventing debtors from transferring assets and preventing creditors from recovering against debtors' assets. Under the laws, creditors can sue to set aside an improper transfer and obtain a lien on the transferred property.

Under Federal Bankruptcy Code, trustees in bankruptcy and debtors in possession can act on behalf of other creditors to recover assets (or their value) transferred fraudulently.[40] A trustee in bankruptcy can also rely on state fraudulent conveyance laws to cancel prebankruptcy transfers.

Under the UFTA, which has been adopted by a majority of the states, fraud can be based on actual or constructive fraud. The latter can be found if

- reasonable equivalent value was not given;
- debtor was financially weak at the time transfer was made or obligation incurred as measured by;
  - seller was or became insolvent in the balance sheet sense;
  - seller was left with unreasonably small assets for its business;
  - seller had intent to incur debts beyond its ability to pay.[41]
  - seller had intent to incur debts beyond its ability to pay.

Bulk Sales

A bulk sale is a transfer of a major part of a business' materials, supplies, merchandise or inventory, which is not in the ordinary course of business. The Uniform Commercial Code (UCC), which has been adopted in nearly every state, contains a section (Article 6) regulating bulk sales.[42]

If the bulk sale meets certain criteria, acquirer does not assume the target's liabilities. First, the target gives acquirer a list of creditors, and together they prepare an inventory of the products transferred. The acquirer must keep the list and schedule for a fixed period, such as six months, and permit inspection or file them in a public office.

Acquirer must give written notice of the proposed transfer,[43] such as 45 days before taking possession or paying for the goods being purchased. The notice must be given to creditors on the list provided by the target, unless the number of creditors is too numerous, in which case public notice in a local newspaper is sufficient.

Second, acquirer must assure that consideration being paid is applied to target's debts listed on the creditors' schedule provided to it. The amount paid does not have to cover the debts. If not, debts must be paid on a pro rata basis.

The UCC does not apply to transfers if acquirer agrees to be liable for target's debts. Target must be solvent after the transfer. Also exempted is a transfer to a new business organized to take over and continue the business, which assumes target's liabilities. In both cases, notices of such an assumption must be published once a week for two consecutive weeks in a general circulation newspaper. The paper must be circulated where target had its principal place of business and must include the names and addresses of target and acquirer and the effective date of transfer.

In 1988, the National Conference of Commissioners on Uniform State Laws, now known as the Uniform Law Commissioners (ULC), and the American Law Institute (ALI) recommended that states repeal Article 6 of the UCC since bulk sale rules were unnecessary due to changes in business and legal practices. In 1996, Delaware repealed its Bulk Transfers code sections.[44] Other states followed. For states wishing to continue regulating bulk sales, ULC and ALI a revised Article 6 was proposed. To date, only a few states have adopted the new rules.

In light of there being two versions of Article 6 and some states having revoked their adoption, it is particularly important for companies involved in mergers and acquisitions to check relevant state rules.

Lender Liability

In most acquisitions, most of the financing will come from lenders. If the acquisition is not successful and lenders take over management of acquirer, they could become responsible for target's liabilities. This theory is called lender liability.

Lease Terms

Lease terms provide the primary protection for lessors. They will establish minimum periods for the lease. Alternatively, they might permit early termination, that is, before a previously scheduled date of termination, but only on the payment of a penalty. In cases of an asset acquisition, the lease might prohibit such transfer, require lessor's approval or require the payment of an assignment fee. The same three alternatives—prohibition, approval or fee—might even apply in case of a stock acquisition.

Shareholders

In this section, we look at target and acquirer's shareholders and what their role is during the acquisition stage. The first area we consider is when their approval of the transaction is required. Governing law or rules of exchange where the company's stock is traded might require approval by target or acquirer's shareholders. The two related questions that must be considered are: (1) When is such approval required?, and (2) What percentage of approval is necessary?

Approval Required by Statute

Corporations are creations of the state. They are created under state law. Therefore, the rights of corporations and their stockholders are primarily a reflection of the state's laws.

In the area of approval of acquisitions the ability of stockholders to vote depends on the type of transaction.

In stock purchases a separate vote of target's shareholders is not required, since target is not a party to the transaction. Acquirer is dealing directly with target's shareholders, and they vote on an individual basis when they decide to sell or not.

Complicating this answer, however, are **control share acquisition statutes**, which began to be adopted by states in the 1980s as antitakeover devices.[45] These laws do not prevent takeovers; they merely limit acquirer's ability to vote the shares it acquires unless the acquisition has been approved by a majority of target's disinterested shares.

Other than short-form mergers where an owner of a very high percentage such as 90 percent seeks to force out the remaining shareholders, generally the shareholders of both companies in a merger must approve the transaction. This also applies in cases of transactions structured in another form, but a court finds are de facto mergers.[46]

Although traditionally the approval of all shareholders was required, at present the usual rule is a majority of outstanding shares. In some states, a two-thirds approval is required.

There are two exceptions. First, in some states acquirer does not have to obtain its shareholders' approval if acquirer is not issuing stock and merger will not necessitate a change in its certificate of incorporation or the shares held by its shareholders[47]

Second, some companies have supermajority requirements. For instance in a merger with an interested shareholder or its affiliate, approval may be required by a very high percent, such as 80 percent of target's shareholders or a majority of its disinterested shareholders. Under some state's **fair price provisions**[48] these supermajority requirements only apply when a fair price is not received. Under

freeze statutes[49] any business combination between target and an interested shareholder or an affiliate is prohibited for a long period, such as five years, unless the acquisition was approved by target's board of directors before the interested shareholder purchased its shares in target.

In asset purchases, approval of target's shareholders is required in all states when substantially all assets are being acquired. Approval of acquirer's shareholders is generally not required.

In share exchanges (or stock purchase binding on all target stockholders if the required number of stockholders have approved) approval of target's shareholders but not of acquirer, is generally required.

If these requirements are not met, the underlying transaction is invalid.

Approval Required by Stock Exchanges

Before issuing common stock, many stock exchanges require that companies listed by them obtain the approval of their stockholders. The New York Stock Exchange (NYSE) and American Stock Exchanges (AMEX), as well as the National Association of Securities (NASD) require that issuers listed on them or on NASD's automated quotation system, NASDAQ, obtain such approval. The requirements apply to both acquirers and targets.

The NYSE requirements apply to all issuance of common stock or securities convertible into common stock if

- amount of stock will have at least 20 percent of the voting power;
- there will be a change of control of acquirer;
- property is being acquired from a director, officer or substantial security holder.[50]

There are exceptions for financially troubled companies and re-issuance of treasury stock, that is, stock that had been issued and reacquired by the company.

The NYSE rules apply to asset purchases, stock purchases and mergers, and require majority approval of the shares voted, not of those entitled to vote, as long as 50 percent voted.

AMEX has a similar rule: 50 percent of the shares voting, although the quorum depends on issuer's bylaws.[51]

In 1989, NASD adopted rules similar to the NYSE. For listing securities on NASDAQ, shareholder approval is required of

- acquisitions of assets, securities, business or companies that increase common stock by 20 percent;
- increase in the common stock or voting power of at least 5 percent by a substantial stockholder holding 5 percent interest in acquirer;

- actions that result in a change of control, and issuance of common stock representing 20 percent or more of common stock or voting power at less than the greater of book or market value.[52]

Beyond effect on stock, control or voting impact, stock exchange rules may also require shareholder approval in other cases, such as an amendment of a certificate of incorporation to increase number of shares, a name change of acquirer or an adoption of a new stock benefit plan.

Unlike the statutory approval discussed above, the transaction is not invalid if the requirements are not met. Instead, the company's stock will be delisted from the exchange or NASDAQ. In some cases, the delisting might be an acceptable cost.

Approval of Parent Company

Suppose a parent company is selling a subsidiary, whose approval is required? Whether a sale of all or substantially all assets, a stock sale or a merger, approval must be obtained from the boards of directors of both companies and from shareholders of the subsidiary other than the parent company.

In addition, if the subsidiary is a substantial asset or the parent's sole asset, then the sale of the subsidiary is a sale of all or substantially all of parent's assets. Whether parent stockholder approval is required depends on the type of transaction.

- In a stock sale, approval of the parent's stockholders is required.
- In an asset sale, however, less than half the states require such approval since a physical asset has only been exchanged for another—cash. Some writers have argued that parent shareholder approval should be obtained even in asset sales.
- In a merger, parent stockholder approval is probably required if a sale is involved, since it would constitute a sale of all or substantially all its assets.

Appraisal Rights

Appraisal rights are also called dissenters rights or dissenters appraisal rights. Their original purpose was to protect minority shareholders and give them a chance to get their money back if the company they had been invested in was sold, merged or if a fundamental change was taking place. The rights are granted by statute and enable shareholders to receive the cash value of their stock rather than participate in an asset acquisition, stock acquisition or merger.

These rights usually track voting rights. This has three implications. First, a shareholder is unlikely to have appraisal rights unless it or its class can vote on the transaction. Second, the shareholder seeking to exercise its appraisal rights must not have voted in favor of the acquisition. In some states, it must have voted against it. Third, the holder can seek appraisal only for all its shares, not a part of it.

Appraisal rights of target's shareholders depend on the type of transaction.

- In a stock sale, there is no such right. Instead, the shareholders vote when they decide to sell or not.
- In a binding share exchange, appraisal rights apply.
- In an asset sale, most states grant appraisal rights to target's shareholders, particularly if the sale is not in the ordinary course of business. Some states and the Revised Model Business Corporation Act, deny appraisal rights if target receives cash and the cash is distributed within one year to shareholders.[53]
- In a merger, appraisal rights will generally be available to target's shareholders. A few states give the surviving stockholders appraisal rights.

Many states have established the **market out** exception to appraisal rights.[54] It applies to companies with stock listed on a national securities exchange or with more than a certain number of stockholders. The belief is that their stockholders already have appraisal rights and they can sell their shares on the market and get their money out.

In recent years, a number of commentators have criticized appraisal rights and questioned whether they achieve their purpose. Some states have begun to reconsider them.

The method of appraisal has been a difficult issue for states and courts. Under Delaware law, shareholders must be given 20 days' notice. Dissenters must notify the company of their objection before the shareholders vote on the transaction. Within 10 days of the acquisition or merger being approved, the company must notify dissenters of their right to exercise their appraisal rights. The dissenters then have 20 days to demand appraisal of their shares. If they are unsatisfied with the appraisal they can file a petition in the court of chancery within 120 days of the transaction, asking for a value determination. A trial on the valuation could take several years.[55]

The Model Act adopts a different approach and tries to get money to the dissenter faster. The dissenter must demand purchase of its shares before the transaction occurs. The corporation must notify the dissenters of its willingness to purchase the dissenter's shares within 10 days of the acquisition or merger being approved. If the dissenter then demands payment, the corporation must pay the fair market value. If dissatisfied with the amount offered, the dissenter can counter with its offer within 30 days. The company must pay this amount or petition the court for a determination.[56]

States are also divided on whether dissenters should benefit from the impact of the acquisition or merger on their shares. Is the value to be paid to the dissenter fixed as of a date before any announcement of the acquisition or merger, and thus at a lower price, or after the transaction is announced, meaning after target's stock rises? Some statutes provide a specific answer to this question. In other states, the courts have provided the answer.

Controlling Shareholders

Controlling shareholder issues arise in two cases: (1) when controlling shareholders sell their controlling interest to acquirer and (2) when acquirers become controlling shareholders. In both cases, their dealings with minority shareholders raise legal issues.

Selling Controlling Interest

The courts have paid careful attention to controlling shareholders who sell their majority interest in target knowing acquirer is likely to strip or loot target of its assets. This is likely to happen if the transaction is a highly leveraged asset acquisition, which means acquirer has borrowed a great deal to finance it. Acquirer might need to strip target of some of its assets to pay for the acquisition. The assets may be cash or noncash assets.

Initially, the courts did not feel that a controlling shareholder owed any duty to target or minority shareholders of target when selling its shares. More modern cases, however, require controlling shareholders to exercise good faith and fairness toward target and its shareholders.[57] This obligation is often summarized as having two aspects—fair dealing and fair price.[58] If controlling shareholders selling their interests possess facts that would put a prudent person on its guard that a potential buyer of its shares might loot target, it must conduct a reasonably adequate investigation.

Over the years, the courts have expanded the obligations of controlling shareholders to not loot the company,[59] not convert or seize for themselves a corporate opportunity that the company had,[60] and not commit fraud or other acts of bad faith.[61] The courts have not required controlling shareholders to share with minority shareholders any premium they receive for their shares from acquirer over the prevailing market price.[62]

On the other hand, the courts have long held that a controlling shareholder cannot sell an officer position or board position to an outsider. It can, however, sell its shares, which might entitle the holder to elect an officer or board member.[63]

Acquiring Controlling Interest

Now, let's consider the reverse situation—actions by acquiring company's shareholders rather than target's shareholders.

In highly leveraged asset acquisitions, as noted, acquirer might need cash to finance its purchase. If acquirer is the only shareholder of target, it will be relatively simple to distribute the needed asset as a dividend. The difficulty occurs when there are minority shareholders, since acquirer does not want to share or lose any of the asset value.

There are two methods available to isolate such assets from the minority shareholders. In a **freeze-in**, acquirer as the majority shareholder of target will transfer value to itself from target in various forms—lease payments, salaries, consulting or management fees. The difficulty is that it takes time to make such distributions and only a reasonable amount of assets may be withdrawn at a time. For a highly leveraged deal with immediate cash needs, a fair amount over a reasonable time may be too late.

In a **freeze-out**, acquirer forces out target's minority shareholders, paying them something other than cash, such as notes or preferred stock of acquirer. In cases that have considered the validity of such actions, courts have looked to see if they violate the fiduciary obligations owed by majority shareholders to minority shareholders, especially where the majority stockholder holds a board position. The courts have required the freeze-out to have a legitimate corporate purpose.[64]

Establishing fairness has depended on whether the minority shareholders received reasonable consideration. Interpreting reasonableness has not been easy. One theory is that the consideration need only be a substantial equivalent in value to what they had before the merger. This is called the **give-get test**.[65] Others have required a proportional sharing with the minority shareholders of the increase in value created by the merger.

Boards of Directors

The necessity of board approval depends on the type of transaction.

- In asset purchases, including sale of a subsidiary, target must usually obtain approval of its board. This will be required by statute for a sale of all or substantially all of its assets or not in the ordinary course of business. For acquirer, board approval will usually be required if it is material.
- In stock purchases, board approval of acquirer and each corporate selling shareholder will be required if the transaction is material to it. The board of target must also approve the transaction if target is a party to the agreement.
- In mergers, the boards of both parties must approve. In forward or reverse subsidiary mergers, board approval of the parent will also be obtained if the parent is a party to the agreement or issues its securities to finance the transaction.
- In binding share exchanges, approvals of boards of both companies will be obtained.

While actions of both acquirer's and target's board of directors may be reviewed by the courts, the courts are more likely to consider decisions of target's board.

Tests

Traditionally, directors were held to two standards. Depending on the state, they are based on common law, statute or a combination.

- **Duty of care** under which directors prior to making a business decision have a duty to inform themselves of all material information reasonably available to them.[66] Having informed themselves, they must act with requisite care in discharging their duties. This includes informing themselves of alternatives. Some jurisdictions interpret this rule as requiring directors to exercise the care of an ordinarily prudent person. Many states include a negligence standard, while others apply a gross negligence rule. Some writers have argued that there is little difference between the two.
- **Duty of loyalty** under which directors have an affirmative duty to protect the interests of the company and an obligation to refrain from conduct that would injure the company or its shareholders or deprive them of a profit or advantage.[67] Examples include fraud, bad faith, self-dealing, and action designed to remain in office.

  Delaware has interpreted this duty to mean that directors must be independent and disinterested.[68] Independence means the director's action must be based on the corporate merits of the transaction. Disinterested means directors cannot be on both sides of a transaction or derive personal financial benefit other than what shareholders receive. In measuring disinterest, the test is subjective—was the particular director affected by self-interest when considering a transaction? It need not be a cash benefit. Goodwill, such as wishing to get in someone's good graces, has been sufficient.

  Directors who are not disinterested should not vote or consider an acquisition. Instead, the matter should be referred to a committee of disinterested directors. This usually means outside directors, as discussed below.

  Many states have applied a good faith standard to this duty. This usually means that there must be a plausible business purpose.[69]

  This duty does not require that directors comply with the wishes of the majority of directors. They might make their own decisions based on their own evaluation.
- **Duty of good faith**, which Delaware courts have interpreted as being different from duties of care and loyalty and applied to severe and deliberate duty

of care violations. The significance is that unlike the other duties, violators cannot be indemnified by the company for their actions.[70]

More recent than duties of care and loyalty, states and courts have turned to the business judgment rule when reviewing the actions of directors. In the 1980s, this rule was interpreted and extended in many cases involving leading takeover specialists.

- **Business judgment rule** (*Smith v. Van Gorkom* case[71] involving Jay Pritzker) under which directors are presumed to have acted on an informed basis, in good faith, and in the honest belief the action was taken in the best interests of the company. This is the reverse of the duty of care, since the courts presume the directors have acted correctly. Under this rule, prior to making the decision, directors must inform themselves of all material information reasonably available to them. It has been interpreted in the nature of a duty of care. Directors' actions may not be the result of fraud, gross negligence, bad faith or self-dealing.

  Since it is presumed that directors reached their business judgment in good faith, the plaintiff must overcome this presumption by proving lack of due care, bad faith or intention to maintain their board positions.

  Applying this test to mergers, directors must act in an informed and deliberate manner in determining whether to approve a merger agreement before submitting it to shareholders. They cannot defer to the shareholders to approve the agreement or not. The board must play an active role in structuring, negotiating and evaluating the proposal.

  In the typical acquisition not involving a hostile tender offer, the board cannot rely on internal estimates of value, yet it need not go so far as to actively solicit other bids or conduct an auction. It should be sufficient for the board to informally solicit potential acquirers. Lock-ups—agreements not to negotiate with other parties—and high termination fees—charged if target negotiates with someone else—are acceptable if the board reasonably believes the transaction is in the best available or the price is the highest value reasonably available under the circumstances. Similarly, the board does not need the right to back out of the acquisition agreement with the first acquirer if a second, higher bid is received, but it should have the right to withdraw its recommendation to shareholders if such a bid is received. Valuation to confirm director's decision can occur after signing the agreement. To conduct a meaningful valuation, directors must have the ability to show confidential business information to potential bidders.

- **Enhanced business judgment rule** (*Unocal v. Mesa Petroleum* case [72] and T. Boone Pickens) under which the court shifted the burden of proof to the board when faced with a hostile tender offer. Before the court can apply the business judgement rule, the board must show reasonable grounds for believing a danger existed to corporate policy and effectiveness and that the defensive action was reasonable. The first part of the presumption can be shown by good faith, while the second is shown by a review of the competing tender offers. After establishing both parts of the presumption, the burden of proof shifts to the plaintiff under the business judgment rule.

- **Fair auction test** (*Revlon v. MacAndrews* case[73] with Ron Perelman) limited the business judgment rule in auctions. If an auction is held with bidders making relatively similar offers or dissolution of the company becomes inevitable, directors cannot show favoritism for a white knight to the exclusion of a hostile bidder, even when the hostile bidder's offer adversely affects shareholders' interests. In such instances, market forces must be allowed to operate freely to bring target's shareholders the best price available. Under this rule, it is often said that the board must maximize short-term profits, meaning get the highest price obtainable.

  Applying this test to competing tender offers, a board cannot grant a lock-up option to one bidder over another for only a slight increase in price. The directors must show that the lock-up provides the greatest short-term value, is advantageous to shareholders, was worth the grant, and did not deter higher competing bids. Its decision does not have to be correct, only reasonable.

  The auction itself must be conducted fairly and is subject to the business judgment rule. This means, for instance, that both bidders must be given the same confidential financial information.

- **Intrinsic fairness test** (*Mills Acquisition v. MacMillan* case[74] with Robert Maxwell, the Bass Group and KKR, an investment firm specializing in leveraged buyouts) under which directors are not required to conduct an auction according to any standards, but once they do so it must be fair. The plaintiff has the burden of proof to show that directors treated one or more of the bidders unequally.

  The courts continue to expand the application of these tests. In *Roberts v. General Instrument Corp,*[75] a Delaware lower court extended the fairness test to privately negotiated nonauction transactions if a competing bid is subsequently received. In *Paramount Communications Inc. v. QVC Network Inc.*[76] the court applied the fairness test to a nonauction when a change in control occurs.

  In mergers between two companies of equivalent size, the courts have indicated that they will not impose the higher fairness tests. They continue to apply the duty of care standard. This means that the board must fully investigate the transaction and, before approving it, determine that it is in the best interests of stockholders. Lock-up devices can be used in such cases, and board members are not required to abandon the merger even if a tender offer is received.

  The courts have been willing to extend the fairness test to preferred shareholders. Even when being cashed out in a merger, nonvoting preferred shares cannot vote on the merger. Without such court protection, they have no right to a fair allocation of the merger price but must rely on the limited distribution rights granted to them under their stock.

In summary, particularly where there are competing tender offers or auctions, the courts are moving from a duty of care under which the price must not be reckless to a higher standard that requires the highest price obtainable. Failure to comply with this standard will enable disgruntled shareholders or disappointed bidders to seek damages based on the value of the company at the time of the judgment.

Independent Directors

In takeovers, many boards appoint a special committee of outside directors to evaluate tenders. If such a committee is appointed, the plaintiff rather than the board has the burden of proving fairness under the fairness tests used by many courts.[77]

Opinions are divided on the effectiveness of such committees. Peter Drucker, a leading management consultant, believes most boards, much less independent boards and directors, are "impotent ceremonial and legal fiction" and certainly [do] "not conduct the affairs of the enterprise."[78] He and others believe that boards are more likely to rubber stamp the actions of management. One case found that the committee of outside directors functioned as little more than a charade.

Other writers have argued that such committees function quite independently and adversarially. In the RJR Nabisco buy-out, the board acted energetically and exercised informed and independent judgment. The courts gave great weight to their decision. To ensure such independence, the Sarbanes-Oxley Act of 2002[79] requires that companies listed on national security exchanges have audit committees composed of independent directors.

To receive the benefit of this test, the independent special committee must be composed of independent directors. Interested directors must not appoint them. The independent directors, in turn, should appoint their own outside advisors, such as independent investment bankers and attorneys not previously involved in the proposed transaction. Their advisors must give them a clear understanding of the new role they play and the degree of independence from other board members that they must exercise.

In conclusion, in an acquisition, there are many things directors can do to perform their duties and meet the tests applied by the courts:

- Take time to consider actions. This includes reasonable prior notice of meetings, prior distribution of materials, and time to review.

- Hold several meetings. Courts are less likely to believe that the board has adequately reviewed the transaction if they do so at only one meeting.
- Exclude interested directors from discussions. If necessary, a special committee of independent outside directors should be organized.
- Require detailed reports from management on the transaction, including background and meetings with acquirer.
- Have independent advisors review the transaction with the board. On the record, positive and negative factors should be discussed, and special features should be carefully explained and discussed.
- Consider and discuss alternatives.
- Distribute and discuss detailed financial statements, especially valuation and fairness of price.
- Obtain outside opinion on fairness of price (fairness opinion).[80]

Protection, Waiver and Insurance

To reduce their exposure in approving acquisitions, many boards now require **fairness opinions** from investment bankers. Independent directors are especially fond of such opinions as support for their decisions.

Unfortunately, even such opinions are not always sufficient to protect directors from liability. In response to the above cases and what was perceived as courts second guessing directors, many states adopted laws allowing corporations to release directors from liability for decisions they made in acquisitions.

Many states and corporate bylaws also allow companies to indemnify directors for their actions in general. Many go further and authorize companies to purchase director and officer liability insurance. In the 1980s, the cost of such insurance rose dramatically, reflecting the perceived increased liability of directors. In the mid-2000s, however, the rates began to decrease somewhat as more companies began to offer such insurance. Regardless of cost, many companies have such insurance. Many outside directors refuse to—and the firms they work for will not allow them to—join boards without such insurance.

Liability to Acquirers

In some states, directors can be liable to more than their shareholders. In broken deals, they can sometimes be liable to the frustrated acquirer.

To be liable, they must first have the right to bind the company without shareholder approval. If they have that right most states will allow them to enter into exclusive merger agreements under which they agree not to negotiate with other parties. Even though subsequent market conditions might increase the value of the company, courts are unlikely to second-guess the board. Courts usually feel it is up to the board to determine the best contract at a given time.

Since such agreements can be binding on the company, directors can be held liable for breach of them if they negotiate with another bidder or refuse to submit the present proposal to the shareholders for their approval. The most famous case in this area is the *Texaco v. Pennzoil* case in which the jury found a binding agreement between sellers of Getty Oil and Pennzoil as buyer and that Texaco had knowingly interfered with the agreement.[81]

A few states, however, have held that notwithstanding binding merger agreements, directors must exercise their fiduciary duty to target if a subsequent tender is received.

Other Parties—Managers, ESOP and Third Parties

Beyond successors, employers, creditors, shareholders and boards of directors, the role and consent of others may be critical to the success of the acquisition. In this section we look at managers and others, such as lessors, lenders, suppliers, customers and government agencies.

Managers

The courts have been reluctant to impose restrictions on the ability of managers to undertake acquisitions. The courts have relied on the **business judgment rule**, as discussed above, and refused to prevent the acquisition unless they could find fraud there. Mere inadequacy of price was not enough to show fraud.

Investment Bankers

In a previous section, I noted that many boards request fairness opinions from investment bankers to confirm that acquisitions are fair. In a few cases, investment bankers have been held liable for issuing fairness opinions without a reasonable basis. The courts have pointed out that investment bankers should have been aware that their opinions would be used to help boards and shareholders decide on the fairness of an offer.[82] If acquirer's offer was not fair, bankers who express a fairness opinion can be liable to shareholders.

ESOP Trustees

If the company has established an employee stock ownership plan (ESOP) to hold shares in the company, the trustees of such plans must be careful when evaluating tender offers—whether friendly or hostile. They are not required to automatically tender shares because the tender price is above the current stock market price.

Trustees can exercise prudence and decide what is in the economic best interest of a plan's participants and beneficiaries. Trustees must evaluate tender offers based on their merits. They can weigh the tender offer against the underlying intrinsic value of target and the likelihood of that value being realized by present management or a future tender offer. They can also weigh the long-term value of the company against the tender offer and ability to invest proceeds elsewhere.

The trustees must transfer shares as instructed by holders of such shares. Shares for which the trustees do not receive instructions must remain invested in the company's common stock. Trustees must also transfer to acquirer a percentage of the unallocated shares (those that have not yet been allocated to specific employees) equal to the percentage of the allocated shares for which they received instructions to transfer to acquirer.

In all their actions, trustees must act as fiduciaries. Nevertheless, if the plan provides that assets are to be managed by a specific person or investment manager, trustees can defer to such persons. This means that a plan might grant participants the authority to instruct trustees what to do regarding tenders.

Under its plan asset rules, the Department of Labor has stated that it will be particularly watchful of attempts by management to use plan assets as offensive or defensive tools in tender offers. The Department of Labor feels that such actions would violate the requirement that pension funds be managed solely in the interest of plan participants and beneficiaries.[83]

Third Parties

Target will be a party to many contracts, possibly hundreds or thousands depending on its size. Many may be material to its business. Equipment and land may even be leased. Relationships with suppliers and customers will usually be reflected in agreements. Loan agreements are important to fund its ongoing operations. Acquirer will want to make certain that these contracts are still in effect after the transaction is completed. Whether they are in effect or not depends on the type of transaction and the wording of the contracts.

In a stock purchase, target remains in existence. Only the stockholders change. Unless the agreement prevents changes in control, the transaction will not affect such agreements.

In direct mergers and forward subsidiary mergers, target merges into acquirer or its subsidiary. The survivor succeeds to the assets and liabilities of the subsidiary. The effect on a third party agreement depends on the agreement's terms.

- If the agreement prohibits an assignment, some courts have not permitted the prohibition to apply to assignments by law in mergers, while some courts have permitted it. Even when the prohibition applies, in the view of most courts, the third party cannot unreasonably withhold its consent.
- If the agreement prohibits any merger, the third party's consent would be required for direct mergers, forward subsidiary mergers and reverse subsidiary mergers.
- If the agreement prohibits any change of control, all acquisitions involving a change of control would be prohibited.

In an asset sale, target's assets and businesses are transferred to acquirer. In most states, such transfers would require the consent of the other parties to target's agreements, particularly if the agreement prohibits any transfers of the asset. Under the Model Business Corporation Act[84], if acquirer succeeds to the ownership of target's assets and target disappears, the transaction is not deemed to be a transfer or assignment necessitating the consent of other parties.

While in a later section I discuss governmental consent to acquisitions under the antitrust laws, the need for other government consents should not be ignored. Target might also possess key government licenses, permits, approvals, patents, copyrights, trademarks or trade names. Acquirer must investigate what consents are needed for each and be certain to obtain each. For instance, a government contract might require consent under the same rules described with other third parties, or the applicable statute might require government consent.

3

Legal: Part 2

In Chapter 2, I described a number of legal issues that impact mergers and acquisitions, including rights and responsibilities of successors, creditors, shareholders, boards, controlling parties and employees. In this chapter, I focus on specific sectors, including securities, anti-takeover, antitrust and industries rules.

Securities

Under the Securities Act of 1933,[1] all securities issued or sold must be registered or qualify for an exemption. Under the Securities Exchange Act of 1934,[2] companies must register if they have assets exceeding $1 million and 500 or more shareholders. States also have laws regulating securities.

These laws can affect the structure and timing of an acquisition. It is important, therefore, for securities laws to be considered early in the process if stock is to be issued. If so, the possibility of an exemption must be evaluated. If none exists, security must be registered or in some states qualified.

1933 Securities Act

Under Rule 145 by the Securities Exchange Commission (SEC), mergers, consolidations, asset acquisitions and securities reclassifications are considered sales of securities if they are submitted to shareholders for approval and a distribution follows that approval.[3] This means several types of acquisitions are covered by Rule 145.

For instance, in a stock for stock exchange, acquirer issues its stock to target as consideration, and target sells its stock to acquirer. Both transactions must be studied for compliance with securities laws. In a stock for assets exchange, acquirer's issuance of stock to target must comply with securities laws.

Similarly, an earn-out—that is, a delayed payment of a part of the purchase price based on target's operation after the closing—may be a security. Securities laws might also apply to submissions to shareholders for their approval of a merger or consolidation or stock for assets exchange, followed by target's dissolution.

Rule 145 also allows companies to place securities **on the shelf** by preregistering securities in advance of acquisition. In such cases, an amendment must be filed containing information on target and transaction.

In the following sections, I describe rules applicable to securities issued by an acquirer and restrictions on what target can do with securities it receives.

Exemptions for Acquirers

Not all securities issued by acquirer must be registered under the 1933 act and under regulations issued by the SEC. It need not register in the following instances:

Accredited Investors under Section 4(6)[4]
Applies to sales to accredited investors if:

- aggregate offering price of securities does not exceed $5 million;
- there is no advertising or public solicitation;
- notice is filed with the SEC using Form D.

Accredited investors include:

- Bank
- Insurance company
- Investment company registered under Investment Company Act of 1940
- Business development company
- Small business investment company
- Tax exempt organization with assets of $5 million
- Director or executive officer of issuer
- Person whose net worth exceeds $1 million or income in excess of $200,00 in each the past two years and expects the same income in the present years
- Trust with assets in excess of $5 million

An offer or sale to one unaccredited investor will disqualify the offering under this exemption even when issuer believed investor was accredited.

Limited Offering under Regulation D[5]
Applies to three types of limited, nonpublic offerings and sales:

- not exceeding $1 million by nonpublic and noninvestment companies (Rule 504);
- not exceeding $5 million by noninvestment companies up to 35 purchasers, excluding accredited investors and related persons (Rule 505);
- unlimited in amount up to 35 purchasers, excluding accredited investors and related persons (Rule 506).

There are other obligations under Regulation D, including:

- Disclosure
- Limitations on offering method
- Resale limitations
- Maximum number of permissible purchasers
- Filing notice with the SEC using Form D

This exemption is based on objective standards and is therefore often called a **safe harbor** exemption.

Limited Offering under Regulation A[6]
Applies to offerings up to $5 million in a 12-month period. This exemption is not available to investment companies. Unless the offering is below $100,000 and by a seasoned and profitable issuer, an offering circular must be distributed and filed with the SEC.

Private Placement under Sections 4(2)[7]
Applies to nonpublic offerings to sophisticated purchasers able to "fend for themselves" and who have access to the kind of information which registration would disclose. Several factors are considered in determining whether this test is met:

- Number of offerees
- Relationship of offerees to issuer
- Relationship of offerees to each other
- Sophistication of offerees
- Size of offering
- Number of units offered
- Manner of offering
- Resale of units

This exemption is more subjective than the Regulation D exemption.

Government Approved under Section 3(a)(10)[8]
Applies to exchanges of securities approved by a federal or state agency or court after a hearing at which interested persons could participate. Under this exemption,

the issuance and exchange must meet the fairness test. This exemption is most likely to apply to mergers and stock-for-stock acquisitions and purchases by regulated businesses such as insurance companies. Acquirers qualifying under this exemption can resell without limitation.

Intrastate Offering under Section 3(a)(11) and Rule 147[9]

Covers sales to purchasers within the same state by a company incorporated or doing business in the state and with its principal office in the state. Doing business means a minimum of 80 percent of the company's assets and sales. In addition, at least 80 percent of the funds raised must be used in the state.

Rule 147 imposes resale restrictions of nine months and requires legends on the stock certificates limiting resale. Stop transfer orders to transfer agents for attempted violations of the Rule are also mandated. Since Rule 147 offerings must be integrated with any offers by the issuer within the past six months, offerings under this Rule could lose their exemption.

This Rule is also based on objective standards and is a safe harbor exemption.

Miscellaneous Exemptions

There are a number of other exemptions from registration by acquirers under the Securities Act:

- Securities issued by a bank
- Securities issued by a savings and loan association
- Certificates issued by a bankruptcy trustee

Filings by Acquirers

If an exemption does not exist, acquirer must file a report or notice with the SEC. The form depends on the transaction's size of offering, experience of issuer and type of transaction.

SEC Form S-1

Used by registrants if no exemption exists and no other form applies. This form does not allow any incorporation of previously filed material. It is, therefore, the most time-consuming report to be filed.

SEC Form S-2

Used by registrants:

- organized and having principal business operations in United States;

- with securities registered under Sections 12(b) or (g) of Securities Exchange Act or required to file reports under Section 15(d) of Securities Exchange Act;
- subject to requirements of Sections 12 or 15(d) of Securities Exchange Act;
- filing reports required under Sections 13, 14 or 15(d) of Securities Exchange Act for at least 36 months;
- not failing to pay dividends since the filing of its most recent report under Securities Exchange Act.

Although not as good as SEC Form S-3 in allowing incorporation by reference of information included in other filings, it does allow significant incorporation. This form cannot be used with an exchange offer for securities of another person.

SEC Form S-3
Used by the same registrants as with SEC Form S-2. In addition, the form can only be used for certain transactions, such as:

- primary offerings for cash but market value of voting stock held by nonaffiliates is $75 million or more;
- primary offerings of nonconvertible debt or preferred, investment-grade securities offered for cash;
- securities offerings with dividend, interest, reinvestment and warrants on a pro rata basis.

This form allows issuers to incorporate the greatest amount of information contained in previous filings by reference, without refiling, attaching or including the information on this form. For this reason it is the easiest to file.

SEC Form S-4
Used to register securities issued in:

- a Rule 145(a) transaction;
- a merger where state law does not require approval of security holders;
- an exchange offer for securities of issuer;
- a public re-offering or resale of securities acquired under this form.

This form requires less information than SEC Form S-1 does.

SEC Forms SB-1 and SB-2
Small business issuers with annual revenues of, and voting stock held by nonaffiliates valued at, less than $25 million can file simplified forms. SB-1 can be used for cash sales of up to $10 million in any 12-month period. SB-2 can be

used for companies that do not have financial statements complying with other SEC rules.

Restrictions on Transfer by Targets

If target received securities in payment even though target is not an issuer, it may be subject to the Securities Act or Securities Exchange Act. If so, it may not be able to resell securities it received. Let's consider a number of transactions.

Securities received in a registered offering

If target received securities issued in a registered offering, it will usually be able to sell them without restriction. This exemption does not apply if target and acquirer are affiliates unless they sell in accordance with SEC Rule 144, which is discussed below. To avoid having to rely on SEC Rule 144, many targets will insist that acquirer register any securities it receives.

SEC Rule 144[10]

If target is an affiliate of acquirer or if securities are restricted, then any resale must be in accordance with this Rule. Securities sold under this rule:

- must be held for one-year;
- are limited in the amount that can be sold in each three-month period, which is usually the greater of 1 percent of the outstanding shares or the average weekly trading volume;
- are limited in how they can be sold, such as by brokers or market maker;
- must be accompanied by filing a Form 144 notice with the SEC;
- must have current public information available on the issuer.

If securities have been held for two or more years by someone who has been unaffiliated for three months then there are no restrictions on resale.

SEC Rule 145[11]

Any unaffiliated party that publicly offers securities it received in a merger, consolidation or asset sale that was approved by shareholders are deemed to be underwriters. As an underwriter it is subject to public information disclosure obligations and restrictions on sales volume and methods. However, there are no requirements similar to the one-year holding period and an SEC filing notice under Rule 144.

Nevertheless, the seller can transfer its shares with no limitation on volume or sales method if it has held securities for one year or met the requirements of Rule 144 (c) regarding availability of current public information.

Exemptions for Targets' Shareholders
Securities received by shareholders of targets usually do not need to be registered under Securities Act. For instance, in stock-for-stock exchanges under Section 4(1) of Securities Act,[12] no registration is generally required.

In addition, affiliates unable to rely on Section 4(1) and persons selling other restricted securities may be able to rely on one of the following exemptions (the first three have been described):

- Section 3(a)(11)
- SEC Rule 144
- Regulation A
- The so-called 4(1 1/2) exemption covering purchasers of securities in an exempt transaction who subsequently sell those securities[13]

If no exemption applies, target's shareholders must register the stock they received before selling.

1934 Securities Exchange Act

The purpose of this law is to provide investors with full and fair disclosure of material information about both the issuer and its securities. The act imposes specific standards and liabilities for anyone involved in preparing a registration statement. They are liable for any material fact included or omitted from the statement. Anyone trading on inside material information is also liable under the act.

Disclosure Obligations
One of the most famous securities rules is Rule 10b-5 under Securities Exchange Act.[14] The Rule states that it is illegal for anyone to:

- use any device or scheme to defraud;
- make any untrue statement of a material fact that is misleading;
- omit to state a material fact necessary to make any statements that were made not misleading;
- engage in any act, practice or course of business that is a fraud or deceit.

The rule applies not only to securities registered under the act but also to any sale of a security.
Form 8-K must be filed within 4 business days after:[15]

- acquisition;
- sale of an asset with a book value or purchase price of more than 10 percent of the company's total assets;
- sale of a business that generates 10 percent of the company's total income.

The form includes the date and method of acquisition, description of assets, business involved, consideration paid, names of acquirer and target, and source of funds. Attached to the form must be a balance sheet, an income statement and changes of financial position.

Timing of Disclosures

The 1934 Act does not require companies to disclose all information, including material information. It is acceptable if there are business reasons for nondisclosure so long as no one is trading on the information. During an acquisition, the nondisclosure of any negotiations must be evaluated regularly.

No disclosure is necessary if a few people closely hold target. If target is publicly traded, any potential acquisition is a material fact. Directors of target must consider at each stage of the negotiations whether they must disclose. The usual rule is not to unless information about the acquisition is leaked and a few begin trading on it.

Under Regulation M-A[16] adopted by the SEC in 1999, parties to an announced merger are permitted to make public statements before any registration statement and proxy statements become effective. Public statements made in the form of written communications must be filed with the SEC. Filing is not required for oral statements such as speeches, phone calls and slide shows. SEC staff, however, recommends filing any scripts for oral communications.

Disclosure is also affected by Regulation FD,[17] which regulates information disclosed selectively to investors. Under the regulation, such information must be filed publicly and available to all stockholders promptly after any inadvertent disclosure.

Proxy Solicitations

If acquirer or target management solicits proxies, that is, the right to vote on specific issues from target's shareholders, it must comply with Regulation 14A, the 1934 Act's proxy rules.[18] The same requirement applies if target solicits proxies from its shareholders to defend against an acquisition.

The act requires that the proxy solicitation materials be filed with the SEC at least ten days before the shareholders mailing. When finally sent to shareholders, copies must simultaneously be sent to the SEC and each exchange where the company's stock is listed.

The mailing must contain information on the proposed acquisition or merger. This includes a summary of the transaction, usually with the main agreement attached. The solicitation must also describe the parties involved and their business, products or services, production, markets, distribution, supply sources, plant locations, and key properties. Financial information must also be included, such as existing and pro-forma capitalization, earnings summaries including per-share amounts, book value including per-share amounts, dividend and value per-share at end of most recent period, unpaid dividends, loans in default, and quarterly sales prices for past two years. Information on new board members must also be included.

The proxy request must indicate in bold face whether it is being solicited on behalf of the firm's board. Proxies can be valid for only one meeting. They must identify clearly and impartially any acquisition or reorganization question being submitted for vote and give the shareholder the opportunity to vote for or against. Discretion can be granted to proxy holders only within narrow limits to:

- Matters incident to the meeting
- Approval of minutes
- Shareholder proposals not included in the proxy materials
- Matters for which the shareholder does not indicate a preference as long as the proxy clearly states how the proxy holder intends to vote on such issues

The proxy solicitation must also describe the revocability of any executed proxy, dissenters' appraisal rights, identity of those soliciting proxy, special interest of those soliciting proxies, description of issuer's outstanding securities and principal holders.

Because of concerns that predictions might turn out to be wrong, most proxy solicitation materials contain only basic information and reasonably certain predictions.

Short Swing Profits

Officers, directors, and 10-percent shareholders are considered insiders. They cannot purchase and sell—or sell and purchase—securities of their associated company during any six-month period. If they do, the issuer or its shareholders can recover profits they earn. [19] This is a strict rule of liability and cannot be rebutted.

This can create problems for insiders who might have sold or purchased shares if an acquisition of their company occurs within six months.

1940 Investment Company Act

This act regulates investment companies, which are defined as a company engaged in the business of investing, reinvesting, loaning, holding or trading in securities, and has more than 40 percent of its assets composed of investment securities.[20] If acquirer or target meets this definition, it must have registered as an investment company.

Companies meeting the definition must register with the SEC and comply with regulations similar to those applicable to mutual funds.

State Securities Laws

While each state has its own securities laws, many of them are based on the Uniform Securities Act,[21] one of the many uniform laws recommended by the Uniform Law Commissioners, which is a national association that tries to bring consistency to state rules by drafting and recommending standard laws in key areas. Although I will use it as the basis for the discussion that follows, when undertaking a transaction the laws of each state where securities will be sold must be carefully studied.

The Uniform Securities Act tracks the federal securities laws in many ways. It contemplates, for instance, a registration or qualification system but establishes certain exemptions.

Exemptions for Acquirers

Some of the exemptions under the Uniform Securities Act are similar to those under federal laws. Others are very different or new, reflecting the greater number of exemptions under state laws than federal laws. Some of the state exemptions not found in the federal system are exemptions for securities:

- issued by financial institutions, insurance companies and public utilities;[22]
- listed on a stock exchange—NYSE or in some cases a regional stock exchange—or on the NASDAQ National Market System.[23]

There are also transaction-based exemptions:[24]

- Sales to institutional buyers
- Limited offerings
- Offerings to existing holders

Filings by Acquirers

If one of the above exemptions does not apply, issuer must register or qualify security with the state securities agency. State review of such registrations falls into four categories:

- Coordination: for securities also being registered with the SEC. The state conducts limited review, since it defers to the SEC to evaluate the registration.[25]
- Notification: for securities issued by seasoned issuers, who simply notify the state agency of its issuance[26]
- Qualification: for other securities under which the state makes its own determination that security meets state requirements[27]
- Merit Review: rather than merely qualifying stock, some states conduct a careful review and analysis of the stock. This includes checking the disclosures and fairness of the terms.

Exemptions for Targets' Shareholders
Whether registered or not, a key question is whether the security is subject to a minimum holding period before its holder can resell it. This should be determined before closing, since the existence of a holding period will reduce a security's value.

Most state laws do not have an exemption similar to Section 4(1) of the Securities Act, which allows target's shareholders to resell securities received by them in the acquisition. Therefore, they must see if another state exemption applies, such as one of the state exemptions available to acquirers discussed above. If no exemption exists, target's shareholders must register before they can sell.

Antitakeover—Williams Act, Federal Reserve and State Regulation

Two sets of laws regulate the takeover of companies. On the federal level is the Williams Act. On the state level most have their own rules.

Williams Act

Passed in 1968, the Williams Act[28] amended the Securities Exchange Act. The amendment created substantive rules governing takeovers while delegating to the SEC the right to establish other rules.

The goal of the act is to give target's shareholders the information they need to make an informed decision. By creating minimum offering and withdrawal periods and pro rata acceptance of oversubscribed tenders, thus taking pressure off to make an early tender so as not to be left out, the act seeks to give shareholders time to consider tender offers.

Critics argue that it hinders the ability of acquirers to replace inefficient managers. According to one study takeovers declined following the passage of the act, which in some ways was the unstated intention of the act. Critics also argue that the act drives up purchase prices by giving other potential purchasers notice of acquirer's intention and gives competitors a chance to make competing bids. Since the act was passed, takeover premiums rose from 32 percent to 53 percent above current market price.

In tender offers, acquirers publicly announce that they are willing to buy a certain percent of target's stock at a fixed price. To encourage target's shareholders to sell, the fixed price is well above the prevailing market price. Target's shareholders have a fixed period in which to tender their shares. Target's shareholders are advised to turn their shares into acquirer's agent, usually an investment bank.

The principal advantage of the tender offer is that acquirer can buy up the shares it wants in one transaction in a brief period rather than accumulating shares over several months or years from holders of large blocks. Concentrating its efforts in one transaction usually means lower transaction costs. It also reduces carrying costs—how long acquirer has to hold shares until it gets control and can take steps to pay off the money it borrowed to buy the shares. Such pay-off steps could include selling off some of target's assets, divisions or business.

The tender amount may be a minimum number (unless the tendered shares reach the minimum, none will be bought), a fixed number (no more or less will be bought), or a maximum number (acquirer will buy as much as target's share-holders are willing to sell up to a certain percentage, which could be 100 per-cent). Acquirer usually wants to acquire at least 51 percent to gain control.

Reflecting these thresholds, there are several types of tender offers. In a **partial tender offer**, acquirer is willing to buy less than 100 percent and will buy no more than the amount announced—even if offered. In an **any-and-all tender offer**, acquirer is willing to buy whatever is offered although there may be a high minimum.

Another type of self-tender offer is the **buyback** in which the company offers to buy a large percentage of its stock for cash. Buybacks are often used in con-nection with earning distributions, restructurings to avoid unwanted third-party tender offers (**defensive buybacks**), and restructurings to avoid loan covenant defaults.

In the 1990s, many companies began to buy back high-cost debt, particularly junk bonds, issued in the 1980s. The holders of such debt were not pleased to lose their high returns. Unfortunately for the holders, the Williams Act does not apply to such **debt buybacks** for cash or stock. Their only remedy was the contractual terms of the debt.

If enough shares are bought back the company might not have enough shares publicly traded to be listed on the public exchanges. In such a case, the company would have used a stock buyback for **going private**.

Buybacks can be used other than in self-tender offers. They are also used in open market purchases, privately negotiated acquisitions, exercise of redemption rights on outstanding stock, and issue of transferable put rights (**TPR**) on out-standing stock. In a TPR, if the company wants to repurchase 20 percent of its shares it issues to shareholders two TPR for each ten shares they own. The TPR gives the shareholder the right to sell back two shares at a fixed price during a fixed period. By setting the exercise price above the prevailing market rate, it can increase the likelihood that all puts will be exercised at the end of the option period.

Rules
The Williams Act applies to both self-tenders and third-party tenders. In a **self-tender offer** the company offers to buy shares from its shareholders. In a **third-party tender offer** acquirer is unrelated. It derives its name from target and its shareholders being the other two parties. Self-tenders are subject to Section 13(e) and Rule 13e-4 of the Securities Exchange Act.[29] Third party tenders are subject to Section 14(d) and Regulation 14D of the Securities Exchange Act.[30] Both types are

subject to the disclosure requirements of Regulation M-A, a new subpart of Regulation S-K, as well as Section 14(e) and Rule 14e of the Securities Exchange Act.[31]

Section 13(e) and Rule 13e-4 apply to tenders of issuer's own equity securities if issuer:

- has class of equity securities registered under Section 12 of the Securities Exchange Act;
- is required to file periodic reports under Section 15(d) of the Securities Exchange Act;
- is a closed-end investment company under the Investment Company Act.[32]

Issuers might conduct **Dutch auctions** under which they invite holders of securities to tender their securities at prices specified by the holders. They might also conduct **modified Dutch auctions** under which the issuer specifies the number of securities it wishes to acquire and the price range within which it is willing to purchase.[33]

Otherwise, many of the rules applicable to self-tenders parallel those applicable to third-party tenders, and since third-party tenders are the basis for mergers and acquisitions I will focus on the latter rules.

Section 14(d) and Regulation 14D apply to tenders for:

- any class of equity securities registered under Section 12 of the Securities Exchange Act;
- any equity security of an insurance company exempt from registration under the Securities Exchange Act by Section 12(g)(2)(G);
- any equity security of a closed-end investment company under the Investment Company Act.[34]

In addition, the tender must result in the acquirer becoming the beneficial owner of more than 5 percent of the class of securities subject to the tender. In such case the acquirer must file with the SEC a Tender Offer Statement on Schedule TO.

Third party acquirers wishing to make **cash tender offers** must file Schedule TO with the SEC, target, other bidders and exchanges where the target stock is listed. The filing must be made as soon as practicable on the date of the tender offer. If there is any material change in information on the schedule, an amendment must be filed.[35] Third party acquirers wishing to make **exchange tender offers** of their stock for stock of target must file registration statements with the SEC, who reviews it and usually issues a comment letter. Once the changes are agreed upon by the acquirer and the SEC, the acquirer can begin the exchange offer.[36]

There are several time limits under the Williams Act. Tender offers must be open for 20 business days—a period during which they can be accepted by target's shareholders. Any increase in price extends the time for another 10 business days.[37]

If more shares are tendered than acquirer has indicated it will accept, shares must be accepted on a pro rata basis[38] under the "all holders" rule that requires equal treatment for all security holders of the same class.[39] The rule also requires acquirers to pay all sellers the best price paid to any security holder. Acquirer must pay for the shares tendered promptly after the close of the offer period.

When undertaking a tender offer under Section 14(e),[40] it is illegal to:

- make a false or misleading statement or omission;
- engage in any fraudulent, deceptive or manipulative act.

Under Rule 14e-1,[41] the following actions are deemed to be fraudulent, deceptive or manipulative:

- holding tender offer open for less than 20 business days;
- increasing or decreasing percentage of the class of securities being sought or consideration being offered without extending the period for 10 business days;
- failure to pay consideration offered or return securities promptly.

Rule 14e-3[42] creates a "disclose or abstain from trading" rule for any person in possession of material information relating to a tender offer.

Disclosure Obligations

Several types of information in a tender offer must be disclosed in Schedule TO:

- Material terms of proposed offer (Item 1)
- Target and stock being acquired (Item 2)
- Acquirer (Item 3)
- Material terms of transaction (Item 4)
- Past agreements between acquirer and bidder (Item 5)
- Purpose of acquisition, including frustrate another tender offer (Item 6)
- Source of funds (Item 7)
- Acquirer's beneficial ownership of target (Item 8)
- Identity and compensation of all advisors (Item 9)
- Financial statements of acquirer (Item 10)
- Other material information (Item 11)
- Exhibits including tender offer, loan agreements and tax opinion[43]

Target must send the tender offer materials to its shareholders or give acquirer a list of its shareholders. Most prefer to deliver the materials themselves.

Within ten days of tender offer being made public, target's management must indicate whether it recommends acceptance or rejection, is neutral, or cannot take a position by filing a Tender Offer Solicitation/Recommendation Statement on Schedule 14D-9,[44] which describes:

- target and stock being acquired;
- acquirer;
- recommendation and reasons;
- description of any understanding regarding the tender offer, including person and compensation;
- transactions during the past 60 days by target and its officers and directors concerning a merger or material transfer of assets;
- copies of solicitation materials.

Considerable litigation has arisen over the adequacy of disclosures in the tender offer documents. While intentions or hypothetical scenarios need not be disclosed, intentions must be disclosed. Even when future actions have not been disclosed in other SEC filings, it is necessary to disclose such intentions in tender offer filings. For instance, an intention to merge the companies at a later date— that is, a second-step merger—which might normally be covered by an SEC filing just before the merger, must be described in the tender offer.

Courts can issue injunctions to prevent tender offers that violate the Williams Act. Competing acquirers, however, cannot sue to recover damages if they lose out in a tender offer battle.

Exclusions
Privately negotiated acquisitions are not covered by the act. One type is the **street sweep** in which acquirer concentrates on institutional holders of large blocks. Distinguishing between public and private acquisitions is not necessarily easy. The courts use eight factors to help:

- Active and widespread solicitation of public shareholders
- Solicitation for a substantial percentage
- Offer to purchase at a premium over prevailing market price
- Terms fixed and not negotiable
- Offer contingent on tender of a minimum and possibly a maximum number of shares
- Offer open for limited time
- Holder pressured to sell
- Public announcement accompanied by rapid accumulation of shares

A number of techniques have been adopted to avoid the Williams Act, although the SEC has not always found them acceptable:

- Cash options: holder has option to choose cash or stock.
- Waffling: bidder hides its future intentions by listing many possible acquisitions.
- Parking: bidder orally contracts with many stockbrokers and dealers, asking each to buy 4.9 percent of target. Each dealer agrees to sell its purchased

shares to bidder at the future market price. Bidder agrees to reimburse each dealer for any losses. Dealers are protected against downside risks and can reap upswings.

- Proxy solicitations: bidder solicits proxies but not stock in an attempt to oust target's board.
- Warehousing: bidder informs institutional investors of its interest in target, expecting them to buy for resale to it at future market price.

Federal Reserve Bank

The Federal Reserve Bank has established rules limiting financing, which are particularly applicable to acquisitions.

Regulation U[45] limits loans that banks can make secured by stock when the money will be used to purchase stock registered on a national exchange or over the counter. The amount is limited to a percentage of the pledged security, which is usually around 50 percent. The regulation applies even if the company acquired is not public when the loan is received, such as when it is used for a reverse subsidiary merger. It also applies to unsecured loans indirectly secured by stock, such as negative pledges in the loan agreement regarding borrower's ability to sell certain stock.

Regulation T[46] limits the ability of broker-dealers to extend or arrange credit other than that covered by Regulation U.

Regulation X[47] requires domestic and international borrowers to comply with the margin rules.

State Regulation

The states have attempted to regulate takeovers since the 1970s. Their attempts fall into four phases that reflect decisions of the U.S. Supreme Court on the constitutionality of their laws.

Prior to 1982 various states attempted to limit takeovers. Some rules were very severe, particularly in regulated industries. Under the Illinois statute, for instance, acquirers of state chartered banks had to get the approval of state banking authorities. In that year the U.S. Supreme Court in *Edgar v. Mite Corp.*[48] held the Illinois statute unconstitutional. Prior approval by the state of takeovers was not possible.

Not willing to give up, states tried again. Up to 1987 most observers assumed that they would meet the same fate as in the Edgar case. In the lower courts they were routinely found unconstitutional. Nevertheless states continued to adopt them. It was felt that they gave local targets another arrow in their defense arsenal. If nothing else, they could use the possibly unconstitutional rules to sue in local courts to delay the takeover.

There were two types of these second-generation statutes:

- **Control share acts:**[49] These laws prohibited the acquisition of a controlling block of shares without the approval of disinterested shareholders. Others allow the acquisition but prevent their voting without such approval. Some states allow target to redeem shares that are not allowed to vote.
- **Fair price acts:**[50] These acts apply to an acquirer who is successful in its tender offer, purchases the shares it wants, and wants to back-end merge target into it. Under these laws the consideration paid by acquirer to the remaining shareholders in the merger must meet certain price criteria or be approved by a majority or even two-thirds of remaining shareholders.

  The merger price must usually be the greater of the price offered in the tender offer, the market price prevailing on date transaction is announced, or the market price prevailing on the date acquirer becomes a 20 percent owner.

  These laws prevent acquirers from front-end loading acquisitions by offering a high price in the tender and then, once it has control, offering a low price for remaining shares.

  In a surprise to most observers, in 1987 the U.S. Supreme Court upheld one of the second-generation statutes: the Indiana Control Share Acquisitions Act.[51] Taking advantage of the situation, states began to push the envelope by adopting stronger takeover statutes. There are several types of these third-generation rules, which I describe next.
- **Business combination (freeze-out) acts:**[52] If acquirer purchases a certain percentage of target's shares, such as 20 percent, a majority of disinterested shareholders must approve any merger with acquirer under these laws. The acts often require acquirers to hold their shares for a lengthy cooling-off period before they can merge with target. The period could be as much as five years. In two cases acquirer might not have to obtain the majority vote or wait the lengthy period. It can avoid the requirements if target's board approves the acquisition and merger or if it pays a fair price.
- **Appraisal or cash-out acts:**[53] Similar to fair price acts, if acquirer purchases the shares tendered to it and subsequently tries to merge the company into it, the remaining shareholders have the right to a fair price. Fair price is usually calculated as the highest price acquirer paid in the previous 90 days. The difference with fair price acts is that if the remaining shareholders object to the price, a court-appointed appraiser sets the price.

  Federal courts learned from the 1987 decision and reversed course. They began to routinely uphold many of the third generation statutes. Their new attitude was strengthened when the U.S. Supreme Court refused to hear a challenge to a business combination act.

  With that decision some states felt that they could extend the envelope even further. The most popular statute in this fourth generation is the **disgorgement act**[54] under which controlling shareholders selling their shares must return or disgorge profits received from an acquirer.

Many of these statutes have been passed in haste, often within a few days. When a leading employer in a state is rumored to be a target, governors and legislatures have shown a remarkable ability to draft, adopt and sign bills protecting them.

Antitrust—Clayton Act, Hart-Scott-Rodino and Other Nations

The laws and rules discussed so far regulated the impact on internal groups. But acquisitions affect more than internal groups such as shareholders, directors, officers and employees. They affect external groups dealing with target, such as suppliers and customers, and external groups not dealing with target such as competitors. In this section I describe rules that restrict the impact on external groups.

Clayton Act

The Clayton Act[55] prohibits two types of actions. Under Section 7 no person can acquire another company if the transaction could lessen competition substantially or create a monopoly.

The Federal Trade Commission (FTC) and the Department of Justice (DOJ) were given responsibility for enforcing the act. The FTC and DOJ have issued a series of merger guidelines. In 1982 the FTC issued a Statement Concerning Horizontal Merger Guidelines while the DOJ issued merger guidelines, which were revised in 1984. In 1992 they issued joint Horizontal Merger Guidelines, which were revised in 1997.[56] In March 2006, the FTC and DOJ issued a joint commentary on the Horizontal Merger Guidelines explaining how the agencies have applied particular guidelines' principles.[57] As the guidelines note, the focus is on mergers that create or enhance market power. Market power, which is the ability to affect the price paid for supplies and charged to consumers, applies to purchasing power and selling power.

To measure market power the FTC and DOJ measure the impact of the merger within economically meaningful markets. To do so, the FTC and DOJ look at the impact of a price increase on each product (product market) of each firm in the geographical area where it is sold (geographical market).

The treatment of acquisitions depends on whether they are horizontal—between competitors in the same product and geographical market—or vertical—between parties in the same manufacturing or distribution chain. In horizontal mergers the FTC and DOJ first look at the amount of concentration. If there is low market concentration or only a slight increase, the FTC and DOJ will quickly review the merger. In other cases, the FTC and DOJ will examine a number of factors.

To measure the amount of concentration, the FTC and DOJ use the Herfind-ahl-Hirschman Index (HHI). The HHI is calculated by adding the square of the parties' individual market shares. The FTC and DOJ have three thresholds of review based on the HHI:

- Unconcentrated markets (below 1,000): The FTC and DOJ will not challenge mergers in this area.
- Moderately concentrated markets (1,000–1,800): In this range the FTC and DOJ are unlikely to challenge a merger increasing the HHI by less than 100 points. Above that level, they will likely challenge.
- Highly concentrated markets (above 1,800): Above this level, the FTC and DOJ are unlikely to challenge a merger increasing the HHI by less than 50 points. A merger increasing the HHI by more than 100 points is unlikely to be permitted, however they are likely to challenge mergers between 50 and 100 points.[58]

    Under the HHI, the definition of the market is important. The broader it is defined, the lower the HHI will be. For instance, if Coca-Cola's market is defined as soft drinks it will have a very high HHI. On the other hand, if its market is defined as drinks—including milk, water, etc.—it will be quite low.

There are a number of exceptions to the HHI treatment.

- Leading firm: if target is small, usually a market share of less than 1 percent, the FTC and DOJ is unlikely to challenge an acquisition by the leading firm even when it has a market share of 35 percent or more.
- Changing market conditions: recent or ongoing changes in the market might indicate the current market share is not a good reflection of competitiveness. For instance, the market share of a company with new technology may be understated while a company without it may be overstated.
- Financial difficulties: if the financial difficulties of a firm reflect an underlying structural weakness rather than a business cycle, its market share may be overstated.
- Ease of entry: if entry into a market is so easy that existing competitors could not raise prices without new competitors appearing, the FTC and DOJ is unlikely to challenge the merger.
- Increased efficiency: if the parties can establish by clear and convincing evidence that the merger will result in increased efficiencies and lower prices to consumers, the FTC and DOJ will consider the efficiencies in deciding to challenge.
- Failing firm: the FTC and DOJ will not challenge anticompetitive mergers if one of the firms is failing. A failing firm is one that is unable to meet its financial obligations in the near future, unable to successfully reorganize under Chapter 11 of the Bankruptcy Act, and has made unsuccessful good

faith efforts to obtain reasonable tender offers from parties posing a lower anticompetitive effect.[59]

Hart-Scott-Rodino

In 1976, Congress added a new section to the Clayton Act. Section 7A was intended to give federal agencies a chance to review mergers before they took place. Under the law called the Hart-Scott-Rodino Antitrust Improvements Act (HSR),[60] no merger of over a certain size can be completed unless the parties give the FTC and the DOJ prior notice.

Since compiling the necessary data covered by the filing can take several weeks, it is important to consider the filing early in the acquisition stage.

HSR filings contain important and confidential business information. When passing the law Congress exempted such information from disclosure under the Freedom of Information Act, which ordinarily gives the public access to documents filed with the government. The information can only be disclosed in an administrative or judicial action or to Congress. The form itself, without attachments, can be released in any civil action challenging the merger. In some cases, parties can refuse to disclose information but must submit reasons.

Except in cash tender offers when only acquirer files, both acquirer and target must make a HSR filing. Depending on size of the deal the buyer might have to pay a substantial filing fee. More information on the fees appears in Table 3.1. The reason for transaction sizes being in odd numbers is that the original amount, such as $50 and $100 million, was subject to increase based on gross national product changes since September 30, 2004.

After filing with the FTC and DOJ, the parties must wait 30 days to close—15 days for cash tender offers. The government can extend the waiting period if it issues a "second request." On December 15, 2006, the DOJ revised the rules for second requests to make it easier for companies to comply.[61] As shown in Table 3.2, the new rules limit the number of employees whose files must be searched and the default period for which documents must be produced. Unfortunately, the numbers vary between the FTC and DOJ.

If a second request is issued, the waiting period is extended for 30 days—10 days for cash tender offers. A U.S. District Court must approve further extensions. In reality, if government needs more time it will advise buyer and seller

Table 3.1 HSR Filing Fees

Transaction size	Filing fee
Over $53.1 million to less than $106.2 million	$45,000
$106.2 million to less than $530.7 million	$125,000
$530.7 million or more	$280,000

Table 3.2 HSR Second Requests

	FTC	DOJ
Number of key employees whose records must be searched	35	30
Default search period (years)	2	2

that it intends to reject the application unless they agree to an extension or refile and start the waiting period running again.

Failure to make a filing can be very dangerous. Fines run up to $11,000 per day for the companies and their officers and directors.[62] The government can also seek to unwind an acquisition.

There are three tests that must be met before HSR applies. There are also several exemptions.

Under the **commerce test**, acquirer or target must be engaged in interstate commerce—that is, business between states or with foreign countries—or in activity affecting commerce. Having regular customers in another state meets the first criteria. Owning a gas station alongside the interstate probably meets the second. Unless you sell a product for local customers you will likely meet the test.

Under the **transaction test** some transactions are not reportable, some are reportable in certain instances, while others are reportable in all cases:

- Transactions valued at $59.8 million or less are not reportable, regardless of the size of the parties.
- Transactions valued at $59.8 million but not more than $239.2 million are reportable if the "size-of-the-parties test" is met.
- Transactions valued at more than $239.2 million are always reportable.

Under **the size of the parties test**, parties involved in the second category of transactions must meet one of the following tests:[63]

- Voting securities or assets of manufacturer with annual net sales or total assets of $12 million or more are being acquired by business with annual net sales or total assets of $119.6 million or more.
- Voting securities or assets of nonmanufacturer with total assets of $12 million or more are being acquired by business with annual net sales or total assets of $119.6 million or more.
- Voting securities or assets of business with annual net sales or total assets of $119.6 million or more are being acquired by business with annual net sales or total assets of $12 million or more.

Even if the above tests have been met, there are several **exemptions** for mergers to which HSR does not apply:

- Posing no substantive antitrust risks
- Already subject to antitrust review
- Bonds, mortgages, or other nonvoting securities
- Real estate
- Voting securities made solely for investment as long as acquirer does not own 10 percent of issuer's voting securities
- Foreign assets if target's assets did not generate sales in the United States of more than $50 million
- Foreign assets if target's assets located in United States are valued at $50 million and target had sales of $50 million or less
- If both parties are foreign[64]

Other Nations

A number of other nations have adopted laws similar to HSR. This can cause difficulties for parties to acquisitions. They must compare lists of countries where they are doing business. Where they overlap they might have to make HSR-type filings. For instance, if both acquirer and target have subsidiaries or operations in Japan, they might both have to make a filing there.[65]

Many nations have become aggressive in monitoring such acquisitions. While it used to be that a merger acceptable in the United States was unlikely to be challenged elsewhere, this is no longer the case. In the past few years the European Union has rejected acquisitions accepted in the United States.[66]

Since the waiting period varies from nation to nation, it is advisable to discuss this issue as soon as possible.

Special Industries—Regulated Industries, Foreign Investment and National Security

Acquirers must pay careful attention to target's business. It may be operating under government permits at the federal, state or local levels that must be transferred. For instance, it may be operating in an industry sector licensed by a governmental agency, and the license might have to be transferred, if possible, to acquirer.

In addition, depending on the size of the transaction and the national security importance of target's business, if acquirer is a foreign party it might have to file a notice of its acquisition.

Regulated Industries

The U.S. government and most states have separate rules for particular industries. The most common are transportation, banking and insurance, communications, public utilities, and alcohol. When purchasing a target operating in any of these and similar sectors, acquirer might need to obtain specific approval for the acquisition from the agency regulating the sector.

Transportation

Transportation has traditionally been one of the most protected and regulated industries in the United States. At the federal level, there are five key agencies:

- The Department of Transportation regulates acquisitions of air carriers.
- The Federal Aviation Authority regulates air commerce, safety of air carriers and use of navigable airspace.
- The Surface Transportation Board regulates railroad rate and service issues, railroad restructuring transactions including mergers, certain trucking company rate matters, certain intercity passenger bus company structure, and rates and services of certain pipelines.
- The Federal Highway Administration develops and implements motor carrier requirements, safety regulations, licensing, registration and inspection requirements, and taxation programs.
- The Federal Maritime Administration and Coast Guard regulate merchant marine and water carriers.

At the state level equivalent agencies exist, which regulate carriers only transporting goods inside the state. Where both federal and state agencies are involved, there are three ways that responsibilities may be allocated between them. In some cases the federal and state jurisdiction might overlap, and approval from both is required. In other cases the federal agency might push the state agency aside and issue all rules in the area. In the third scenario the federal agency might delegate their authority to the state agency and allow the state to issue all rules.

In addition to federal and state regulation, some local agencies regulate carriers. The best examples are taxis and buses.

Banking and Insurance

Up until recently, banking was one of the most protected industries in the United States. Depending on whether they are national or local and on the type of organizational structure they chose, banks are regulated by federal or states agencies. The first antitakeover statutes, for instance, required the approval of state banking authorities for the acquisition of a state-chartered bank.

Agencies at the federal level in the case of national banks and at the state level in the case of state charter banks and most insurance companies scrutinize acquisitions of banks and insurance companies. The relevant federal authority is the Federal Reserve Board while most states have state banking commissions and state insurance commissions.

For many years banks in most states could only operate in the insurance market through separate subsidiaries or affiliates. In 1999 the Gramm-Leach-Bliley Act[67] repealed the Glass-Steagall Act of 1933,[68] which had kept banks out of the stock market, and the Banking Act of 1933, which had separated commercial banks and securities firms.[69] As a result, the banking, insurance, and securities sectors (and the parties operating in each of them) are blurring.

Communications and Public Utilities

Federal and state governments carefully regulate and monitor communication companies. At the federal level the responsible agency is the Federal Communications Commission (FCC), which has bureaus regulating different industries:

- The Media Bureau regulates AM/FM radio and television broadcast stations, as well as cable television and satellite services.
- The Wireless Telecommunications Bureau oversees cellular and PCS phones, pagers two-way radios, as well as the use of radio spectrum for communications by business, local and state governments, public safety service providers, aircraft and ship operators, and individuals.
- The Wireline Competition Bureau is responsible for rules and policies concerning telephone companies that provide interstate and, under certain circumstances, intrastate, telecommunications services to the public through the use of wire-based transmission facilities, such as corded and cordless telephones.
- The International Bureau represents the FCC in satellite and international matters.
- The Public Safety and Homeland Security Bureau addresses public safety, homeland security, national security, emergency management and preparedness, disaster management and related issues.

    At the state level, the agency is usually called a Public Utilities Commission.

    The right to operate companies providing electricity, natural gas and water is usually only regulated at the state level. There are two exceptions:

- The Nuclear Regulatory Commission regulates the use of nuclear materials and facilities. It issues licenses and permits for construction, maintenance and operation of such facilities.
- The Federal Energy Regulatory Commission (FERC) regulates the transmission of energy or energy production in interstate commerce. It monitors transmission and resale of natural gas; regulates pipeline transmission of oil; regulates transmission and wholesale of electricity; grants licenses and inspects private, municipal and state hydroelectric projects; monitors

environmental issues of utilities; and overseas accounting and financial reporting regulations of utilities.

In addition there are, of course, federal environmental regulations applicable to electric, gas and water providers, and some permits issued to them at the federal level might need to be transferred to acquirer.

Alcohol

Acquirers face four types of problems in the alcohol area. First, several agencies at the same level of government might regulate the business. At the federal level the Bureau of Alcohol, Tobacco and Firearms (ATF) is dominant, but other agencies are involved. Second, the jurisdiction of federal, state and local agencies can overlap. Third, in the case of a diversified target with operations in many sectors, several different agencies at the same government level may be involved. Fourth, government approvals held by target might require acquirer to submit an amendment in case target is acquired.

As part of their due diligence, acquirers and their attorneys must determine sectors where target is operating, which government agencies regulate its business, and whether the approval of any agencies is required. If approval is required, they should quickly move to obtain it. As a precaution, the purchase agreement should give acquirer flexibility to postpone the closing, adjust the price or walk away from the deal without penalty in case approval is not obtained.

Foreign Investors

Under the International Investment and Trade in Services Survey Act,[70] the president has authority to survey foreign investment. That authority has been delegated to the Secretary of Commerce who issued regulations covering the types of information to be collected. Under the regulations, reports must be filed as transactions occur and periodically.

On a transaction basis, within 45 days of acquiring a U.S. company, foreign acquirers must file Form BE-13. The report must be filed by either a U.S. affiliate if the foreign acquirer purchases directly—or indirectly through an existing U.S. affiliate—at least 10 percent of the voting interest of a U.S. target or an existing U.S. affiliate if it acquires a U.S. target, including its assets, and merges it into its own operations. Each foreign parent or U.S. affiliate that is a party to the transaction must file.

There are exemptions for small acquisitions, such as acquisitions with a total cost of $3 million or less or acquirer's total assets are $3 million or less, and less than 200 acres.[71]

In addition, a Form BE-14 must be filed by either·a U.S. person assisting a foreign person or its U.S. affiliate in acquiring 10 percent or more voting interest in a U.S. business or a U.S. person that enters into a joint venture with a foreign person to create a U.S. business.[72]

On a periodic basis the Commerce Department requires foreign acquirers to make periodic reports. U.S. affiliates that are owned by 10 percent or more by foreign acquirers must file these reports:

- BE-605 must be filed quarterly within 30 days of the end of each of its first three calendar quarters and within 45 days of the end of its last calendar quarter.[73]
- BE-15 must be filed by May 31 each year.[74]

The U.S. affiliate is exempt from the above reports if none of the following exceed $30 million for the calendar year:

- Total assets
- Annual sales or gross operating revenues, excluding sales taxes
- Annual net income after U.S. taxes[75]

It must, nevertheless, file BE-605 and BE-15(C) certifying that it is exempt. If any one of the above items exceeds $30 million, the U.S. affiliate must file BE-605 quarterly report and a short or long form of the BE-15 depending on how much the affiliate exceeds one of the above tests.

Another periodic report is the BEA-12, which must be filed every 5 years since 1987.[76] This survey is more comprehensive than the others are.

National Security

In 1988, the United States passed the Exon-Florio amendments to the Omnibus Trade and Competitiveness Act.[77] The amendments became Section 721 of the Defense Production Act of 1950. They authorized the president to investigate proposed acquisitions by foreign persons of U.S. businesses. If the acquisitions threatened to impair national security, the president was authorized to suspend or prohibit them.

Regulations under the amendments authorize either party to the acquisition to voluntarily file a notice describing the transaction with the Committee on Foreign Investment in the United States (CFIUS), an inter-agency committee of 12 chaired by the Secretary of Treasury that includes the Secretaries of Homeland Security, State, Defense, Commerce, Justice and others.[78]

CFIUS has 30 days in which to review the notice and make a determination:

- if the acquisition could result in foreign control of a U.S. entity;
- if control could threaten U.S. security;
- if other laws do not adequately protect U.S. security interests.

In 1993, the Byrd Amendment to the National Defense Authorization Act[79] revised the Exon-Florio provision by requiring investigations in cases where acquirer is controlled by or acting on behalf of a foreign government and acquisition could result in control of a person engaged in interstate commerce in the United States that could affect U.S. national security.

If CFIUS determines that there is a threat to U.S. national security, its investigation of the transaction can postpone the 30-day review period for another 45 days. Upon completing its investigation, CFIUS files its recommendation with the president who has 15 days to act. He can approve, take no action, prevent the acquisition, or order divestiture. There is no judicial review of his decision.

The voluntary report must describe the acquisition, acquirer (especially any foreign government ownership), target and affiliated companies. CFIUS will be particularly interested in whether any goods or technology manufactured or developed by target are sold to the U.S. government—particularly those having military, munitions or national security relevance. CFIUS will also want to know acquirer's intention on how it will run target's business.

There are certain exemptions:

- Purchases of stock of U.S. target solely for investment, if the foreign acquirer holds 10 percent or less
- Direct purchases by a financial entity in the ordinary course of business for its own account, if a significant portion of its business is not the acquisition of companies
- Purchases of assets, such as inventory, real estate or equipment
- Purchases of voting securities by a securities underwriter

In July 2007, President George Bush signed the Foreign Investment and National Security Act of 2007. The new law expands the ability of the President to prevent or undo acquisitions, mergers or takeovers. It also tightens formal review procedures, particularly for government-owned or -controlled entities, and increases Congressional reporting requirements.

4

Finance

There are two basic sources of finance: (1) equity with ownership rights, and (2) debt with an obligation to pay back the amount borrowed (principal) and a rental charge for use of the money (interest). In between there are a number of financing techniques—options, warrants and equity kickers.

In this section, I describe these sources of financing. I also discuss some of the financing issues of particular interest to acquisitions—junk bonds, buy-outs and valuation.

The discussion focuses on corporate finance, since most acquirers who must raise money for their acquisitions are corporations.

General

Regardless of the financing source chosen, a number of common issues must be addressed:

- Economic participation to be given to funding source
- Management participation to be given to funding source
- Cost of funds
- Duration of funds
- Security to be provided[1]

I will consider each issue before turning to specific funding alternatives.

Economic Role

The basic question of each financing is the same, What kind of economic participation will the financing source receive? Will it be equity? If so, the funding source is an investor and will usually be entitled to ownership, voting, profits and any increase in value of the company through appreciated stock.

Alternatively, will it be a loan? If so, the funding source is a lender and only receives a fixed fee above return of the amount lent. It is not entitled to any ownership, and it does not share in any increase in value. Banks are the primary sources of loans.

To give lenders a chance to participate in some of the increase in value, convertible instruments were developed. The best example is the convertible debt, which is a loan but at the option of the lender can convert into an equity interest.

Management Role

The next basic question is, how much management participation the financing source will be given? Or will it be allowed not only to participate but also to control management? And will the control be of all issues, certain major issues, or only when the acquirer is in financial difficulty?

Management participation is almost always given to majority investors. It can also be given to minority investors and lenders in certain cases and for certain issues. For instance, minority shareholders may have voting rights on key issues (such as, asset sales, mergers or new securities issues) and the ability to appoint board members. Most debt instruments contain restrictions on how the company can be run. These are contained in positive (what the company must do while the loan is outstanding) and negative (what it cannot do) covenants.

Cost

The cost of funds is the rent charged by the funding source for using its money. In equity, the investor wants to participate in the increased value of the money. For this right, it is willing to take a position subordinate to debt. In an acquisition, it means the acquirer must share any increase in value with investors. This giving up of future gains makes equity the most expensive form of financing when the company increases in value.

In debt, the lender is less willing to gamble on an increase in value. It wants a fixed rental charge or interest. Such a limited return is great for a company increasing in value at a faster rate than interest. On the other hand, a fixed return can be a difficult burden for a company not growing or generating sufficient cash to meet its obligations.

In some cases, a lender might want a bonus or equity kicker, such as a warrant entitling it to receive shares in the company. Such a warrant would be separate from the loan, since the warrant might remain even after the loan is repaid. Other lenders provide funds as convertible debt. In such a case the loan is not repaid, but the amount of the loan is converted into equity.

Another issue to consider is the interim charge by financing sources for the use of their money. Investors might want quarterly dividends. Lenders might want monthly or annual interest payments. The acquirer must be able to meet those payments or restructure the payments in a way that it can realistically meet. This could include an agreed deferral of dividends during the early years or a balloon payment of interest at the loan's maturity.

Duration

The duration and term of financings varies. Equity is practically permanent. An investor wanting his or her money back must generally sell its shares to another investor. The company is not required to repurchase them.

Debt, on the other hand, is usually for a fixed period. It must then be repaid, although in some cases if the acquirer has met certain standards it will be permitted to roll over or continue the loan.

Debt generally has three durations:

- demand, which requires repayment when demanded by lender;
- short term for up to one year;
- long term for over one year.

With debt, acquirer must be certain to have cash when the loan or interest becomes due. A similar concern applies to dividends on equity. In both cases, the payment schedule must be matched to company's cash flow, so money will be there when needed. A loan, for instance, should not come due at a low point in a business cycle.

Risk and Security

All financings involve risk. The higher the risk, the higher the return that must be paid. There are certain things that can be done to reduce risk and thus the return that must be paid. A particular asset can secure a loan. If not repaid, lender has the right to seize the asset. Equity can also be secured. Preferred shares entitle holder to a priority over other investors if the company is liquidated. And in the case of tracking stock, the equity tracks, or is based on, the income of a particular business unit.

Security should be neither given easily nor more than necessary, since it will limit acquirer's ability to borrow and use security in the future.

Equity Financing

In this section, I describe basic equity types, issues to consider in issuing equity, specific types of securities and sources of securities funding.

Types of Securities

There are two basic types of stock—common and preferred.[2] Unless the company's organizational documents provide otherwise, all stock is common and has the same rights and privileges. Most companies, however, have several types of stock with different rights regarding dividends, liquidation, redemption, conversion and voting. Usually these different types are established as one class of common stock with the other separated as preferred stock.

The most typical form of equity is common stock. It has no special rights or privileges. Among shares, the dividends, assets on liquidation and voting are equal. Unless other classes are created, it represents all ownership of the company.

Stock issued with priorities over common stock is called preferred stock. Under Revised Model Business Corporations Act (RMBCA) and most state laws, these preferences are usually for distributions—both regular dividends and on dissolution. As discussed below, the dividend preferences may be cumulative, noncumulative or partially cumulative.

In exchange for greater rights to distributions, preferred stock is often subject to certain limitations, as discussed below, regarding voting, dividend, participation, redemption and convertibility.

Straight preferred stock is the basic form. This entitles holder to a fixed return in dividends with the right to receive a preferred amount on liquidation before common shareholders. The liquidated amount is usually par value or a designated value of the stock plus any unpaid dividends. There is no opportunity to share in any increased value, since the dividend return and liquidation value is fixed.

In this sense it is close to a debt instrument, except in two ways. Debt has a higher priority and gets paid before preferred stock, and preferred stock cannot

Table 4.1 Types of Stock

Type	Category	Sharing of Dividends, Assets and Voting
Common		Equally
Preferred	Straight	Different from common
	Classes	Different among preferred classes and from common

receive dividends if it is insolvent. If it did receive dividends while insolvent, it would have to refund any amount received.

Preferred stock is often divided into two or more classes. The priority among preferred classes is set in the offering memorandum and share certificates. Subsequent classes may be given greater priority than earlier shares, if allowed by organizational or earlier share documents.

Types of Rights—Voting, Dividend, Participation, Redemption and Convertibility

Founders and owners have great flexibility in designing their equity structure. They can grant certain rights but not others. They can give one class of equity more rights than others. And, they can transfer rights from one equity group to another from time to time.

When designing their equity structure, there are a number of rights and privileges to be considered and allocated. The allocation is usually determined by the negotiating leverage of the parties.

The more important rights are voting, dividend, participation, redemption and convertibility.[3]

Voting

Voting rights of a security are critically important. They must, therefore, be clearly described in the organizational and issuing documents. In addition, outside the company, shareholders may enter into voting agreements on how they will vote. Unless limited in one of these ways, each share has one vote. Two areas are particularly significant—the right to vote for directors and on issues important to holder.

Voting rights can be conditional, limited or excluded. Conditional voting means that the holder can vote only if certain events have occurred, such as a failure to pay a debt or a filing of a bankruptcy petition. Limited voting means that the holder can only vote on certain issues. At a minimum, these issues will include merger, acquisition, dissolution, sale of significant assets and dissipation of shares by issuing more or changing rights.

Voting can be on a per share basis or can be limited to certain classes on designated issues. For instance, all shares may be able to vote on mergers and acquisitions, but only those classes affected may vote on changes in share rights.

Dividend

Most investors desire a rental fee for the use of their money. They expect regular payments, which are usually quarterly. The timing of these payments or dividends must be clearly described in organizational and offering documents. Issues to be addressed include rate—whether flat, a percentage of purchase price or liquidation value—and preferences over other classes or for missed payments.

The right to missed dividends can be cumulative, noncumulative or partially cumulative. Cumulative means the company must make up any fixed dividend that was not paid as soon as it has the available cash. Noncumulative means the company does not need to make up any missed dividends, unless the board had officially declared it would pay a dividend and then found it could not. Partially cumulative involves a limited right to receive missed dividends.

Participation

Preferred stock is frequently entitled to a fixed return of dividends a fixed amount on dissolution. In such cases, it is nonparticipating. Other preferred stocks, and nearly all cases of common stock, have the right to receive a percentage of total dividends and a percentage of assets on liquidation. They are participating.

One variation of participation is tracking stock, which bases distributions on the performance of a particular subsidiary or business unit rather than the entire company. Since the unit is usually a higher performer than the overall business, this type gives greater participation.

Redemption

Redemption refers to turning in one's shares and getting back what you paid for them. This can be at the option of the holder or the company, and can be exercised only on fixed dates or during certain periods. If the holder has the redemption right, the security becomes more of a debt instrument. If the company has the right, it can refinance at the times allowed and frequently on more favorable terms.

The two big issues are timing—when can or must it be redeemed—and price—what premium must be paid.

Convertibility

Convertible securities are shares that can be converted into another class of security, usually preferred shares convertible into common shares. Sometimes, they can be converted into cash, debt or an asset owned by the company. In some cases, they are convertible into shares of another company.

Until conversion, such shares are usually treated the same as other stock of the same class with the same dividend and dissolution rights. Voting rights, however, may be treated differently. Convertible preferred stock might have voting that is equal to common stock on a share for share basis;·equal to the number of common stock into which it is convertible;·or as a class to designate a fixed number of directors.

When issuing convertible stock, the company must carefully describe:

- when convertibility is allowed (fixed date, certain period or on certain events);

- who can exercise the right (all, majority or some of the holders);
- how converted (automatically or on exercise of right);
- what it is converted into;
- how to calculate the conversion ratio.

The company must also understand what impact a conversion will have on its financial statements.

Specific Types of Securities

We have seen that there are two basic types of securities, common and preferred, and that they can have five main characteristics—voting, dividend, participation, redemption and convertibility. Now let's put the types and characteristics together and describe the principal alternatives.[4]

- Founders stock: the organizers of a company usually care most about participation. They want the right to a higher percentage of dividends and liquidation value. Being first in and therefore at most risk, they want the largest share of gains. They will also want voting control, at least initially and possibly later over certain issues. Redemption and convertibility are not usually granted.
- Voting common stock: this is the most common form of stock. Common has equal rights to voting, dividends and participation. There is usually no redemption or convertibility.
- Nonvoting common stock: holders of this stock have the same rights to dividend participation as other common stock. They just do not have any right to vote except perhaps under certain conditions, such as default, or on certain issues, such as dilution or major decisions. As with voting common stock, there is usually no redemption or convertibility. Founders and management issue these shares to investors to maintain control of the company.
- Multiple classes of voting common stock: there can be more than one class of voting common stock. Each class might have the right to elect its own directors. The number elected does not have to be equal. For instance, if founders cannot raise money by nonvoting common stock, they might sell to a new investor a separate class of common stock with the right to elect one director while founders elect the others. Alternatively, if the company does not have cumulative voting, an investor might want to make certain it has at least one board seat by insisting on a separate class. Other than separate voting rights, the multiple classes usually have the same rights to dividends and participation with no redemption or convertibility.
- Nonvoting noncumulative preferred stock: holders of this stock are most concerned about getting their money back with some gain. They are willing

to give up voting rights, the ability to participate in any upswing, as well as any missed dividend payments. They are only entitled to a fixed return as holders of preferred stock and missed dividends that were declared but not paid. Their fixed return must be paid before payments to any common stockholders. Redemption and convertibility rights may be given to preferred stockholders.

- Nonvoting fully cumulative preferred stock: holders of this stock are primarily concerned about getting their stock back with some gain. They are also willing to give up voting rights and the ability to participate in any upswing. However, they have not given up, and are entitled to receive, missed dividends. Often, if dividends are missed, the nonvoting aspect might change to voting entitling holders to appoint a director. Any missed dividends must be paid as soon as money is available. In some cases, missed dividends may be paid in installments. As with liquidation value, dividends are fixed amounts. Holders may be given redemption and convertibility rights.

- Nonvoting partially cumulative preferred stock: since the company might not want to go back and make up all missed dividends, it might agree to a limited make up obligation. The partially cumulative aspect of this stock might mean the company only goes back a certain time, such as two years, or a certain percentage, such as 50 percent. These shares might also have redemption and convertibility rights.

- Adjustable rate preferred stock: holders of preferred stock receive a fixed rate of dividends. Holders of this type of stock have the rate adjusted from time to time. The adjustments can be tied to changes in interest or bond rates, such as 1 percent over prime. If so, holders are assured of a return higher than what they could have received from a bank. If the rate is adjusted for some other measure, such as the performance of a stock market, holders can protect themselves from falling behind the general market. Rates are usually adjusted at fixed intervals, such as once a year, and are limited on how high or low they can change at any one time or over the life of the stock. Redemption and convertibility rights can be granted to these shares.

- Voting preferred stock: this is the second major class of stock after voting common stock. Holders of this stock can vote for directors, with voting on an existing per share basis (one stock, one vote), convertible per share basis (if one preferred stock could be converted into four common, the holder has four votes), or by class (each class elects its own director). Major changes such as mergers, acquisitions, sales of substantial assets and dilution might require the vote of preferred stockholders. Such stock might have redemption and convertibility rights.

- Convertible preferred stock: these preferred shares have voting and fixed dividend rights. Although there is no participation right for the shares themselves, they can be converted into something else that might give the holder the ability to participate in the upswing. The shares might also have redemption rights.

- Participating preferred stock: these preferred shares have voting rights. In addition to fixed dividend rights, they also have the right to participate in increased value through dividends and on liquidation. For instance, after receiving its fixed dividend, these shares may be entitled to share with common stock in any remaining funds. Since they can share in the upswing through their participating rights, they do not need convertibility. The shares might also have redemption rights.

- Redeemable preferred stock: these shares have voting and dividend rights. Depending on their other features, they may also be participating and convertible. The redeemable feature involves turning them in for cash. The redemption can be at the option of the holder (a put) or the company (a call), can be voluntary or mandatory and can be available on certain dates or periods. The company may be required to establish a sinking fund, making it the obligation of the company to set aside funds on a regular basis so that sufficient cash will be available to retire the stock. The price, timing of the redemption and security will be governed by the offering documents.

Funding Sources—Nonregistered and Registered Primary Offering

Assuming the company cannot raise money from existing shareholders, managers or employees, in an acquisition it might have to look to outside sources for equity. As discussed in Chapter 3 under the securities laws, money from such sources can be raised in two ways:[5]

Companies raising money from outsiders must usually register the securities being offered with the federal Securities and Exchange Commission (SEC) or file with one of the state securities administrators. There are a few exceptions to this requirement, which are called **nonregistered primary offerings**.

These exceptions are generally referred to as private placement or exempt offerings made to sophisticated investors, such as insurance companies, pension funds and venture funds. They are exempted principally because the administrators believe such investors have sufficient specialized knowledge to take care of themselves.

A private placement can be an offering of an equity or debt security. Usually, an unlimited number of "sophisticated" investors meeting certain requirements under the securities laws can be approached. The dollar amount raised, however, may be limited. While usually used by small companies, a few large public companies have relied on nonregistered offerings to raise money in strategic, specific transactions.

If an exemption does not apply, the acquirer must register its securities with the SEC and file with appropriate state agencies. In **registered primary offerings**, the acquirer will usually retain a group of investment bankers who will agree to market or underwrite the offering.

Debt Financing

Debt does not give the lender any ownership interest in the borrower. The lender is only entitled to the return of its money plus a rental charge (interest) for the use of it. Interest can be paid periodically or when the principal is repaid.

Lenders are more concerned about the return of their money plus interest. They are less interested in taking a risk on the future of the borrower by acquiring an ownership interest. Instead they settle for a fixed return.

For the borrower, debt is cheaper than equity if the company's value is growing or will grow faster than the rate of interest. On the down side, fixed obligations to repay borrowed amounts, as well as possible fixed periodic payments of interest, create an inflexible obligation for the company. It must be able to make the payments when due.

Types of Debt—Secured and Unsecured

There are two types of debt—secured and unsecured.[6] They can also be categorized by the underlying security.

Secured debt is called a bond. The company's obligation to repay is secured by the pledge of specific assets. If the company defaults, the lender can sell the assets and keep what is owed to it. Anything extra is turned over to any other lender with a secondary secured interest in the same asset, then to unsecured creditors and finally to the company. If the asset does not cover the debt, the lender becomes an unsecured creditor for the shortfall.

For many companies, secured debt is the only method to raise debt. Lenders are unwilling to lend money without some security. Even for those with other methods, secured debt is cheaper than unsecured—since the risk is lower, the return can be lower.

As with preferred stock, secured lenders can have different priorities. First priority lenders receive a first or senior lien on the asset pledged. Those coming later receive junior liens. Later lenders can have priority over prior lenders with the consent of their predecessors. In most cases, subsequent liens on the same property are prohibited. These lien priorities and any prohibitions are established in the debt instrument.

Senior and junior liens deal with timing or who gets the money first. Another common allocation between lenders is based on the asset. Different lenders may be given liens on different assets.

As discussed below, debt secured by the pledge of real estate is known as mortgages.

Unsecured debt is called a debenture. The company's obligation to repay is not secured by the pledge of any specific asset. The company's obligation is secured by the company's general financial condition. If the company defaults, secured creditors have a prior claim and can sell assets on which they have liens. Anything left over is divided among unsecured creditors who take priority only over equity holders.

For companies, unsecured debt has the advantage of not tying up company assets. They can be sold or pledged in the future. Additionally, more unsecured assets will make it easier to attract future unsecured lenders.

The disadvantage for companies is that unsecured debt is more expensive than secured debt. There is more risk since unsecured lenders receive payment after secured creditors, and more risk means more return demanded by unsecured lenders. Because of the greater risk they are exposed to, unsecured lenders might also impose restrictions on how the company can run its business. They are likely to include restrictions on sales of substantial assets, new stock issuance and even new financing.

Types of Rights—Repayment, Interest Rate, Security, Subordination, Conversion, Covenants and Default

Debt involves a number of issues. The most important issues are repayment of principal, payment and amount of interest, optional prepayment, security, subordination, conversion, covenants and events of default.[7]

The first right of debt is to be repaid. This raises the question of when that will happen. Will it be on a fixed date (balloon payment) or in installments over a period of time? If repaid in installments, when will they start, and how often will they be made—annually, quarterly or monthly? A related question is whether the installments will be in equal amounts or possibly escalate over time?

Interest is the next great right of a lender, that is, the right to be paid for the use of its money. Interest can be at a fixed rate or adjusted over time. Adjustments are usually based on an objective standard, which is usually a funds rate set by the federal government such as Treasury bill rates. The amount of interest is

Table 4.2 Types of Debt

Type	Category	Obligation to Repay
Bond	Secured	Secured by pledge of specific asset
		Different priorities possible
Mortgage	Secured	Secured by pledge of real estate or equipment
		Different priorities possible
Debenture	Unsecured	Not secured by pledge of specific asset
		Must rely on unsecured assets

based on borrower's financial condition and prevailing financial market conditions. Interest may be payable at maturity along with principal or periodically, such as monthly, quarterly or annually. Depending on borrower's financial condition and cash flow, payments may be postponed for several months or years. A variation of the usual obligation of the issuer to pay interest in cash is the **pay-in-kind bond** that gives the issuer the right to pay interest in cash or additional securities.

In some cases, borrowers want the right to repay the debt prior to its due date. Borrower might have extra cash flow or the interest rate of the existing debt may be higher than current market rates. Lenders, on the other hand, do not want borrowers repaying early in most cases. They might have obtained the lent money from other institutions at a fixed rate and for a fixed term. If the rate is good, that is, higher than existing rates, lenders will certainly not want the money back since they cannot redeploy the money and earn as much. Some lenders might permit repayment as long as the borrower pays a premium to make up for any losses they might incur. The make up fee, however, will be stated in the loan agreement.

As noted, debt can be secured or unsecured. If secured, the loan documentation must carefully describe the asset and whether subsequent liens on the same asset can be granted.

Unsecured debt is subordinate to secured debt. Even within secured debt, one lender might have a lower priority (junior lien) to another (senior lien). The debt instruments must carefully describe the priorities and which lender is subordinate to another. The subordination provisions must also clarify whether repayments can be made to junior lien holders while senior debt is outstanding. In some cases, such repayment may be prohibited; in others it may be possible as long as no default has occurred.

Similar to holders of convertible preferred stock, secured and unsecured lenders might have a right to participate in the upswing if the lender does well. This usually takes two forms:

- Straight debt that is repaid in accordance with its terms and with the lender receiving separate warrants that, for a fee or exercise price, can be converted into stock. In some cases, the debt's principal or interest can be used to pay the exercise price.
- Right to convert debt into stock.

The conversion terms will be fixed in the debt instrument, including the exercise price, number of shares lender is entitled to, and date or period when conversion is permitted. The conversion usually requires notice rather than being automatic.

To reduce their risks, many lenders restrict what the company can do while the loan is outstanding. These restrictions are called covenants and are either affirmative, with the borrower agreeing to do something in the future, such as, maintain certain financial ratios, or negative, with borrower agreeing not to do something, such as, not merge, acquire or sell a substantial portion of its assets.

If something bad happens to borrower or borrower's business, lender might not want to wait, possibly for years, for the debt to be repaid while hoping that borrower's condition does not deteriorate during that time. A lender wants to take immediate action if borrower:

- breaks or breaches a covenant;
- breaches a representation or warranty about its financial condition;
- defaults under another loan instrument (called a cross default);
- is insolvent or becomes bankrupt.

These are called events of default, and after a period of time, called a cure period, entitle lender to take certain action. These include the right to demand immediate payment of outstanding debt (acceleration) and to elect one or more members of the board of directors.

Specific Types of Debt

I have described the two basic forms of corporate debt—secured (bond) and unsecured (debenture). I have also described the basic rights associated with debt—repayment of principal, payment and amount of interest, optional prepayment, security, subordination, conversion, covenant and event of default. Now, lets put them together and describe specific types of corporate debt:[8]

- Demand note: this is the simplest form of corporate note. Lender can demand repayment of principal and payment of interest at any time. This gives holder the greatest flexibility but creates the greatest risk for borrower. At a minimum, borrower should obtain prior notice of the demand so that it has a minimum period to raise money and pay off the debt.
- Unsecured fixed term debenture: as noted, a debenture is unsecured. If the due date for repayment is fixed, it is an unsecured fixed term debenture. The fixed term allows the borrower complete use of all funds borrowed until the end of the term.
- Secured fixed term debenture: while debentures are unsecured, there is one exception. Fixed term debentures can be secured by the pledge of certain assets. Even though they are unsecured, they are usually junior to other secured lenders and in many cases to commercial lenders. These debentures are usually issued to related lenders—founders, managers, employees or affiliated companies.
- Real estate mortgage bond: loans secured by real estate owned by a borrower are mortgages. Since corporate secured loans are called bonds,

secured real property loans by corporate borrowers are called real estate mortgage bonds. The security can be specific property owned by borrower or all real estate owned by it. The security may be limited to property presently owned by borrower or might include "after acquired" real estate. Borrower might want to issue future bonds on the same property. If so, such "after issued" bonds will be subordinate to the first or senior bonds. In many cases, senior bonds might prohibit future bonds on the same asset.

- Equipment mortgage bond: in addition to issuing bonds on real property, a corporate borrower might issue bonds on its other assets, such as equipment. These types of bonds are called equipment mortgage bonds and are issued by companies with substantial investments in equipment. Railroads are the best example.
- Conditional sale bond: a specialized equipment mortgage bond is the conditional sale bond. In this case when a company needs equipment it takes possession, but title is retained by seller or by a trustee if bonds are sold to the public. The company is liable for the bonds and pays them as they become due. To reduce the equipment seller's risks, a large down payment is usually required with the face value of bonds being much lower than the resale value of the equipment.
- Trust certificate: another specialized equipment mortgage bond is the trust certificate. Under this arrangement, a trustee purchases equipment needed by a company and leases that equipment to the company. The trustee pays for the equipment in two ways. It receives from the company a large down payment, which reduces the trustee's risk. For the balance, it sells bonds to the public by issuing trust certificates. The company makes regular rental payments to the trustee, which are sufficient to cover principal and interest on the bond. Although the trustee is primarily liable, the company guarantees the bond.
- Collateral trust bond: so far we have seen two types of security for bonds— real estate and equipment. Intangible assets, such as stocks, bonds, securities and notes, are a third type of bond security and are used as security for collateral trust bonds. The most common intangibles pledged are stocks and bonds of subsidiaries and unrelated companies, accounts receivable and notes receivable. The pledged assets are usually turned over to a trustee, since possession is the only way to obtain a security interest over such assets. Any dividends or interest earned by the pledged assets, however, is turned over to the borrower—at least prior to any default.
- Guaranteed bond: rather than being secured only by the assets of a corporate borrower, a lender might ask for greater security, such as a guarantee by someone else. The guarantee can be of principal only or of both principal and interest. The most common guarantor is the borrower's parent,

although a noncorporate founder or principal shareholder may also be asked to be a guarantor. If there are several founders or principal shareholders, they may all be asked to sign a joint guarantee.

- Convertible debt financing instrument: for lenders, debt has the advantage of priority over equity. It has the disadvantage of a fixed return in exchange for lower risk. Some lenders like to hedge their bets by lending debt but with the right to convert the debt into equity if the company starts to do well. Such an equity kicker often reduces the interest rate on the debt. Convertible debt is similar to convertible preferred stock. The difference though is that convertible debt cannot elect directors nor have any other rights of shareholders. Many convertible debt instruments, however, give holders the right to elect directors in case of default and prohibit certain actions such as mergers, acquisitions and sales of substantial assets.
- Mezzanine debt: this tends to be junior subordinated debt with warrants. Its name derives from being in the middle, similar to the mezzanine section of a theatre and can refer to:
  - Timing: bridge financing occurring between early stage investment and initial public offering
  - Security: equity having security rights between senior secured loans and unsecured equity

Mezzanine finance has become popular lately, in part because of the decline of the junk or high-yield bond market to be discussed in a latter section. This market typically costs investors, meaning they offer investors returns of, 10–25 percent, versus 6–10 percent for debt and 25 percent or more for junk bonds.

Funding Sources—Internal, Vendor, Partner, Private and Commercial

A company has many funding sources to use for an acquisition. Some of them can be used to pay the purchase price. Others can be used to free up other funds. For instance, a company can use vendor financing rather than a bank loan to pay for new equipment and then use the bank loan to pay for an acquisition.[9]

Internal Funds
One of the first places to look for funds to pay for an acquisition is internal funding. Almost all acquisitions rely on internal funds to some extent.

These internal funds are after-tax earnings from the company's prior operations, which have not been distributed to shareholders. Another source is cash accrued for future obligations. If those obligations can be reduced, cash can be freed up. Future taxes are an example. If the company has been conservative in its depreciation practices, it can make cash available for the acquisition by becoming more aggressive.

Each line item of the company's books should be evaluated and means of freeing up cash should be sought.

Vendor Financing

When making an acquisition, cash is cash whether it comes from internal or external sources and whether it is used directly to fund the purchase price or indirectly for other obligations. As noted, if cash can be diverted from paying off vendors to making the acquisition, the company can reduce the additional amount it has to borrow.

Acquirer should evaluate the cost of increased finance charges from vendors, versus borrowing money or giving equity to raise money for the acquisition. Vendor financing and debt can be expensive, but they will be less expensive than equity for a company that might increase in value after an acquisition.

Strategic Partner

Another source of funds is a strategic partner. This can take many forms:

- Acquirer might look for another company to assist it in making an acquisition.
- Two or more companies might agree to acquire a company and split the assets.
- Customer may be willing to enter into a long-term supply contract, which acquirer can use as security for a loan.
- Customer may be willing to prepay or fund product development.
- Customer of target might not be pleased with target's performance and therefore assist acquirer in taking it over.

Private Loan

Founders and major shareholders may be asked to provide funds that can be used to finance the acquisition. Their loans can be secured or unsecured and possibly convertible into equity. Even if secured, they may be subordinate to other secured creditors.

Commercial Loan and Lease

There are a number of commercial lenders and lessors. The terms vary depending on the source and issues I discussed earlier—repayment of principal, payment and amount of interest, optional prepayment, security, subordination, conversion, covenant and event of default.

The most common commercial lenders are:

- commercial banks;
- commercial finance companies;

- thrift institutions;
- syndicates composed of two or more commercial lenders that "participate" in a loan.

They offer a wide variety of financing alternatives:

- Short-term working capital loans
- Long-term lending
- Real estate and mortgage lending
- Inventory and accounts receivable financing
- Equipment leasing
- Specialized forms of debt financing

Commercial banks provide a wide variety of business credit on a secured and unsecured basis. Many specialize in making loans to companies in specific industries.

Commercial finance companies often provide loans to companies that cannot qualify for loans from commercial banks. They reduce credit standards, demand less collateral, provide longer-term loans and agree to higher loan-to-collateral value ratios. In exchange, they demand higher returns than banks.

Thrift institutions such as **savings and loan associations** and **savings banks** can invest a portion of their assets in general commercial loans. They might also finance purchase of assets, such as in an acquisition.

Leasing companies are another possible source. As noted, to the extent acquirers can free up cash by leasing assets rather than paying money to buy them, more funds are available for purchasing target. Leases do not appear on the acquirer's balance sheet and thus do not use up credit lines.

Junk Bonds and High-yield Bonds

One type of corporate bond that is particularly important in acquisitions is the junk or high-yield bond.

Popularized in the 1980s by firms such as Drexel Burnham Lambert and individuals such as Michael Milken, the bonds were known as junk bonds. The term referred to the high risk, but high returns that were associated with them. The high risk was based on the belief that the companies issuing them had a greater risk of default. The high returns were necessary to encourage investors to purchase them.

Before Milken, issuers were companies whose bonds had been rated as investment grade at time of issue but encountered financial difficulties and had their ratings downgraded to noninvestment grade. They were known as **fallen angels**.

It was Milken who popularized them as first-time issuance, rather than postissuance downgrades. He argued that their high risk was more than compensated by their high returns. Through Milken and others at the time, small companies and major investors used junk bonds to finance takeovers. Most purchasers were large, sophisticated investors.

While this aspect of the bonds was an acceptable business practice, some actions associated with them were not. Many of the people involved with them at the time resorted to illegal activities in connection with the acquisitions being funded by the junk bonds. These activities included insider trading, stock manipulation and market rigging. Two things happened as a result: many of the people involved with such activities went to jail, and the name junk bonds became tarnished. A new name became necessary.

While a name change was necessary, the high-risk attribute had not changed. Reflecting this emphasis the name became high-yield bonds. Not surprising, it focussed on the positive aspect (high yield) and not the negative (high risk). It is equivalent to calling a used car a high-ownership car.

Whatever the name, the term refers to corporate bonds and obligations—any evidence of debt, such as notes, debentures or commercial papers—that are rated as noninvestment grade by a major bond-rating agency, such as Moody's or Standard & Poor's. The ratings are the agencies' opinion on the ability of the bond issuer to make principal and interest payments. Table 4.3 shows the credit ratings that are used for investment and noninvestment grade bonds.

According to Moody's, Ba bonds have speculative elements, their future cannot be considered assured, while their protection of principal and interest is moderate and not well safe-guarded. B bonds lack characteristics of a desirable investment and the payment of interest and principal may be small. Caa bonds are of poor standing and may be in default or have elements of danger with respect to principal or interest.

Standard & Poor's, BB bonds have less near term vulnerability to default than B or CCC, but face major ongoing uncertainties . . . which might lead to inadequate capacity to make interest or principal payments. B bonds have a greater

Table 4.3 Credit Ratings

Grade	Moody's Investor Service, Inc.	Standard & Poor's
Investment Grade	Aaa	AAA
	Aa	AA
	A	A
	Baa	BBB
Noninvestment Grade	Ba	BB
Junk or High Yield	B	B
	Caa	CCC
	Ca	C
	C	D

vulnerability to default than BB bonds and the ability to make interest and principal payments is likely to be impaired if adverse business conditions occur. CCC bonds have a currently identifiable vulnerability to default and will be unable to pay interest and principal without favorable business conditions.

Most states prohibit investments by insurance companies in bonds that are rated three or lower by the National Association of Insurance Commissioners (NAIC). This is a national body established in 1871 with its headquarters in Kansas City, Missouri, whose members are state insurance regulators. NAIC rates bonds as well as stocks in its Securities Valuation Manual. Bonds meeting certain credit requirements are carried at face value, plus or minus any purchase discount. NAIC also maintains a Valuation of Securities System (VOS), which is an online database that monitors insurers' solvency by listing securities held by them and their historical financials beginning in 1989.

How safe are junk bonds? On the one hand, the acquirer might not believe it cares as long as it can sell the bonds. On the other hand, the higher the perceived risk of junk bonds in general, the higher interest it will have to pay.

It is generally believed that the savings and loan association (S&L) crisis that struck the United States in the late 1980s and early 1990s was caused by defaults of junk bonds held by the S&Ls. Additionally, a 1989 study of all high-yield bonds issued between 1978 and 1986 showed that 34 percent of the bonds defaulted. It also found that the best high-yield bonds were issued at the beginning of the period with the default rate rising over the time studied.[10]

Some of this has changed in recent years. With the shift of the name to high-yield bonds and the reduction of illegal activities associated with acquisitions, the bonds have become a bit more popular. Additionally, investors have changed. There are more funds purchasing them as a way to spread the risk. Instead of one only investor owning one junk bond, four investors can purchase four bonds with each owning one-fourth.

How good is the market for high-yield bonds? Can acquirers still use them to finance acquisitions? Most people assume that the junk bond market collapsed with the fall of Milken and Drexel Burnham Lambert. It did not. By the mid-1990s, sales had returned to the levels of the 1980s. By 1997, the high-yield bond market had:

- seven years of solid returns;
- a default rate of 1.6 percent;
- a majority of funds, that is, 65 percent, going into junk bonds, with investments in government bonds declining;
- set a record for new sales;
- a declining cost to acquirers issuing the bonds due to the declining default rate. The spread between junk-bond yields and safe Treasury securities was 3.2 percent.

  The culmination was Amazon.com's offer to sell $275 million in 10-year, unrated high-yield bonds

By 1998, sales had risen to $157 billion—almost 16 times the amount issued in 1991. At the turn of the century, sales fell back to $86 billion in 1999 and continued at lower levels for the next several years. There were three reasons:

- Default rates rose.
- Time from issuance to default shortened from three to two years.
- In the late 1990s, investors preferred "dot-com" stocks
- Following the collapse of dot-com stocks, investors pulled away from all high-risk stocks.

In the twenty-first century, sales turned back upward as investors began to look again at high-risk stock to balance their portfolios. According to Thomson Financial, junk bond issuance in the United States rose to near record highs in 2006. U.S. companies sold $150 billion worth of junk bonds in 2006, which was up from $99 billion in 2005. The 2006 total broke the twenty-first-century record of $143 billion set in 2004. According to Raj Dhanda, the head of fixed-income capital markets at Morgan Stanley in New York, the driving force behind the new levels was cheap debt that was driving mergers and acquisitions to higher levels.[11]

The leading underwriter of high-yield bonds in 2006 was J. P. Morgan, while the largest deals were Freescale Semiconductor and HCA Inc.[12]

Leveraged and Management Buy-Out—Debt and Equity

A leveraged buy-out (LBO) is the acquisition of a target business by private investors. The purchase price is primarily financed by debt arranged by investors. A smaller portion will be equity contributed by the investors.

Consider a private group of investors who agree to purchase a target for $100 million, billion or, someday no doubt, trillion. They might contribute $5–15, with the balance raised as debt to be secured by target's assets from closing. As I discussed in the previous section, the debt will be junk or high-yield bonds.

Owners, management, unions or third parties can initiate buy-outs. When initiated by owners, including their board of directors, the sale can be conducted by private sale negotiated with just one buyer or by private auction negotiated with a limited number of buyers.

Debt Portion

The debt raised to finance the buy-out is borrowed against target's assets and projected cash flows. The debt is usually in layers of senior and subordinated debt and is repaid by target out of its future earnings.

Senior Debt

Senior debt usually makes up 50–70 percent of LBO financings. First liens or claims on targets' assets secure such loans. The most common lenders are banks. To a lesser extent, acquirers use privately placed notes to institutional investors and public issuance of bonds. There are usually two types of senior debt.

- **Revolving Line of Credit** is made available to a target based on a percentage of the appraised liquidation value of its inventory and accounts receivable. There may be a maximum based on its available cash flow to service senior debt. Between 15–35 percent of the funds will be from such a line of credit. The term is usually for one year and is subject to renewal if certain conditions, called covenants, are met. The cost is usually between prime and 2 percent over prime. This is usually the lowest cost funding for buy-outs.
- **Term Debt** is a loan based on a certain percentage of the appraised fair market value of target's land and buildings plus the liquidation value of its machinery and equipment. A maximum based on cash flow needed to service senior debt is usually established. Between 25–50 percent of the buy-out funds will be term debt. The term is usually five to eight years with interest at prime to 3 percent over prime. This is the second lowest cost buy-out funding.

Subordinated Debt

Subordinated debt usually makes up 15–30 percent of LBO financings. These funds are subordinated to senior debt and are only secured by excess cash flow. As noted in the previous section most buy-outs include public issuance of high-yield or junk bonds, which are purchased by insurance companies, pension funds and other institutional investors. They traditionally rely on subordinated debt. In many cases, target's selling shareholders might take debt for their former equity. Since repayment is subordinated to senior debt and is at greater risk, these funds are more expensive—from 2–8 percent over senior debt. In addition, an equity kicker giving lender equity in the target might raise the return to the lender to 15–30 percent.

One reason buy-outs are heavily leveraged is so equity can reap a higher return. The more debt, the less equity, and the less equity, the more each share receives in dividends and increased value.

Debt is also cheaper than equity. Since debt, including subordinate debt, receives distributions on liquidation before equity, it is less at risk. The lower risk means lower return. Additionally, payments to debt holders are deductible expenses. Payments to equity holders are nondeductible distributions.

Equity Portion

Between 10–20 percent of the total funds in a buy-out is equity, which is only repaid after all debt. Equity comes from private investors whose name reflects the restricted trading of their equity. The shares they receive are not publicly traded on an exchange. After the buy-out, the target will be privately owned, even if it had been a public company, and will no longer have its shares publicly traded.

There are two basic types of private investors involved in LBOs. There are outsiders, for whom the term LBOs applies. Outside investors, such as institutional investors or funds, usually expect a 20–40 percent annual return.

And then there are insiders, primarily members of management, for whom the term MBO or management buy-out applies. In many cases, the buy-out might include both outsiders and insiders.

In recent years, there has been a trend for buy-outs by employees or unions not just managers. These acquisitions are frequently funded in part by employee benefit plans, such as employee stock ownership plans (ESOP). ESOP ownership offers several advantages:

- Contributions to the ESOP by target are deductible, reducing taxes by about 40 percent of the amount contributed.
- Interest rate on senior debt will be reduced on average by 15 percent. As a result of the above tax savings, more cash flow is available to service debt. This gives more comfort to lenders who reduce their rates to reflect the lower risk.
- As owners, employees and unions might become more willing to make reduce wages, accept reductions in force (RIF), and reduce employee benefits. Wage reductions between 5 and 15 percent are possible.
- With their vested interest in the company, employee productivity often rises.
- From the above savings, buy-out debt can be paid off sooner, thus saving the target significant money.
- Net result of these savings is increased net worth and enterprise value.

Influences

Why are LBOs and MBOs happening? What is driving them?

First is purchase opportunity. More companies are willing to spin off subsidiaries, divisions or business units to concentrate on their core business. They are divesting segments that are not central to their operations or that can be better handled by others. Additionally, in a world of limited resources, companies will allocate their management, finance and technology to areas that they believe offer more opportunity.

Second is finance opportunity. In the past 20 years, the availability of funds to purchase large businesses has increased tremendously. In large buy-outs, lenders provide billions of dollars. This had not happened before.

Third is the climate. Buy-outs are acceptable. Each year they get bigger, and each instance encourages other companies to consider the possibility.

Fourth, in the case of MBOs, is incentive. Managers and employees may be more motivated when they own a piece of the business. Direct ownership also frequently allows an extra layer of outside supervision to be eliminated.

Fifth, more so in the case of MBOs, is focus. Businesses owned by managers may be more capable of concentrating on the long-term health of the company. There is less need to worry about short-term returns or using up cash reserves to make dividend distributions.

Case Studies

To highlight the differences between buy-outs, I will describe two case studies. One of them is a quite famous LBO, the other is a little known MBO.

Many writers describe buy-outs as a post–World War II phenomena. It has been around for a long time, however. For as long as companies and businesses have existed, individuals have wanted to buy them and owners have been willing to sell.

Although it is not well known, one of the earliest examples of an MBO in the last century was by Henry Ford.[13] In 1916 he looked for ways to fund the development of the River Rouge plant—a facility that would be a completely integrated vertical producer of automobiles, from processing steel to manufacturing cars. To pay for the plant he slashed dividends from $60 million in 1915 to $1.2 million the next year. His minority shareholders were not pleased—especially John and Horace Dodge who had been using their share of the dividends since 1913 to build a competing company. Henry was equally displeased when they sued to force him to pay dividends.

After considerable dispute, the courts ultimately allowed Henry to proceed with his development plan, as long as he paid his minority shareholders a dividend of $19 million.[14] Henry did not like having to give up $19 million—money that he could use to develop the River Rouge plant—to what he called parasites. He decided to take action.

He first started saying that he might go out and develop another automobile company that would make cars, especially his Model-T, cheaper than the existing Ford Motor Company did. He also had agents in late 1918 and early 1919 offering to buy shares held by minority stockholders.

On July 11, 1919, he closed his deal to buy out minority shareholders for $105.8 million.[15] In true MBO form, he borrowed most of the purchase price, which was $75 million, from a syndicate led by Chase Securities. Henry celebrated by dancing a jig around the room when the deal was signed.

Over the next several years, Henry reinvested his money in the River Rouge plant. Between 1918 and 1920, he ploughed $60.5 million into the facility. The result was a modern manufacturing wonder—90 buildings, 42,000 employees and 93 miles of railroad track. All of it was able to turn iron and steel into a car within one day, and it demonstrated the future of mass production.[16] His MBO is also an example of management having a greater appreciation of future opportunities than did existing owners who cared more for short-term dividends than long-term growth.

The next example is better known and started out with insiders in an MBO but quickly involved outsiders in an LBO. In many ways it is the epitome of LBOs during their heyday in the 1980s. The example is RJR Nabisco and was popularized in a book and movie called *Barbarians at the Gate*.

The acquisition started as an MBO when Ross Johnson, CEO of RJR Nabisco, a manufacturer of cigarettes and consumer-products, persuaded Shearson Lehman Hutton to back him in a $75-per-share, $17 billion management buyout of his own firm. Unfortunately for Ross, within a week an outsider, Kohlberg Kravis Roberts & Co. (KKR), recognized the value of RJR Nabisco, arranged the necessary financing and bid $90-per-share. The next five bidding rounds brought in such figures as Bruce Wasserstein and the Forstmann brothers.

Ultimately KKR won the most expensive LBO of its time with financing provided by Merrill Lynch, Morgan Stanley, and Michael Milken junk bonds. The win was expensive, however. The cost was almost double the starting bid—$109 per share, $31.5 billion. In LBO fashion most of the purchase price, $30 billion, was debt.[17]

The story did not end there, however. Months after the deal closed in February 1989, Congress considered changing the tax status of debt raised for LBOs. Moody's responded by downgrading RJR's debt. To keep RJR afloat, KKR in July 1990 injected another $1.7 billion in equity.

In the long run, the investment was not a good one for KKR. By the time it sold its remaining shares in RJR in March 1995, RJR's stock price had inched up only 2.3 percent to $5.75 not counting dividends from its original cost of $5.62 a share.[18]

Valuation

One of the more difficult areas in acquisitions is valuation.

We have discussed a number of areas, such as legal, tax and accounting. Each has difficult rules, and for many of them there are disagreements on how they are to be interpreted. With valuation the problem is a bit different. The rules are pretty clear, but what rule to apply is less certain.

The difference may be visualized as a fork in the road. With valuation the branches are clearly defined but with equivalent arguments for taking each fork. Once the choice is made, however, the paths are pretty well defined. With legal, tax and accounting, the forks are more confusing and less defined along their course.

In valuation we are faced with many different methods to value a business. The choice among them depends not on what is right but on which one will give the highest numbers if you are selling or the lowest numbers if you are buying. Whose choice will be used then depends on negotiation leverage.

Let's start with some background and then move to the different approaches.

Standards and Appraisers

Several bodies have tried to establish valuation standards. The most important are:

- USPAP: Uniform Standards of Professional Appraisal Practice of the Appraisal Standards Board;
- ASA: American Society of Appraisers;
- IBA: Institute of Business Appraisers;
- NACVA: National Association of Certified Valuation Analysts;
- AICPA: American Institute of Certified Public Accountants;
- IRS: Internal Revenue Service.

Courts can also be added to the list, since various court decisions have created valuation rules.

At present, there is no governmental appraisal license required. However, most appraisers have one of the following professional certificates:

- ASA: Accredited Senior Appraiser, issued by ASA
- CBA: Certified Business Appraiser, issued by IBA
- CVA: Certified Valuation Analyst, issued by NACVA
- ABV: Accredited in Business Valuation, issued by AICPA

There are two types of appraisals: complete and limited. Complete appraisal is in compliance with the agreedupon standards. Limited appraisal relies on permitted exceptions under the agreed upon standard. For instance, USPAP allows appraisers to perform assignments in which the scope of work is less than or different from USPAP standards. However, such change cannot reduce the credibility of the results.

Definitions

According to the above standards, the basic definition of value is the worth of something. There are, however, five different definitions of worth:

- Fair market value: amount at which property would change hands between a willing seller and a willing buyer when neither is acting under compulsion and when both have reasonable knowledge of the relevant facts (ASA, following IRS Revenue Ruling 59–60).
- Fair value: value determined by courts as to what is fair, particularly when trying to protect minority shareholders in a merger or acquisition.
- Liquidation or break-up value: value of assets if business ceases and individual assets are liquidated either orderly, selling over reasonable time to obtain highest price, or forced, selling as quickly as possible such as at auction.
- Book value: for an asset, its capitalized cost, less accumulated depreciation, depletion and amortization as it appears on company's books. For a business, it is the difference between total assets—less depreciation, depletion and amortization—and total liabilities, which is also known as net book value, net worth and shareholders' equity.
- Investment or intrinsic value: value of a business or asset to a specific purchaser, thus taking into account synergy.

Because of this basic disagreement over worth, the usual result in valuation is a range of values rather than a specific amount.

Theory

In valuation the goal is to identify for the buyer the present value or worth of an asset based on its future benefits. Based on this theory the value depends on estimating the future values and discounting them back to the present.

Translating this theory into reality is more difficult. It is difficult to identify with certainty what the future will bring. If it was easy we could all invest wisely if not perfectly. Getting two groups, buyer and seller, with vested interests in different conclusions to agree on such a number is even more difficult. Similarly, getting consensus on the discounted value of future benefits also creates problems.

Estimated or Historical Numbers

To reduce some of the disagreement about predicting the future, one solution is to base the valuation on past performance. Take an easy example. Suppose that last year's earnings were $1 million. Assuming the economy, market and competition did not change, under this method this year's earnings would be projected to be $1 million.[19]

A variation is to project those numbers into the future rather than making pure predictions of future benefits. For instance, revenues last year were $10 million, but a new customer has agreed to place an order for $2 million. In such a case, the projection for this year would be $12 million. Similar adjustments to expense items would be made, for instance a key supplier might increase its prices by 10 percent. If so, the pro forma projection should show a 10 percent increase in this expense item.

Venture capitalists investing in start-up companies prefer historical sales figures. They argue that for a start-up it is the only reliable number. Of course, it does not hurt that such numbers are to their benefit when valuing a company that may soon be taking off with sales rising significantly.

Variables

Regardless of whether the decision is to use actual historical numbers or estimates, some type of numbers must be used.[20] The most common types of numbers used in valuations are based on internal and external factors:

- Earnings or cash flow
  - From operations
  - From investments
- Liquidation or mortgage of assets
- Sales price

These internal variables will be affected by what is being sold, such as:

- minority, controlling or majority;
- voting rights;
- restrictions on transfer;
- other rights associated with shares;
- method of payment—cash or deferred;
- timing of sale—urgent or in due course.

External factors will also affect the value, such as market for shares. The most important external factor, however, is risk.

Risk

Risk is one of the most important variables affecting valuation. Envision an x-y axis chart with return on the vertical axis and risk on the horizontal axis. Next, draw a line in the chart starting at the bottom left corner and rising to the top right corner. The line represents the relationship between risk and return, with risk on the vertical line and return on the horizontal. When risk is low, such as in the bottom left corner, return is also low. When risk is high, such as in the upper right corner, return is also high.

In valuation, lower risk means return is more certain and present value is higher. On the other hand, higher risk means present value is lower. Risk is reflected in the discount or capitalization rate used to bring the estimated future earnings back to the present.

Risk comes from many sources. Some of the more important factors are the economy, market, competitors and even demand for company's products.

Methods

Valuation methods can be divided into four categories: assets, sales and income, market comparisons and discounted cash flow. The latter two are the primary valuation methods used.

Asset Based

Asset based valuations are the most conservative methods. The four most important ones are:

- **Adjusted Net Book Value**: This method bases the valuation on the historical cost of the asset, or net book value.[21] That value can then be adjusted as necessary, for instance, upwards for excessive depreciation and LIFO (last in, first out) reserves and downwards for unfunded pension and retirement benefits.

  Tangible assets are the first and easiest to value. They usually have a purchased value that, after depreciation, is reflected on target's financial statements. Intangible assets, such as customer lists and patents, are more difficult. These might not have been purchased, and there may not be a readily determinable market value for them.

- **Replacement Cost**: This approach can be used on a stand-alone basis or to supplement another. For instance, the replacement cost can be used in lieu of the adjusted net book value, or it can be used to check the adjusted net book value. It can also be used as the starting point for estimating liquidation value, which I will soon discuss.

  This method usually results in a higher value than the adjusted net book value, since the book value might reflect several years of depreciation. The depreciated value may be below what it would cost to replace the asset. As a result, sellers prefer this method when starting negotiations. Most appraisers object to this method, preferring instead to adjust any replacement cost by depreciation and obsolescence.

Consider software purchased a year ago. It may already be fully depreciated and show a zero value under the adjusted net book value method. To replace the software, there will be some cost to buy new software. That cost would be the replacement cost. However, this may not be a realistic number since the new software would have many new attributes. Under the modified replacement cost method, the cost of the new software would be reduced to reflect the old software not containing those features.

- **Liquidation Value**: This is also a conservative approach since it ignores the value of the business as an operating business. Instead, it looks at what those assets would bring if they were sold at an auction as the company is being dissolved. This is likely to be a low number. Nevertheless, it is commonly calculated and used by buyers and sellers as a base line number or floor for negotiations.

  Liquidation value is calculated by estimating what the assets would bring if sold for cash. As noted, it can be assumed that the assets are being sold on an orderly or forced basis. The shorter the assumed period, the less money is likely to be received.

  All liabilities are deducted from the cash received. This includes costs of selling the assets, such as appraisal fees, real estate fees, brokerage commissions, attorney fees and accounting fees.

- **Secured Loan Value**: Under this approach, a reverse calculation is made. For instance, banks will lend up to 90 percent of the value of land and accounts receivable. Therefore, the value of such assets is based on the assumption that any loan on them is at 90 percent of the value. If a bank has lent $90,000 on a piece of land, even though the outstanding balance has been paid down under this approach the value is assumed to be $100,000.

  A similar calculation is made for inventory, although the percentage is lower. Banks are usually only willing to lend 10–60 percent depending on raw materials, work-in-process or finished goods. Such percentage also depends on historical turnover and salability.

Sale and Income Based

There are two valuation methods based on target's sales or income:

- **Price/Earnings Ratios**: This method considers target's stock price as traded and divides it by target's earnings per share.[22] Thus, if target's stock is traded at $10, and target earned $5 per share last year, its ratio is 2. This derived ratio is then multiplied by projected earnings. If target anticipates earning $10 million, its value would be $20 million. The method is commonly used for publicly traded companies.

  Acquirer can reverse this ratio to determine what it is willing to pay for a target. For example, assume acquirer wants a return on investment (ROI), which is measured by earnings divided by investment, of 5. Also assume that the above numbers still apply. In this case, acquirer can determine what it is willing to pay in order to accomplish its ROI objective.

A related approach is the comparative price-earnings ratio method. Under this approach an acquirer determines the price-earnings ratio of similar companies in the industry. The acquirer then multiplies that value by the sales of the target. If another company in the same industry was recently acquired at a price-earnings ratio of 5, the assumption is that the same ratio applies to a target in the same industry.

- **Rules of Thumb**: Executives often make quick, informal valuations based on industry-wide formulas rather than basing them on a particular company. These methods are usually based on a multiple of sales, earnings and customers. Examples of these are beliefs that radio and television stations sell for 8 to 12 times operating cash flow, insurance agencies sell for 150 percent of annual commissions, and automotive repair facilities sell for 3 times average monthly receipts. These are helpful rules for quick analysis but should not be relied on for more than giving rough estimates.

Market Comparisons
There are two valuation methods based on market comparisons:

- **Stock Market Comparisons**: Start-ups and privately held companies lack values assigned by the market to their shares. Publicly traded companies, on the other hand, have stock market assigned values. In some cases, start-ups can rely on those public market assessed values to determine their own.

  If a start-ups' principal competitors have traded stock, it can argue that their price/earnings ratios should apply to it. Before potential investors will accept this argument, however, they will want start-up's financial statements adjusted to conform to its competitors' statements. In addition, the value will have to be reduced to reflect the lack of a market for a privately held company (illiquidity) and any lack of control.
- **Merger Market Comparisons**: One problem with looking at regular market share trades is that they represent daily trades of minority interests. As I noted above, minority interests are worth less than majority interests. In an acquisition, acquirer usually purchases control of target. Therefore, rather than looking at minority interest trades on the exchanges, a more realistic comparison for an acquirer may be recent mergers or takeovers of companies in the same industry. Such information is usually available and adjustments made as required.

Discounted Cash Flow
The final valuation method is the discounted cash flow (DCF) method. In this approach, a company's estimated future cash flows are brought back or discounted to the present.[23] The advantage of this method is that the future cash flow

reflects management's perception of anticipated earnings, cost savings and technology improvements. It does not reflect the stock market's perception of those earnings.

A key variable under this method is the discount rate or the amount by which the future earnings are discounted. Take an easy example. If your bank is paying 3 percent interest and you leave your money with them, you are saying that $100 today is worth $103 in a year. Your discount rate is 3 percent.

When dealing with businesses, the discount rate is not so clear. It can be affected by a number of factors, such as:

- acquirer's assessment or risk;
- acquirer's required ROI and cost of capital;
- current interest rates;
- current and projected inflation;
- target's cost of capital.

This valuation method also brings down the future or residual value of target at the end of the forecast period. Any of the other methods can be used to calculate this value, including book value, multiple of earnings, cash flow, or other factors.

5

Accounting

Traditionally, two basic accounting questions arose in any acquisition: what accounting method to use and how to apply it. Due to changes in accounting rules, the first question is no longer relevant.

General

As to method, there are several possible accounting methods depending on whether a merger or acquisition or stock acquisition is involved.

In mergers and consolidations, the purchase accounting method must be used. Under this method, the acquisition is treated as if acquirer purchases target. The accounting treatment is similar to that used in the purchase of assets in the ordinary course of business. This meant that:

- Common ownership is only from closing.
- Asset and liability values are recorded at fair market value.
- Purchase price is allocated to the net assets (assets less liabilities) purchased.
- Difference between purchase price and fair market value of the net assets is treated as goodwill.
- Depreciation is based on higher current fair market value.
- Higher depreciation means lower income.

Up to June 30, 2001, pooling of interests accounting method was permitted for mergers and consolidations.[1] Under this method, the acquisition was treated as a merger or pooling of the ownership of the assets into a single business with no change in status. This meant that:

- Common ownership was treated as having always existed;
- Assets and liabilities were carried forward at their recorded values;
- No goodwill was recognized;
- Depreciation was based on lower carry-forward value;
- Lower depreciation meant higher income.

Although the pooling of interests method is no longer permitted, it is important to understand its requirements, recording, disclosures and tax treatment since a present target might have previously acquired and be carrying businesses under this method. The differences between the two methods are summarized in Table 5.1.

Acquisitions of stock are treated differently and more simply. They require relatively little accounting on the part of acquirer. It need only record an investment in target's stock. The acquisition remains on acquirer's books for as long as it holds target's shares. In subsequent periods investment income must be recorded.

If controlling interest, usually over 50 percent, of target's voting common stock is acquired, consolidated financial statements covering acquirer and target must be prepared. In acquisitions of 20–50 percent of target's stock, the equity method must be used. This means that investments are recorded at cost, and acquirer records its percentage of target's assets, liabilities, earnings and losses. In investments under 20 percent, acquirer does not need to reflect target on its financial statements. Table 5.2 summarizes the key elements of accounting for acquisition of stock.

Purchase Method

Purchase method accounting follows historical cost accounting principles. The method is a very flexible one. It applies whether the acquisition is of all or a part of a business, assets or stock are acquired or consideration is cash, another asset, debt or equity.

Table 5.1 Accounting Methods in Mergers

Differences	Purchase	Pooling of interests
Ownership of target	From closing	Deemed always existed
Assets and liabilities recorded at	Fair market value	Recorded values
Goodwill	Recognized	Not recognized
Depreciation based on	Higher fair market value	Lower carry-forward value
Income	Lower	Higher

Table 5.2 Accounting Methods in Acquisition of Stock

Acquire	
Controlling interest (over 50%)	Acquirer record investment and future income
Equity (20–50%)	Consolidate target on its financial statements
Less than controlling interest (under 20%)	Record its % of assets, liabilities, earnings losses
	Not reflect target on its financial statements

Requirements

To apply the purchase method two steps are involved. They concern acquirer and acquisition cost.

Acquirer

The first step in applying the purchase method is to determine the acquirer. Usually it is fairly easy:

- If cash or some other asset or debt is paid, acquirer is paying.
- If stock is issued, acquirer is issuing.
- In a merger it may be more difficult. Acquirer is presumed to be the company whose shareholders end up holding a majority of the voting control of the combined business. This presumption can be overcome if:
  - majority ownership does not include control of board of directors and management;
  - majority holders do not receive a majority of the market value of the shares issued;
  - assets, revenues and earnings of the company owned by minority shareholders are greater than that owned by the majority.

If two companies of equivalent size merge, determining acquirer is important. Problems are most likely to arise if the two have vastly different price/earnings multiples or if one has a book value well above market value while the other's market value is higher.

Acquisition Cost

The second step is calculating the acquisition cost. This is normally determined as of the closing date, which is when assets are exchanged. An earlier date is possible if control was previously obtained. If an earlier date is chosen, profits and losses must be calculated as of then. In addition, interest on the compensation must be calculated and attributed to acquirer, since it did not have to pay when it took control.

The acquisition cost must usually be measured by the fair market value of the consideration paid. Traded securities are based on the current market price as of the date of transfer. In some cases the value may have to be reduced. Examples are if:

- securities are restricted in some way, such as limitations on subsequent transfer;
- securities represent a large block, particularly if compared to normal trading volume;
- there is a thin or no market for the securities.

In such cases, a valuation from investment bankers may be required. If the value of the securities cannot be easily determined, the value must be based on the value of the assets being acquired. Goodwill will not normally be recognized in such cases.

If the consideration includes future **kickers**, that is, additional payments if target does well in the future by meeting certain performance criteria, their value should be recorded at the acquisition date if it is determinable beyond a reasonable doubt. If not, additional consideration must be included when the contingency is resolved.

If the value of stock given as consideration is guaranteed, the purchase price is the greater of the guaranteed amount or the fair value of the securities originally issued. Any additional consideration given after the closing as part of the guarantee is treated as an adjustment to paid-in-capital. It does not change the acquisition cost.

Outside acquisition costs, such as finder fees, investment banker fees, legal and accounting fees, are added to the cost of the assets acquired. Inside acquisition costs must be expensed. Financing fees for funds borrowed to finance the acquisition should be amortized over the life of the finance.

Other Issues
There are a number of other issues involved with using the purchase method.

- Push-down accounting[2]: if substantially all of the common stock of target is acquired, the Securities and Exchange Commission (SEC) requires the purchase price to be pushed down to target's financial statements if they are included in any SEC filing.[3] For instance, debt incurred to finance the acquisition must be pushed down to target's balance sheet if:
  - the debt is assumed by target;
  - the debt will be retired by target making an offering;
  - target guarantees or pledges its assets as collateral for the debt.

If push-down accounting applies, the financial statements should be prepared on both an historical and push-down basis.

- Leveraged buyout: the SEC[4] and Financial Accounting Standards Board (FASB),[5] which establishes accounting standards, have developed guidelines for the accounting of leveraged buyouts. The treatment depends on whether it is a purchase or recapitalization, which is a distribution of cash and stock to existing shareholders without any real change in control. If a purchase has occurred, the rules discussed above apply. If a recapitalization has occurred, the historical values of assets and liabilities will be continued with cash distributions treated as dividends.
- Pension accounting: in recent years, one of the leading stumbling blocks for proposed acquisitions has been the pension liabilities of targets and

whether they are fully funded. This has been less of an issue for targets having defined contribution plans that specify the amounts they must contribute to pension trusts each period based on formulas. It has been more likely to arise with defined benefit plans that specify the benefits that employees will receive at retirement. Under the usual formula for such plans, the benefits are a function of employees' years of service and compensation level at retirement.

Recording

The acquisition cost must be allocated to the assets acquired. To do so all assets must be listed at current or fair market values. As part of this process assets must be reviewed to see if they are properly funded or valued. This includes the previously noted pension funds as well as retirement benefits, leases and inventories.

The purchase price must then be allocated to the fair market values of the acquired assets. Any excess of the purchase price over the fair market value of the purchased assets is allocated to goodwill. On the other hand, if the fair market value is greater than the purchase price, meaning acquirer is getting a bargain by paying less than what they are worth, the difference is treated as negative goodwill and recognized as an extraordinary gain.

Goodwill and other indefinite life intangibles, such as renewable trademarks, are not amortized. However, they must be periodically tested for impairment in accordance with FASB Statements.[6] Limited life intangibles such as patents and copyrights are recorded at cost and amortized over their remaining useful life—up to 40 years. Most acquirers use the straight-line method of amortization.

Target's liabilities assumed by acquirer should be recorded at the present value of the amounts. If the amount is less than the book value of the debt, the difference should be used to reduce goodwill and amortized over the period of the debt. This means an accelerated reduction in revenues after the acquisition, since the amount must be amortized over the duration of the debt.

The treatment of unresolved contingencies is also important. Often called "pre-acquisition contingencies," they refer to uncertainties existing before and at closing and include unsettled litigation, contract disputes and contested tax liabilities. The fair value of any such contingencies should be allocated to the purchase price if determinable. If the determination is made more than one year after the closing, the difference between the estimate at the closing and the finally determined amount should be included in net income in the period when determined.

Net operating loss carryforwards (NOLs) acquired from target may be recognized at the time of acquisition to reduce acquirer's deferred tax liability to zero. Anything left over will be used to reduce goodwill to zero then noncurrent assets to zero, with the balance used to reduce goodwill below zero. On the other hand, NOLs realized after the acquisition but not recorded at that time will be retroactively recorded as above—adjustments to goodwill to zero, noncurrent assets to zero, and then goodwill below zero.

Disclosures

All material details of a purchase method acquisition must be disclosed. In addition, summary pro forma results of operations must be shown for the acquisition period and for the prior period if comparative statements are issued. Statements must treat the combination as if occurring at the beginning of the acquisition period.

Tax Treatment

Simply stated, transactions under this method are partially or fully taxable.

The difficulty with such a simple statement is that the tax treatment of acquired assets or liabilities might differ from the accounting treatment. This is often due to different valuation and allocation practices. Since most acquisitions are at premiums over book or even market value, from a tax standpoint, acquirers prefer to allocate the premium to target's intangible assets that are short-lived and tax-deductible. This will allow them to reduce income and taxes. From an accounting standpoint, however, they prefer to assign the difference to goodwill where the impact on earnings is minimal.

Under an APB Opinion[7] issued by the Accounting Principles Board, FASB's predecessor, the tax value was to be used with the accounting cost reduced to reflect the effective loss of tax benefit. This was called the "net-of-tax" approach with the amount of the reduction assigned to goodwill or noncurrent assets.

In 1987, FASB issued a statement[8] prohibiting use of the net-of-tax approach. Instead, companies were required to use the 'liability method" under which a deferred tax asset or liability is recognized for differences between accounting and tax values. Deferred taxes were not recognized in such cases and goodwill was not adjusted. Instead, the difference was retained permanently.

Pooling of Interests Method

Under the no-longer permitted pooling of interests method, acquisitions were treated as if the shareholders of two companies were combined. Since the acquisition only involved shareholders, the assets and liabilities of their companies were not changed and retained their preclosing value. The two companies were treated as if they had always been combined.

This method was advantageous if the purchase price exceeded the book value. Book value refers to historical acquisition value less depreciation as carried on the books rather than present fair market value. The reason for this advantage was that companies preferred to retain the lower book value rather than writing up the value to reflect purchase cost. This enabled the combined company to show lower depreciation charges after the closing, since it was depreciating the lower value. This, in turn, meant higher profits.

Requirements

An APB Opinion[9] established detailed criteria that had to be met before pooling of interests could be used. If they were not met purchase method had to be used. The rules were complex and intended to prevent pooling of interests if shareholder interests changed. Such changes included use of cash, changes in equity interests, extraordinary dividends, asset distributions and spin-offs, greenmail, and sales of significant portion of assets. Normal dividends were not covered. If shareholder interests were changed, there was no simple merger of interests, and pooling of interest treatment was not available.

The Opinion created three sets of conditions. They applied to the pre-acquisition, acquisition and postacquisition periods.

- Pre-acquisition Period: Three requirements applied to this period.
  - Another company could not have owned more than 50 percent of acquirer or target within two years of the closing. This requirement did not apply to a new company established within this period or to a subsidiary being sold to comply with a government order.
  - Acquirer and target had to be independent. Neither could own more than 10 percent of the other's voting common stock. This included purchases of treasury shares, although the SEC had issued detailed rules[10] on when treasury share purchases were acceptable. These included acquisitions to settle lawsuits under a contract or as a result of a stockholder's death, and purchases under option plans, stock purchase plans or convertible securities.
  - Within two years of the closing, acquirer and target could not have changed the equity interests of their shareholders in contemplation of the acquisition. Based on these rules, many normal transactions within the two-year period preceding the acquisition disqualified companies from using pooling of interests method. These included stock acquisition plans to reduce capitalization or dilution of earnings per share, acquisitions of stock when prices was low, and defenses against takeovers.
- Acquisition Period: Four requirements applied to this period.
  - The acquisition had to occur in a single transaction or within one year under a planned acquisition. The one-year period was extended for any delays beyond the control of the parties, such as due to litigation or the

government. Any substantive changes in the agreement restarted the one-year period.

- Acquirer could only issue to target common stock with the same rights as those of a majority of its outstanding voting common stock. Such stock of acquirer had to be issued in exchange for substantially all—90 percent or more—of target's voting common stock. No cash distribution was permitted except to purchase fractional shares and shares held by dissident shareholders. This rule did not apply to target's nonvoting common stock. Such stock had to be acquired for cash, debt, similar securities or acquirer's common stock. The rule applied to warrants and options for target's voting common stock.
- Target's shareholders had to receive stock in proportion to their holdings before the closing. If the value of target was 10 percent of acquirer's new combined value, they had to receive 10 percent of combined shares. Their proportion had to be fixed in reference to their holding before the closing. It could not be varied even by reference to objective standards. This meant earnings or market price contingency agreements could not be used under pooling of interest method. However, earn-outs were acceptable if they only affected whether the closing occurred and not the value of the shares.
- Postclosing Period: Three requirements applied to this period. There could be no agreement between acquirer and target for certain things:
  - Retire or require any common stock issues at closing
  - Give acquirer's shareholders any special benefit that changed the ratio of shareholding between acquirer's and target's shareholders. This included guarantee of loans secured by stock issued at closing.
  - Dispose of a significant part of the combined assets within two years of closing. This did not cover sales in the ordinary course of business, disposal of duplicate assets or operations, or as required by government. Although treasury shares could be sold in the postclosing period to avoid the appearance that they were in contemplation of closing, they should have been delayed until at least 30–90 days after closing.

There were other instances where the pooling of interests method was permitted. It could be used if the sum of:

- inter-corporate investments beyond 20 percent;
- impermissible treasury shares;
- shares paid for in cash;
- minority interests of acquired company was greater than 10 percent of the voting common stock of target.

Table 5.3 Key Requirements for Pooling of Interest

Securities used by acquirer as consideration	Must be voting common stock with rights identical to those of the majority of its outstanding voting common stock
Postclosing contingencies	Not permitted
Tainted treasury shares	Not permitted, including shares reacquired within prior two years
Each combining company	Must have been independent from the other for past two years
Acquisition	Must have been completed in one closing within a year of the acquisition plan being adopted
All shareholders	Must be treated equally
Planned postclosing transactions	Not permitted

In summary, the most important of the pooling of interest requirements and the ones most often involved are summarized in Table 5.3.

The biggest disadvantage of the pooling method was that transaction costs such as legal, accounting and investment banker expenses had to be treated as current expenses. The recognition of more expenses meant income was reduced. In the purchase method they could be amortized over the life of the acquired assets, resulting in lower expenses and higher income.

Recording

In pooling of interests method, acquirer's and target's book or historical asset values had to be used after the closing. Adjustments, however, were permitted if the companies would have made them if they were still separate.

There were several rules concerning the treatment of equity. First, the separate equity accounts and retained earnings had to be combined. Second, if the par or stated value of any shares issued in the acquisition was less than the acquiring company's, the difference had to be added to additional paid-in capital. On the other hand, if it was more, the difference had to reduce target's paid-in-capital with anything left over used to reduce acquirer's.

The pooling had to be recorded as of completion of the combination. This was usually the closing date. However, the combination had to be treated as having occurred at the beginning of any financial statement period.

As noted, any costs of the transactions, including the pooling, had to be treated as expenses. On-going integration costs also had to be treated as expenses as they occurred.

Disclosures

An APB Opinion[11] required significant disclosures about pooling acquisitions. This included revenue and net income of each company from beginning of period to closing. The acquiring company also had to reconcile previously reported revenue and earnings to those reported for the combined companies.

Tax Treatment

Most transactions qualifying as pooling of interests were treated as tax-free reorganizations. In such cases, no taxes arose as a result of the acquisition. However, there were some differences in the tax and accounting treatments of acquisitions.

Additionally, in some cases the accounting and tax impacts differed and led to different decisions. From an accounting standpoint, if pooling of interests applied, acquirer kept the book value of the acquired assets. Any depreciation was reduced and the effect on earnings was also minimized. From a tax standpoint, however, purchase method might have been better since assets would be recorded at their higher purchased value. This would mean higher depreciation and lower earnings, but it would also mean lower income taxes.

Acquisition of Stock Methods

There are three types of stock acquisitions—passive investments, substantial influence investments and controlled investments.

Passive investments are acquisitions of stock that do not give acquirer substantial influence over target's board of directors or control of the election of directors. Such acquisitions are initially recorded at cost. On the date of financial statements, the acquisition must be revalued to reflect the then prevailing fair market value. This revaluation process is called mark-to-market. The amount of such revaluation is treated as gain or loss and included in income if the shares are trading securities or deferred to stockholders' equity if the shares are available for sale. Trading securities are bought and held primarily for sale in the near term to generate income on short-term price differences, while available for sale securities are defined negatively. They are securities that are not trading securities or that acquirer has the positive intent and ability to hold to maturity. Dividends received on stock investments are recorded as dividend income. Table 5.4 summarizes the differences among these two forms of passive investments.

Under an APB Opinion,[12] the equity method must be used for **substantial influence investments**. As with passive investments, the acquisition is recorded at cost when purchased. Earnings of target are treated as if received, whether or not they are, by reducing the investment by the amount of acquirer's share of target's earnings. When dividends are actually received they are treated as a return of capital, which means the investment is increased by that amount. The equity

Table 5.4 Passive Security Investments

Method	Purpose	Revaluation is gain or loss
Trading securities	Bought and sold primarily for sale in near term	Include in income
Available for sale	Not trading securities, or	
Positive intent to hold to maturity	Defer to stockholders' equity	

method cannot be used for common stock investments held by companies registered under the Investment Company Act[13] or by nonbusinesses such as individuals, trusts or estates.

Under an FASB Statement,[14] if acquirer has a **controlled investment**—usually meaning it owns a majority of target—the investment must be consolidated in acquirer's financial statements. Consolidation means target's assets, liabilities, earnings and losses are combined with acquirer's.

Because of the complexity of the equity method for substantial influence investments, I will describe its requirements, recordings and disclosures.

Requirements

An APB Opinion[15] created several requirements for use of the equity method. Although acquirer cannot have majority ownership, it must still exercise "significant influence" over target's operating and financial policies. Such influence can be established by seats on the board of directors and through participation in the decision making. The influence is more likely to be found if other shareholding is dispersed and therefore held by many different holders. The Opinion presumes such influence, however, if acquirer holds 20–50 percent of target's voting stock. Other examples when equity method must be used are corporate joint ventures and nonconsolidated investments separately reported in parent-company financial statements.

Table 5.5 Acquisition of Stock Methods

Method	Treatment
Passive	Record investment at cost
	Revalue investment on date of statement
	Treat revaluation as gain or loss
Substantial influence investments	Equity method
	Record investment at cost
	Earnings reduce investment when earn
	Earnings return of capital when receive
Controlled investment	Investment consolidated in acquirer's statements

The SEC has taken an even more aggressive view.[16] Although the equity method under accounting rules is usually limited to common stock ownership, the SEC has indicated that the equity method might have to be used for SEC filing purposes if acquirer owns convertible debt or preferred stock. This requirement is more likely to apply if the convertible debt or preferred stock could be converted into common stock and, if so, would give acquirer 20–50 percent of target's common stock and significant influence over its operations. The SEC is concerned that companies might try to avoid the application of the equity method so as not to record losses of an unconsolidated subsidiary.

Recording

In recording its investment in target, three main issues arise under the equity method—carrying amount, earnings and restatement.

As to **carrying amount**, acquirer must record its investment in target's common stock at the purchase price. Any undistributed earnings by target after the closing must be added to the purchase price. A permanent drop in the value of the investment must be recorded with the carrying purchase price reduced. Any difference between the purchase price paid by acquirer and the underlying net value of the assets must be allocated to specific assets purchased. If this is not possible, the difference must be treated as goodwill.

As to **earnings**, acquirer must show its share of target's ordinary earnings or losses as a single line item. Extraordinary items must be separately stated unless they are not material in which case they can be consolidated with ordinary line items.

Acquirer should not show dividends, intercompany transfers, or intercompany profits and losses between it and target. Earnings per share for acquirer on its investment in target must be based on all common stock of target plus any stock equivalents and preferred stock.

Acquirer should record deferred taxes on target's undistributed earnings and current taxes on distributed earnings. The application of ordinary or capital gains tax rates depends on how the gain will be realized.

If acquirer sells target's stock, at the time of sale it should report the difference between sales price and the value of the stock carried on its books. Acquirer can treat the sale as a capital transaction or recognize the gain or loss as if the shares had been sold.

As to **restatement**, if acquirer's investment in target falls below 20 percent, it must stop recording its share of target's earnings or losses. The value of the investment does not need to be adjusted, but any amounts received after falling below 20 percent should be used to reduce the value of the investment.

Disclosures

As with pooling of interests and purchase methods, investments accounted for by the equity method are subject to significant disclosure requirements. An APB Opinion[17] describes those obligations in great detail.

Divestitures

Now lets consider the accounting treatment of the flip side of an acquisition—divestitures. There are two possible treatments depending on whether or not the business being sold qualifies as a "segment of a business."

Requirements

According to an APB Opinion,[18] "segment of a business" means a unit that represents a separate major line of business or customers. It can be a subsidiary, division or department, as long as its assets, operations and activities are clearly distinguishable. The separateness must be established by physical location, operations and financing reporting.

If acquirer intends to sell off a business that is not being operated as a separate unit, it should spin it off and operate it as a separate business unit before selling.

The segment of a business must actually be disposed. Acquirer cannot remain liable for its operations. Therefore, a divestiture is not entitled to treatment as a sale of a segment of a business unit if:

- acquirer continues to be involved in its operations;
- consideration received by seller is debt whose repayment is dependent on target's operations after the sale;
- seller guarantees target's debt or other performance.

Any costs associated with the disposal of a segment must be treated as expenses and charged against income of the segment being sold. Such costs include severance pay and additional pension costs. If the segment is being shut down instead of sold, any costs to close the segment should be similarly treated.

Recording

If the divested unit qualifies as a segment of a business, its operations should be retroactively isolated and separately reported. The information should be recorded as income before extraordinary items rather than as income from continuing operations.

If the divested unit does not qualify as a segment of a business, assets, liabilities, profits and losses are reported separately but only from the closing. In addition, the information is reported as income from continuing operations, not as income from extraordinary items. If the results are material, however, they should be disclosed as a separate part of income from continuing operations.

If a divestiture plan is adopted but will not take effect until a future reporting period, the anticipated gain or loss should be reported in the financials for the period in which the plan is adopted.

Disclosures

Under an APB Opinion,[19] significant disclosures must be made regarding the disposal of a segment of a business. These include description of the segment, expected disposal date, manner of disposition, remaining assets, liabilities of the segment that will not be sold, applicable taxes, and gain or loss.

Spin Offs

Another type of divestiture is the spin off of a subsidiary by the parent company. The subsidiary could be a long-standing separate company or a recently incorporated segment of a business.

Recording

The SEC requires that the spun-off subsidiary's financial statements include all assets, liabilities, profits and losses attributable to its operations.[20] If the parent has paid any expenses on the subsidiary's behalf, its financial statements must be retroactively revised to reflect such payments. The subsidiary's paid-in-capital must be increased by an equivalent amount.

The expenses of the subsidiary must be based on market rates. Any amount taken out by the parent in excess of what the subsidiary would have paid to unrelated suppliers, such as for financial or management services, must be retroactively treated as a dividend to the parent. Any amounts charged by the parent less than what the subsidiary would have paid to unrelated suppliers must be reflected in notes to the subsidiary's financial statements.

Retained earnings of the business segment prior to incorporation cannot be carried forward into the new company.

Disclosures

Pro-forma financial statements for the subsidiary must be prepared showing its:

- income taxes;
- effect of terminated or revised agreements with the parent;
- dividends declared after date of balance sheet;
- other adjustments.

Historical earnings per share are not permitted.

6

Tax

By Richard Westin

Background

Are taxes an important consideration in a corporation fusion or division? The answer is that they usually start as something of only modest importance, like a patch of clouds on a mariner's distant horizon, but tend to become crucial as the deal moves along. In fact, they often destroy an otherwise viable deal or leave the parties to the deal with responsibility for tax liabilities that might crop up long after the closing. Getting early advice on how taxes are likely to impact the deal can head off these problems. Even then, expect taxes to take center stage for at least some of the later negotiations.

What you are about to read is a simplified version of the basic rules. You will not become a tax whiz by reading what is to come, but it will give you a vocabulary that will help you converse with tax experts and an appreciation of the basic concepts. The good news in this entire area is that the experts in the field can usually find any number of ways to skin the tax cat by structuring the deal to meet the requirements of the federal income tax laws.

From a big picture point of view, there are two basic models of income taxation of an acquisition, namely taxable and nontaxable:

- In the taxable format, the acquirer buys the seller's equity and the seller reports a capital gain or loss that generally pays a 15 percent tax on the capital gain, *or* the acquiring *corporation* buys the selling corporation's assets in which case it is the selling corporation that pays the tax on the gains arising from the sale.

- In the nontaxable format, the acquiring corporation uses its own stock as consideration. Done right, no one pays any taxes and the whole thing is as if nothing happened. The target's shareholders wind up with stock of the acquiring corporation. Their holding period for the acquiring corporation stock is added to the holding period of their former stock in the target. Their gain or loss on the sale of that stock is deferred until they sell the stock of the acquiring company. Likewise, the target pays no taxes and either disappears through a merger or consolidation or carries on as a subsidiary of the acquiring corporation.

Divestitures are also taxable or nontaxable. If the divestiture falls into the nontaxable category, the result to all the parties is no current tax but a potential for future taxes on selling the stock of either the divested company or the company that did the divesting.

In between these two extremes there are mixed cases where the selling shareholders or target corporation engage in a fusion or division that is partly taxable, usually because they have nonqualifying consideration, such as cash, in addition to nontaxable consideration, such as voting common stock of the acquiring corporation.

Likewise in divestitures, the road is generally open to disposing of an existing or newly formed subsidiary in a tax-free or taxable method. It used to be that one could spin off a subsidiary and then let it or the remaining corporation be a target in a corporate acquisition. The U.S. Congress in its wisdom recently decided that was too much of a good thing and has required a two-year cooling off period before a tax-free division can be followed by a tax-free or table acquisition of either corporation. This is discussed further below.

Notice a key fact. These allegedly tax-free deals are really tax deferrals, not tax exemptions. To take a simple example, assume you owned stock of Dell Computer that cost you $1,000 and that IBM took over Dell in exchange for IBM stock. Assume that when the smoke cleared you owned IBM stock worth $6,000. Assume the takeover by IBM was a nontaxable corporate reorganization. As a result your basis (tax investment) in the IBM stock will be the same $1,000 as in your former Dell stock. If you sell the IBM stock a few days after the reorganization for $6,000, you will be taxed on the $5,000 gain. That makes the deal a *tax-deferred* reorganization not a *tax-free* reorganization.

A Little Tax History

The modern corporate income tax was—as are so many taxes—the product of a war. As usual, the tax was not repealed after the war but rather lived on and gained force. However, from the very beginning the U.S. Congress realized that the corporate income tax had to accommodate changes in the business climate, and it has generally accommodated the needs of the business community as it revised the Internal Revenue Code. Incidentally, whenever the term "IRC", "Code" or "tax code" is used here it means the Internal Revenue Code and the Section numbers are all references to sections of the Internal Revenue Code.

The earliest corporate acquisition provisions appeared in the Revenue Act of 1918[1] in anticipation of the end of World War I and of the inevitable restructuring of American industry from its wartime footing to a world at peace. As the Senate Committee of the day put it, the legislation would "negative the assertion of tax in the case of certain purely paper transactions."[2] In other words, it would guarantee that there would be no tax if a corporate restructuring were just a rearrangement of legal forms with the same shareholders and business left standing.

This was an antidote to earlier laws under which a purely technical exchange could be taxed, such as a New Jersey corporation doing nothing more than reincorporating itself as a Delaware corporation and issuing new Delaware stock to its shareholders in exchange for their old New Jersey shares. On the other hand, the 1918 law was very vague; it merely said that a "reorganization" was not taxable. Congress did not take the trouble to stop and tell the world what a reorganization might be. As a result, the courts were forced to develop some of the most important doctrines in the area.

Later revenue acts refined the definition of the term "reorganization" and steadily expanded the kinds of transactions that could qualify but did not explicitly incorporate all these judicial doctrines. Even today the definition of a "reorganization" consists of two elements. One is the mechanical description of various types of qualifying exchanges of stock and assets found in §368 of the Code.[3] The other consists of the four requirements derived from case law that are generally independent of the definitions in §368.

- The reorganization must have a corporate-level business purpose, such as going out of the money-losing Army tent business and into the canvas pants business.
- The target's business must continue to some minimum extent after the reorganization known as the "continuity of business enterprise" requirement.
- The owners of the target must have a continuing stake in the acquiring corporation known as the "continuity of proprietary interest" requirement.
- The reorganization must be structured pursuant to a "plan of reorganization. This is rarely an issue because there is almost always documentation of a plan. The plan need not be written, but it is unwise not to write it up.

As time passed, the number of reorganizations grew from one, namely state law mergers and consolidations, under what is now IRC Section 368(a)(1)(A) to seven and even allows for tax-free cross-border mergers and consolidations. Number seven is IRC Section 368(a)(1)(G) and it involves certain bankruptcy-related transactions. Notice that "G" is the seventh letter of the alphabet. Later Sections tended to add one or more of the four requirements directly into the new law of the day.

Nevertheless, the four requirements are still not all in the Code and were not all included in the Treasury Regulations until 1980.[4] The purpose of the Big Four requirements is to make sure that the reorganization provisions are limited to *bona fide* cases and above all to prevent "astute tax lawyers" from converting what is in substance a taxable sale into a tax-free reorganization by skillful maneuvering of form.

The corporate divestiture rules have much the same history except that the Code and regulations adopted under it are generally clearer as to the requirements for a tax-free transaction.

Pressure of Taxes on Acquisitions

Taxes often set up huge tensions between buyer and seller or between a corporation and its shareholders. There are seemingly endless tax issues that can crop up in an acquisition or divestiture. What follows is a description of some of the more common problems.

Buyer Who Wants Depreciation Deductions

This scenario involves the shrewd buyer that wants to wind up with a lot of depreciation deductions after the deal closes and sets its offering price on that assumption. The typical seller, however, will want to walk off with no income tax liability. This raises complicated bargaining problems and the need for a spirit of compromise. Here is a common example.

> **To illustrate:** Target Corporation is in the furniture business and has one owner: the Wood family. The Wood family advisors tell the Woods that the corporation's stock is worth $6 million. The board of directors of Acquiring Corporation wants to take over Target Corporation and seem willing to spend $6 million to buy it. The assets of Target Corporation have been written down to $0. Now for the hard part: the Wood family insists that it be paid in stock of Acquiring Corporation so as to avoid income taxes on the sale. The board of Acquiring Corporation insists that the $6 million will only be paid if it can buy the assets of Target Corporation for $6 million, thereby allowing it to deduct the cost of the those assets over time via depreciation deductions.

This is a classic. How does one accommodate the parties? It might in fact be impossible. Perhaps the Wood family might be willing to cut their price if the deal is done nontaxably. Perhaps they would be willing to accept a taxable deal if they are paid more.

Buyer Who Wants to Tie Price to Target's Income

Imagine you are the president of a furniture corporation that is in a buying mood. You identify a target corporation that is available for $6 million, payable in common stock. You are intrigued but suspicious of the sellers' claims about the future of the target. You get the seller to agree to take $4 million in stock at the initial closing plus ten year's worth of extra stock computed on the basis of the target's profitability over the coming decade. Can you do it without causing the sellers to be taxed?

The basic answer is "no." One can agree to make contingent payments of stock if, among other things, at least half the stock was issued at the closing *and* the rest of the stock will be issued within five years. Your proposal fails because it lasts a decade. On the other hand, taxes exert only a reasonable influence here; after all, five years is quite a long measuring period.

Conflicted Sellers

So far, we have treated buyers and sellers as if they were monolithic. That is a helpful simplification when starting out, but it overlooks the host of situations where the sellers are in different tax situations. For example, a tax-exempt charity is indifferent to whether the sale of its stock in the target is taxable or nontaxable because it does not pay income taxes anyway.

On the other hand, most shareholders would prefer a nontaxable disposition of their stock. Others might find a taxable sale acceptable because they can use the gain to offset capital loss carryovers, or their stock might have lost value, so they want to report a loss on the sale. In these situations it may be possible for the buyer to offer a mix of taxable and nontaxable consideration such as common stock for the sellers who fear taxes and cash for the rest of them.

In the real world there are seemingly endless variations on the tax postures of the parties. It is the job of the informed tax advisor and the inquisitive, insistent client to optimize everyone's tax situation. By doing so, buyer and seller will generally get their optimum deal.

Estate Taxes

The federal estate tax generally applies to the transfer of property at death, including transfers of shares in closely and widely held corporations. In practice, however, there are practical differences. For one thing the valuation of shares in a closely-held corporation is less certain, so that the amount of estate tax that the Internal Revenue Service (IRS) will ultimately assess is harder to predict. Also, shares in closely held corporations are less liquid, making it difficult for executors to dispose of stock in order to pay estate taxes and other expenses. These considerations often encourage shareholders in a small corporation to exchange their stock in a tax-free reorganization for shares in a publicly traded corporation. This is true even though the Code contains some specialized provisions that are designed to soften the blow of estate taxes on family-owned corporations, such as special valuation rules and a chance to defer paying estate taxes at the price of a low interest charge.

Reorganization

In order to have a tax-free acquisition the transaction must be a so-called "reorganization." The term reorganization in defined in Section 368(a) of the Code and has precise legal definitions. Lack of a "reorganization" means there is a taxable transaction; this is not a problem if the target or its assets are sold at a loss but a big problem if it is sold at a gain by a taxable shareholder that has no losses to shield the gain.

The Code recognizes seven types of nontaxable reorganizations of which five—A, B, C, D, and G—can be used as ways to acquire other companies. The type E reorganization involves an internal recapitalization and an F involves a change of name or place of incorporation. Of the remaining five, types A, B and C are by far the most common.

Here is what the alphabet soup really means:

- Type A reorganization is a merger or consolidation under U.S. or foreign law. The difference between a merger and a consolidation is that in a merger one of the parties survives and one is gone. In a consolidation, both are gone and a new legal entity takes them over.
- Type B reorganization is a stock-for-stock exchange in which the target shareholders surrender voting stock.
- Type C reorganization is an exchange of substantially all of a target corporation's assets for stock of the acquiring corporation.
- Type D acquisition, which is virtually unheard of, involves the transfer of the target corporation's assets to another corporation that the target corporation shareholders already control.
- Type G reorganization is a bankruptcy reorganization, which may be acquisitive or divisive in character.

Table 6.1 summarizes all seven forms of nontaxable reorganizations.

Table 6.1 Nontaxable Reorganizations

Type	Name	Summary
A	Merger	Only one party survives
	Consolidation	New company formed
		Neither party survives
B	Stock for stock	Target shareholders surrender voting stock
C	Assets for stock	Target assets surrendered for stock of acquiring company
D	Assets for stock	Target assets surrendered for stock of company controlled by target stockholders
E	Reorganization	Internal recapitalization
F	Change of incorporation	Same company survives
G	Reorganization	Bankruptcy proceeding

Assuming the transaction fits one of these definitions *and* the additional requirements in the Regulations are met, such as "continuity of business enterprise," the reorganization generally results in the nonrecognition of gain or loss by the acquirer and its shareholders except to the extent that target's shareholders get nonqualifying consideration or "boot," meaning "in addition". Further, the acquired corporation's "basis" for its assets and its tax history carry over.

To illustrate: Assume that the Wood Furniture Corporation is taken over by the Big Furniture Corporation in a merger that qualified as a type A reorganization. Assume Wood Furniture's tax records indicate that it paid $1 million for its equipment and had written the equipment down to $400,000 so that at the time of the merger the "basis" (tax cost) of its assets was only $400,000. In that case, the Big Furniture Corporation's basis in that equipment will also be $400,000. There are plenty of other important tax attributes of the target that can carry over, but basis is often the most important single tax account.

The type A and type C reorganizations are basically asset acquisitions in which the target goes out of existence. Compared to an A reorganization, the type of consideration that can be used in a C reorganization is limited. On the other hand, the acquiring corporation can pick and choose which liabilities it will assume in a C reorganization. In a type A reorganization, the acquiring corporation takes over all of the target corporation's liabilities by operation of law.

Type A Reorganization

The type A reorganization is defined as a statutory merger or consolidation under American or foreign law. The Code does not prescribe the type of consideration that must be used in a statutory merger; but the "continuity of interest" doctrine requires that the consideration include a significant equity interest in the acquiring corporation. In the transaction the target merges into the acquiring corporation, and the merged corporation's shareholders exchange their stock for consideration provided by the acquiring corporation. There are no specific limits on the ability of the target to dispose of unwanted assets before the merger.

Nobody knows exactly how much stock the acquiring corporation must issue to target's shareholders, but the consensus is that the target corporation shareholders as a group must get stock of the acquiring corporation or its parent that is worth at least half of what the target company stock was worth. For example, if the target's stock was worth $1 million, the shareholders of the target must get at least $500,000 worth of acquiring corporation stock. The stock can be preferred or common, voting or nonvoting. This flexibility makes the type A reorganization the acquisition tool of choice, especially because the stock issued by the acquirer can be no vote or preferred stock.

If you read the financial press you will notice that many mergers occur at the subsidiary level. For example, the announcement of the merger may be by a well-known parent corporation, but the actual merger will be into one of its subsidiary corporations.

Forward Subsidiary Merger
As discussed in Chapter 1, this very common deal is known as a "forward" subsidiary merger. The mental image is that of a target corporation that merges forward and disappears into a subsidiary of the corporation that provides the stock used as consideration in the merger. To qualify a forward subsidiary merger as a type A reorganization substantially all of the target's assets must be acquired by the acquiring subsidiary. Thus premerger dispositions by the target have to be minor. Under the IRS ruling guidelines, the "substantially all test" is generally met if the transferred assets constitute 90 percent of the value of the net assets and 70 percent of the value of the gross assets held by the target immediately before the merger.

Are the special rules for forward subsidiary mergers particularly important? Yes. In fact, they are all-important because most acquiring companies are wary of direct mergers, mainly because they cannot be absolutely sure of what liabilities they are taking on in the merger.

> **To illustrate:** Acquiring Corporation makes millions of cars. It wants to acquire the assets of Target Corporation. If it merges under state law with Target Corporation in exchange for one million shares of Acquiring Corporation stock, it can easily achieve a type A reorganization. The trouble is Target Corporation might have liabilities for such things as workers' health claims and environmental pollution. If Target Corporation merges into a subsidiary of Acquiring Corporation, the subsidiary alone picks up the liabilities.

This raises another way to go about a reorganization, namely a "drop down." In a "drop-down" the target's business is first acquired by a parent corporation and then contributed to a subsidiary. For example, in the case of the Acquiring Corporation-Target Corporation merger, Acquiring Corporation might merge Target Corporation into Acquiring Corporation and then Acquiring Corporation might transfer the Target Corporation business to a newly formed subsidiary.

Will this work to rid Acquiring Corporation of the invisible Target Corporation liabilities? Likely not. The law generously allows postreorganization drop-downs to not disturb the tax-free nature of the reorganization. On the other hand, state law can make the acquisition-plus-drop-down something one does only after careful consideration. The good news is that in recent years the government has become progressively more generous about allowing drop-downs into lower tier subsidiaries and even partnerships.

Reverse Subsidiary Merger

As noted in Chapter 1, there is the "reverse" subsidiary merger. In this deal a subsidiary of the acquiring corporation merges *into* the target with the target surviving the merger. Why would one do such a strange thing? The answer is often either to preserve a license to operate a special kind of business or to preserve the famous name of the target. For a reverse subsidiary merger to qualify as a potentially tax-deferred reorganization, the surviving corporation must hold substantially all of the properties of both corporations after the transaction. In the merger, target's shareholders must transfer stock representing "control" of the target in exchange for voting stock of the acquiring corporation. "Control" means ownership of at least 80 percent of the voting stock and at least 80 percent of every other class of the target's stock.

Here is a fairly typical example of a reverse subsidiary merger:

> **To illustrate**: Acquiring Corporation wants the business of Target Corporation. Target Corporation holds a radio station license that has great value and its name is well known by the biggest consumer group of all, 13-year-old girls. It gets the Target Corporation board and shareholders to agree to the following deal: Acquiring Corporation will set up a new subsidiary called Newco and will deliver one million voting of Target Corporation in exchange for their Target Corporation shares. On the same day, Newco merges into Target Corporation. When the smoke clears, Acquiring Corporation owns Target Corporation. Newco is gone.

Table 6.2 summarizes the key issues of forward subsidiary mergers and reverse subsidiary mergers.

Type B Reorganization

A type B reorganization is an acquisition of stock representing control of the target solely in exchange for voting stock of the acquiring corporation or a

Table 6.2 Type A Subsidiary Mergers

Type	Summary	Target
Forward	Target merges into subsidiary of corporation that providing stock used as consideration	Disappears
Reverse	Subsidiary of Acquirer Merges into Target	Survives

corporation in control of the acquiring corporation. Unlike the reverse subsidiary merger where the acquiring corporation must obtain control in the transaction, a type B reorganization can be accomplished by a "creeping acquisition" of the target corporation's stock.

An example is a public tender offer in which a publicly traded corporation offers its voting stock for common stock of the target with the proviso that the deal will only close if the shareholders of the target corporation tender at least 80 percent of the target's stock, meaning 80 percent of all voting stock and 0 percent of each class of no-vote stock. It can also be achieved on a much simpler level, say where a local restaurant corporation offers its voting stock for the stock of a similar restaurant that it wants to combine forces with. In that deal, the acquiring restaurant will issue its stock to the owner of the target restaurant tax-free. The target restaurant winds up as a subsidiary of the acquiring restaurant with both owners now owning stock of the parent, that is, the acquiring restaurant.

The big problem with type B reorganizations is that one has to be careful not to pay the target corporation shareholders for anything other stock than their stock. This issue is extremely dangerous and has to be watched with great care.

Type C Reorganization

A type C reorganization is an acquisition of substantially all of a target corporation's assets solely in exchange for voting stock of the acquiring corporation or of a corporation in control of the acquiring corporation. In determining whether qualified consideration is used the acquiring corporation's assumption of a liability is ignored. In fact, up to 20 percent of the consideration can consist of property other than stock of a party to the reorganization although the 20-percent limitation is reduced by the amount of liabilities assumed by the acquiring corporation. What these confusing rules mean is that one is free to take on target's liabilities without wrecking a type C reorganization, but it has to be with extreme caution about adding any consideration other than stock.

To illustrate: Acquiring Corporation (AC) obtains all the assets of Target Corporation for $10 million worth of AC stock. That is clearly a good type C reorganization. If AC pays with $8 million in stock and $2 million in cash, it is still—just barely—a good type C reorganization. If instead AC paid with $7 million of stock and assumed $3 million of debt it is a good reorganization. However, if AC paid with $8 million of stock, assumed liabilities of $2 million and added one cent of cash, the reorganization would fail to meet the requirements of and would be taxable exchange of stock for assets.[5]

The type C reorganization is intended to apply to transactions that are functionally equivalent to state law mergers. One feature of a statutory merger is that the target is liquidated by operation of law. To keep the symmetry alive Congress generally requires the complete liquidation of the corporation whose assets are acquired in a type C reorganization. The result is that the target corporation necessarily distributes the acquiring company's stock to its shareholders. Type C reorganizations can be done via subsidiaries and drop-downs.

In truth, type C reorganizations are uncommon apparently because of two factors. First, the legal and accounting expenses of conveying properties from one corporation to another tend to be prohibitively high. Second, there is the problem that invisible liabilities might move over to the acquiring corporation along with the target's assets. This requires indemnification agreements, escrows and the like that can complicate the negotiations and even then ultimately prove inadequate.

Type D Reorganization

These are virtually never used as acquisition techniques, so we are all but ignoring them here. They call for one corporation to transfer substantially all of its assets to another corporation provided that the transferor corporation, one or more of its shareholders, or both combined own at least 50 percent of the voting stock of the target when the smoke clears. Perhaps it will catch on some day as an acquisition technique. Right now it lives in obscurity.

Type G Reorganization

The basic structure of a type G reorganization is a transfer by one corporation of some or all of its assets to another corporation in a federal bankruptcy case or in a receivership, foreclosure, or similar proceeding in a federal or state court. Stock or securities, meaning long-term debt, of the acquiring corporation must be distributed in a specified manner. Any transfer of assets must be made by a corporation that is under the jurisdiction of a court in a Title 11 or similar case, and the transfer must be made pursuant to the plan of reorganization approved by the court. It can take the form of a subsidiary merger provided the rules that are otherwise applicable to such reorganizations are met.

A key relaxation of the rules is that for purposes of qualifying the G reorganization, creditors of the target are treated as the proprietary, that is, stock, owners of that entity. This makes it possible for a corporation that is insolvent and has no continuing shareholders to qualify for tax-free reorganization treatment, even though there is no "continuity of proprietary interest," just debt-holders. If it were not for this rule, corporations whose equity was wiped out would never be able to qualify for reorganization treatment because there would be no equity-holding "proprietors" who got stock for their stock.

The type G rules have been most commonly used in the realm of insolvent savings and loan associations (S&L) and have proven to be a useful currency for companies shopping in that graveyard.

Treatment of Reorganization Parties

So far, we have seen what transactions constitute reorganizations, and we know that if the transaction does constitute a reorganization then the door to tax deferral swings open. But what are the details? To answer the question one has to look at the impact on each player, namely the target, the acquirer, and the shareholders and debt-holders of the target.

Target

Section 361 of the tax code guarantees that a corporation does not recognize gain or loss on the transfer of its property for stock or securities of a corporation that is a party to the reorganization.[6] If the target also receives "boot," that is a non-qualifying consideration such as cash, then gain but not loss becomes taxable unless the "boot" is distributed pursuant to the plan of reorganization. In general, the acquiring corporation's assumption of the target corporation's liabilities is not treated as boot.

> **To illustrate:** Acquiring Corporation takes over Target Corporation in a type C reorganization in which Target Corporation gets Acquiring Corporation stock at the closing. There is no tax to Target Corporation when it transfers its assets to Acquiring Corporation in exchange for the stock. What if Acquiring Corporation sweetens the deal with $100,000 in cash? The answer is that the $100,000 is a taxable gain to the extent that there would have been a gain if Target Corporation had simply sold its assets to Acquiring Corporation.

There is also an escape hatch for Target Corporation. It can distribute the $100,000 like a hot potato to its shareholders. In that case the shareholders may be taxable but Target Corporation is freed from tax. We will come to that next.

Share and Security Holders of Target

Section 354 of the tax code generally assures that stockholders or security holders recognize no gain or loss when they exchange their stock or securities solely for stock or securities in a corporation that is a party to the reorganization.[7] As a practical matter, a "party to the reorganization" is the target, the acquiring corporation and the parent of the acquiring corporation if in the last case parent corporation stock is being used as consideration.

If the target's shareholder or security holder receives only qualified consideration, then he or she takes a basis in the qualified consideration that is equal to the basis of the stock or securities surrendered in the exchange. As a result, taxation of the gain is deferred until a subsequent disposition of the stock or securities received in the takeover.

> **To illustrate**: You are a Target Corporation shareholder. Your stock cost you $600 and it is worth $1,000. You have owned it for 17 months. You get $1,000 worth of Acquiring Corporation stock in a state law merger that qualifies as a type A reorganization. The result is that you owe no income tax, your basis in the Acquiring Corporation stock is $600, and you are considered to have held the Acquiring Corporation stock 17 months on the day you got it.

The original appreciation in the target corporation's stock can escape taxation entirely if the shareholder holds the qualified consideration until death. In that case the basis of the stock or securities in the hands of the taxpayer's estate will be stepped up to its fair market value.

If the exchange also involves the receipt of nonqualifying consideration, such as cash, gain but not loss is recognized up to the amount of the boot. Further, part or all of that gain may be taxed as a dividend, ordinarily at capital gains rates, if the exchange has the effect of a dividend to the recipient shareholder. In general, a shareholder or security holder is treated as receiving boot if the principal amount of securities received exceeds the principal amount of securities surrendered if securities are received and no securities are surrendered or if the person receives property other than stock. Security holders are taxed on the receipt of qualified consideration attributable to accrued interest on securities surrendered.

> **To illustrate**: You are a Target Corporation shareholder. Your stock cost you $600 and it is worth $1,000. You have owned it for 17 months. You get $900 worth of Acquiring Corporation stock and $100 of cash in a state law merger that qualifies as a type A reorganization. The result is that you owe income tax on a $100 long-term capital gain, your basis in the Acquiring Corporation stock is $600, and you are considered to have held the Acquiring Corporation stock 17 months on the day you got it. If you had a $1,500 basis in the Target Corporation stock and you got cash of $100, you could not recognize the $500 loss or even a $100 loss. If the $100 boot were treated like a dividend (see the following two paragraphs), you would still have a $100 capital gain.

Here is an example of how a security owner is taxed. It is confusing.

To illustrate: A shareholder exchanged a security with a face amount of $1,000 for 300 shares of stock and a security in the principal amount of $1,500. The security had a fair market value on the date of receipt of $1,575. The excess principal amount is $1,500 (face amount of securities received) minus $1,000 (face amount of securities surrendered), or $500. The taxpayer is then supposed to divide the $500 (excess principal amount) over $1,500 (face amount of securities received) to yield a fraction (one-third). She multiplies that fraction by the $1,575 (fair market value of the securities received) to yield $525. This $525 is the fair market value of the excess principal amount and is treated as "boot."

The determination of whether the receipt of boot has the nature of a dividend is generally made by reference to the principles of IRC Section 302.[8] The issue is too complicated for a book like this and the issue is now rarely important because dividends are generally taxed as capital gains. The practical outcome is that if you are an individual shareholder of the target, you are going to get a capital gain result. If you are a corporate shareholder of the target, your planning efforts will be to characterize the boot as a dividend so as to claim a dividends-received deduction.

Acquirer

Section 1032 of the Code provides for no taxation of an acquiring corporation that issues its stock to acquire property even if the issuance is not part of a tax-free reorganization.[9] Similar treatment is generally provided if a subsidiary corporation issues its parent's stock in a qualifying reorganization.

The acquiring corporation generally takes a carryover basis for assets or stock received in connection with the reorganization, increased by any gain recognized by the transferor on the transfer. In addition, under Section 381 the acquiring corporation in an asset reorganization "steps into the shoes of" the target corporation with respect to earnings and profits, net operating loss (NOL) carry-overs, and other tax attributes of the target corporation.[10]

To illustrate: Acquiring Corporation takes over Target Corporation in a type A reorganization. Target Corporation has business assets with a basis of $1 million and a holding period of one year. In addition, it has tax credit carryforwards of $230,000. Acquiring Corporation's basis in those assets will also be $1 million and it will also have a one-year holding period in them as of the date they shift over to Acquiring Corporation. In addition, Acquiring Corporation will inherit the $230,000 tax credit carryforwards.

Taxable Reorganization

There is no decree that reorganizations have to be tax-free. It is easy to design one's way around a tax-free result by deliberately flunking one of the requirements for a nontaxable reorganization. The easiest way is to stage a state law merger of two corporations but issue too little stock. For example, if the target company's stock was worth $1 million and the acquirer issues only $300,000 worth of stock and $700,000 of cash, the deal is fully taxable because there is not enough "continuity of proprietary interest." As a consequence, all the target's shareholders have a taxable result. That may be fine with them if they have all lost money on their investment because it will allow them to report a tax loss.

On the other hand, the deal may be taxable to some and nontaxable to others. The leading example is the "cash option merger." Here, the acquiring company promises to issue at least $500,000 of stock thereby guaranteeing overall continuity of proprietary interest, but individual shareholders have some freedom to pick and choose whether they want cash, stock or stock plus cash. The people who lost money on their investment can take cash only in which case they are entitled to recognize their losses.

Clever as all this might seem, in today's robust economy most people want nontaxable deals. This has resulted in an increasing use of nontaxable reorganizations, not taxable acquisitions.

Section 351 as Acquisition Technique

Section 351 of the Code says that if one or more people acting in concert transfer assets to a corporation in exchange for stock of that corporation, the transfer is tax-free provided that the transferors as a group wind up with 80 percent stock control of the corporation meaning 80 percent of the voting power plus 80 percent of each class of stock. The tax result is as if nothing happened. The shareholders take a basis in the stock that is the same as their basis in the assets they transferred, and the corporation takes the assets with the shareholders' basis.[11]

To illustrate: Fred, a cab driver, is worried about personal liability if he gets in a traffic accident. On the advice of Percy, his nephew in law school, Fred forms a corporation, Purple Cab Co., to which he transfers the cab. He has owned the cab for 18 months and it has a $3,000 tax basis in Fred's hands. Tax results vary:

- Income tax: no one pays a tax
- Basis of stock: Fred's tax basis in Purple stock is $3,000
- Fred's holding period for the stock: 18 months
- Purple's basis in the cab: $3,000
- Purple's holding period for the cab: 18 months

The details get more complicated if the property is subject to debt or if certain kinds of assets, such as inventory, are transferred to the corporation, but the basic idea is pretty simple. Now let's look at how Section 351 can be used as an acquisition technique. Here is one version of how it works:

To illustrate: Fred is stinking rich. He owns 15 percent of the stock of Purple Cab Co., a huge New York City cab fleet. The Chicago Cab Corporation (CCC) wants to take over the business. Fred wants to retire in serenity and that does not include owning stock of CCC, which he considers volatile. What should he do? One answer is to contribute the 15 percent block of Purple Cab Co. stock to Newco in exchange for Newco preferred stock, offering a cumulative 8 percent dividend. The other party contributing to Newco will be CCC, which will put in quite a lot of cash. Soon thereafter, Purple Cab Co. and CCC will go through a taxable merger. The public shareholders of Purple Cab Co. will have taxable transactions. Fred will be untouched by taxes because he will own preferred stock of Newco that he got in a tax-free transaction covered by Section 351. Newco will pay a tax on its disposition of the Purple Cab Co. stock, but that is Newco's problem, not Fred's.

Another way to use Section 351 to perform a nontaxable acquisition is to put a controlling block of stock of the target company into a new or existing corporation and to take back stock—even preferred stock—of the existing corporation.

To illustrate: Fred owns 90 percent of Purple Cab Co. He contributes his stock to CCC in exchange for preferred stock, common stock or both combined of CCC. If he winds up with 80 percent control of CCC, Section 351 renders the deal nontaxable to Fred. If he cannot end up in control, he can still get the same favorable tax result if he can get the existing shareholders of CCC to make a modest transfer of assets to CCC. If they comply, then the existing shareholders count as "transferors of property" such that the "transferors" as a group have the usual 80 percent control of CCC and everyone's transfer is protected by Section 351.

Section 351 deals often have the merit of being simple to execute and subject especially to simple tax law rules. In this complex area, simpler is better. Warning: one of the complications is that some transactions can fit under both Section 351 and a reorganization rule. It is not always clear what set of rules applies in such cases.

Nonqualified Preferred Stock

The benefits of tax deferral in reorganizations used to be available to people who took back "stock" of any kind. Financially conservative taxpayers found it was possible to design preferred stock that was comfortably similar to debt. Preferred stock is stock, as opposed to debt, that has debt-like features. There is no single definition, but a common example would be stock with a face amount of $1,000 per share that pays a fixed dividend of 5 percent only if the directors determine there is enough cash to allow the corporation to make the payment.

For example, the recipients could bargain for a dividend rate tied to an external index, such as the rate of interest charged on loans to prime customers over a given time period, or they could bargain for a redemption feature forcing the corporation to buy back their preferred stock. Congress felt that such stock was too close to being debt and withdrew the protection of tax-deferral from its receipt. In effect it is now treated as no better than debt. Typical preferred stock generally becomes nonqualified preferred stock in any one of four situations:

- Issuer or a related person must redeem the stock
- Holder has the right to require such a redemption or purchase
- Issuer or related person has a right to redeem or purchase and as of the issue date the right is likely to be exercised
- Dividend rate on the stock varies at least in part with reference to interest rates, commodity prices, or other similar indices

The first three requirements apply only if the right or obligation referred to may be exercised in the 20-year period beginning on the issue date of such stock and the repurchase right or obligation is not subject to a contingency that, as of the issue date, makes the likelihood of the redemption or purchase remote.

Management Buy-outs

As discussed in Chapter 1 management buy-outs—often called leveraged buy-outs because they so often depend on debt—have made a lot of people rich, mainly management and venture capitalists that supported the deals with cash. The basic idea is to let management buy out the remaining shareholders with debt and then use the earnings of the business to service the debt, capitalizing on the fact that the corporation can deduct the interest it pays to the lender. The deals are usually structured as a one or two corporation transaction. We will point out some variations as we go along.

In the one-corporation format the entrepreneurs form Newco, a corporation established to do the deal. Newco gets debt and equity financing and then merges into the target that is being taken over. Target's old shareholders get cash and notes of target in redemption of their target stock and the Newco shareholders get target stock and target debt. This gets the target shareholders out of the way as if they had simply redeemed their stock. For tax purposes, Newco is treated as if it never existed and the target shareholders will basically be treated as if they

Table 6.3 Management Buy-Outs

New Company	Recipient of Target Stock	Target Shareholders Receive
Merges into target	New company shareholders	Cash for Target stock
Forms new sub, which merges into Target	New company	Cash for Target stock

redeemed their target stock—that is, sell it back to target—and will claim capital gains or loses on the "redemptions."

In another model, the venture capitalists and managers contribute equity to Newco with lenders advancing cash to Newco. Newco then forms a new subsidiary (New Sub), which merges into target. In a taxable reverse subsidiary merger, target's old shareholders get cash or cash and notes of Newco and Newco gets target stock. When the smoke clears, Newco owns all of target. For tax purposes New Sub is disregarded and treated as if it never existed. The old target shareholders are treated as if they sold their stock for cash and notes. Target will pay dividends to Newco, and Newco will be entitled to claim a deduction equal to the dividends it receives, which in effect makes the dividends tax-exempt. Newco will deduct the interest payments it makes to the lenders.

As an alternative, the lenders might lend to both Newco and New Sub, which means that both target and Newco will be borrowers in the end. The tax differences are minor. In another version, Newco might buy some target stock and target might borrow money to redeem the remaining stock from the older target shareholder group. Again, the tax variations are minor.

Use of Debt in Acquisition

Debt has two advantages over stock for tax purposes. First, when it is repaid the lender is not taxed on the return of the principal. By contrast when a shareholder cashes in her stock, she is likely to have either a taxable gain if she redeems a large part of her stock or a dividend if she does not. Second, the corporation can, within limits, deduct debt payments. These factors have made debt part of the corporate way of life.

On some occasions the debt may be disregarded and treated as equity, which will generally occur if the company is loaded with debt. The debt is subordinated and is provided by the shareholders to the corporation on a pro rata basis.

Congress has retaliated against the use of excessive debt with several other controls. Here is a thumbnail sketch of the key limits:

- Section 279 disallows interest expense deductions on certain "acquisition indebtedness" meaning subordinated convertible debt issued to provide consideration for the acquisition of stock of another corporation or at least 2/3 by value of another corporation's assets. It only applies if the borrower has a high debt/equity ratio or a low ratio of earnings to interest obligations.[12]
- Section 163(j) restricts interest expense deductions or payments to related tax-exempt organizations, taxable REIT subsidiaries or foreign persons. This is known as the "interest stripping" provision. It only applies if the borrower has a debt to equity ratio of at least 1.5 to 1, the interest payments are free of U.S. income tax, the payee is related to the payer—generally meaning

there is at least 50 percent common ownership of both entities—and the payer has a high level of interest expenses for the year.[13]

- Section 163(d) limits the current deductions that investors can claim for interest used to finance their investments to the income from the investments for the year.[14]
- Section 163(e) and (i) restrict deductions on high-yield debentures issued by corporations. It applies if the obligation has a maturity of at least five years and its yield to maturity is at least five percentage points higher than an objective rate announced monthly by the IRS.[15]

Acquisition Costs

The Code allows deductions for "ordinary and necessary expenses" of carrying on a trade or business or for investment activities. "Necessary" simply means "appropriate and helpful." The usual meaning of "ordinary" is "not a capital expenditure" but instead a current cost, such as the cost of gasoline to run a taxi as opposed to the purchase price of a taxi. An ordinary and necessary expense is currently deductible. A capital expenditure is "capitalized," that is, added to the basis of the asset or treated as a new asset, and if it is deducted it is done over time through depreciation or amortization. Section 263 of the Code explicitly enacts the capitalization rule, but its edges are fuzzy because the law is not sufficiently clear to tell exactly when an expenditure must be capitalized versus deducted. Let's consider some different scenarios.[16]

Acquirer

Generally speaking, all acquisition expenses must be capitalized. The theory is that the acquiring company obtained a new business and the expenses associated with obtaining it are no different from the costs associated with buying a new asset. The costs just have to be identified and added to the basis of the new asset.

Even indirect costs of an acquisition must be capitalized. Thus, expenses incurred in a corporate merger that are necessary to the achievement of a long-term benefit must be capitalized even though they were not incurred as direct costs of facilitating the merger. For example, expenses such as legal fees and officers' salaries that are attributable to investigating a potential merger before its approval have to be capitalized if they allowed the taxpayer to achieve the desired long-term benefits from the transaction. As a planning matter, the usual approach to dealing with this problem is to have all employees involved in the acquisition report on how they used their time during the year of the acquisition. This allows the company's accountants to derive an apportionment formula for allocating in-house expenses to the acquisition.

Target

The Supreme Court's latest foray into the area has sharply cut back the expenses one can deduct in connection with a takeover. Specifically, in *INDOPCO, Inc. v. Commissioner*,[17] the Supreme Court held that certain legal and professional fees incurred by a target to facilitate a friendly merger created significant long-term benefits for the taxpayer and therefore were capital expenditures even though some of those expenses, standing alone, would otherwise be currently deductible.

There are now two rationales for why acquisition-related expenses of the target must be capitalized. First, any change in the corporate capital structure is in itself a transaction, and its expenses must be capitalized. Second, expenses of a takeover might create a benefit that lasts beyond the close of the taxable year. What is so strange about the INDOPCO case is that there was no actual asset that one could identify as associated with the capitalized expenses. The Supreme Court in effect forced the taxpayer to invent a new account and add the capitalized expenses to it. Evidently it would never create a tax benefit for the target because it could never be written off.

Severance payments are often made to employees of the target. Do they have to be capitalized? The IRS has ruled that severance payments are not always capitalized under the INDOPCO doctrine if the origin of the payments is the employment relationship as opposed to the merger.[18] On the other hand, if severance payments are a part of the acquisition of property, the ruling does not protect them. That means taxpayers have to make their own determination as to whether the severance payments are made as severance pay or as payment for property.

Net Operating Losses

Few areas of the tax law are more complicated than those involving the effect of acquiring a company with historical losses. Congress and the Treasury Department have established powerful roadblocks to "trafficking" in loss corporations in order to cash in on their losses. What follows is a thumbnail sketch of the area.

The pot of gold is IRC Section 172, which generally provides that a net operating loss (NOL) may be carried back to the two preceding taxable years and then carried forward for 20 years following the taxable year of the loss.[19] A taxpayer can elect to waive the carry back of NOLs and simply carry the losses forward for the 20-year period. Once the 20-year period expires, the NOL is gone forever. When a target with an NOL is reorganized into an acquiring corporation, Section 381 of the Code initially suggests that the acquiring company gets the loss. That is only true at first blush.[20]

Obstacle One: Section 269

The first obstacle to claiming an NOL is a subjective rule found in Section 269, which lets the IRS deny the benefit of an NOL or any other beneficial tax attribute of the target if the principal purpose of the transaction is to evade or avoid federal income tax by securing the benefit of a deduction, credit or allowance, which the parties to the transaction would otherwise not enjoy.[21] If Section 269 applies, the IRS has broad authority to disallow a deduction, credit, or other allowance in whole or in part or to reshuffle income, deductions, tax credits, or allowances between taxpayers. Section 269 reaches the following three types of transactions:

- A party acquires control of a corporation, meaning the ownership of stock with at least half of the total combined voting power of all classes of stock entitled to vote or at least half of the total value of shares of all classes of stock of the corporation
- A corporation directly or indirectly acquires the assets of a corporation that it did not control immediately before the acquisition, and the acquiring corporation takes a carryover basis in the property acquired. This is a legalistic way of saying that the acquisition was the tax-free variety
- A corporation buys control of the target and then liquidates it into the acquirer pursuant to a plan of liquidation adopted not more than two years after the purchase.

     In general Section 269 turned out to be a disappointment to the IRS, because the courts so often refused to allow the IRS to apply Section 269 in cases where taxpayers came up with plausible business reasons for the acquisition. The government felt, probably correctly, that a lot of taxpayers' explanations were contrived or even bogus.

     As is common in the tax arena, the losing party went to Congress for help. The specific need was for a statute that did not depend on debating the taxpayer's motives but instead established objective standards that either applied to the acquisition or did not. The result was the enactment of Sections 382–384.

Obstacle Two: Objective Limits under Sections 382–384

In general when one company takes over another in a reorganization, the target's tax attributes—meaning things like basis in property and method of accounting—are frozen and "carry over" into the hands of the acquiring corporations.[22] At the same time, the law imposes limitations and conditions on the transfer of

NOL carry-overs. The key limit is that the acquiring corporation can use the target's NOLs to offset only a part of its income in the year of acquisition. For example, if in mid-year a big profitable corporation merged with a small corporation that was running at a loss, then acquiring company could at most use half the target's losses against the corporations' combined income.

> **To illustrate:** Acquiring Corporation makes about $5 million a year in after-tax profits. Target Corporation regularly loses $1 million per year. If Acquiring Corporation and Target Corporation merge in mid-year with Acquiring Corporation the survivor, then Acquiring Corporation can use $500,000 of Target Corporation's losses *generated this year* to offset Acquiring Corporation's own income. All things being equal, the earlier in the year the deal closed the better.

It is also impossible for the acquiring corporation to use its operating losses against the target's premerger income.

Now for the hard part. What about NOLs carry-forwards from years before the acquisition? Can the acquiring company claim them or are they shut off? The basic idea is simple: if more than 50 percent of the stock of any corporation changes hands within a three-year period, the target's NOLs do survive, but they are restricted to offset future income at an annual rate equal to the value of the loss multiplied by a given rate of interest, namely the federal "long-term tax exempt rate."[23] This dollar amount is known as the "Section 382 limitation" and it is the bane of many a corporate acquisition.

Also, the target's business must continue for at least two years; otherwise, the NOLs are forfeited completely.[24] The Congressional plan is to let the loss corporation use its losses at the same rate that it theoretically could have generated income if, instead of being subject to an "ownership change," it sold all its assets and invested the proceeds in long-term tax-exempt debt.

> **To illustrate:** Target Corporation has assets worth $1 million and a $3 million NOL that it can carry forward, assuming there is no ownership change. Acquiring Corporation buys all the stock of Target Corporation and continues Target Corporation's business. Because over 50 percent of the Target Corporation's stock changed hands in less than three years, the Section 382 limit applies. The limit is $1 million times the federal long-term tax-exempt rate, say 4 percent. As a result, only $40,000 per year of the $3 million NOL carryforwards can be used to offset Target Corporation's future income.

Nothing in the law extends the 20-year statutory life of NOLs, so in the above example most of the NOLs will be lost altogether. Multiplying $40,000 per year by the maximum 20-year life yields a total of only $800,000 means that at least $200,000 of the $3 million of NOLs is in effect disallowed for good.

The new rules are rough. For example, if the new owners turn the loss corporation around with new management and an infusion of additional capital, the

Section 382 limit applies even though the NOLs would offset income derived solely from the same business that produced the losses.

Now for some details. First what is an "ownership change?" There are two ways in which an ownership change might occur. The first is through an "owner shift" involving one or more 5 percent shareholders.[25] The second is through an "equity structure shift."

There is an *owner shift involving a 5 percent shareholder* if there is any change in the ownership of the stock of the corporation that affects the percentage of stock owned by any person who is a 5 percent shareholder before or after the change.

There is an *ownership change* just after any owner shift involving a 5 percent shareholder if the percentage of the stock of the loss corporation owned by one or more 5 percent shareholders has increased by more than 50 percentage points over the lowest percentage of stock of the loss corporation owned by such shareholders at any time during the three-year testing period. The testing period concept forces one to identify every stock-related transaction for increases in ownership by major shareholders and then see if—looking backwards three years from each such transaction—there had been more than a 50 percentage point rise in ownership by all such shareholders. This requires looking at subtle transactions, such as stock redemptions, as well as the obvious ones.

> **To illustrate**: A owns all the stock of Target Corporation. On January 1, Year 1, A sells 51 percent of its stock to B. Two "owner shifts" occur on that date, because A and B are both 5 percent shareholders immediately after the sale and both have altered their holdings. B's owner shift causes an "ownership change" triggering the Section 382 limitation, because B's ownership of Target Corporation increased by more than fifty percentage points—from 0 percent to 51 percent—in the three-year period ending just after the sale.

The stock ownership percentage of a shareholder is determined by the value of the stock owned by the shareholder and not by the number of shares. Traditional preferred shares are not treated as "stock,"[26] but warrants, options, and convertible debt are generally treated as "stock."[27] A strikingly one-sided rule provides that rights to acquire stock are treated as "stock" only if it will result in an ownership change, that is, only when it hurts the taxpayer.[28]

For the purpose of testing whether an ownership change has occurred, all less than 5 percent shareholders are treated as a single 5 percent shareholder. This keeps changes of ownership among the small fry, such as typical stock market investors, from confusing the picture. Stock owned by any member of the same family is also treated as owned by a single individual, which means that sales and other transfers within a family are ignored,[29] as are gifts, bequests, and transfers of stock between spouses.

An ownership change also occurs if there is an "equity structure shift" resulting in an increase of more than 50 percent ownership within the testing period.

Equity structure shifts include tax-free reorganizations, taxable reorganizations, public offerings and similar transactions.

> **To illustrate**: Target Corporation, which has 2,000 small shareholders, merges into Acquiring Corporation and the former shareholders of Target Corporation get 25 percent of Acquiring Corporation's stock. The result is an ownership change, which subjects Acquiring Corporation (known as the "new loss corporation") to the Section 382 limitation. The Acquiring Corporation shareholder group, considered as a single less-than-5 percent shareholder, has increased its ownership in Target Corporation from 0 to 75 percent.

There are complicated anti-avoidance rules to prevent such game playing as interposing intermediary corporations to obscure ownership changes.

Business Continuity Requirement

The new loss corporation must continue the business enterprise of the old loss corporation at all times for the two-year period after the ownership change.[30] If not, the loss corporation's NOLs are completely eliminated and Section 382 annual limitation for any postchange year is zero.

There is another "loophole plug." Because the Section 382 limitation is dependent upon the value of the loss corporation at the change date, taxpayers might be tempted to increase its value in order to increase the limitation. This ploy is cut off by an "antistuffing" rule, which ignores capital contributions that were made in order to increase the Section 382 annual limitation and presumes such a forbidden plan if the contributions are made within two years before the change date. There is more, but it is beyond the scope of this book.

Built-in Gains and Losses

What if the target owned assets that had lost value? Could the acquiring corporation merge with the target and sell the loss assets and use those losses to offset the acquiring corporation's gains?

> **To illustrate**: Acquiring Corporation bought stock of Target Corporation some years back. It paid $1 million for the stock and it is now worth $5 million. Target Corporation's stock is valued at $1 million, and Target Corporation's primary asset is $1 million worth of stock of Central Railroad that cost $5 million some years back. Can Acquiring Corporation merge with Target Corporation and promptly sell both blocks of stock for a total of $6 million in cash and pay no tax on the sales? The answer is no, because the loss on the Central Railroad stock arises from a (bad) "net unrealized built-in loss."

Net unrealized built-in losses—meaning losses that can be measured but have not been "cashed in"—that are recognized during the five-year postchange period are treated in the same way as prechange NOLs, and their deductibility is subject to the Section 382 limitation. The prohibition is softened by a "threshold requirement" that exempts small "net unrealized built-in loss," which are those that do not exceed the lesser of•15 percent of the fair market value of the loss corporations assets immediately prior to the ownership change or $10 million.[31]

For example, if the Central Railroad stock that Target Corporation held had only declined by 15 percent, Acquiring Corporation could freely take over Target Corporation and claim the loss.

Well, almost. Notice how the IRS might step in and disallow the loss under Section 269 on the grounds that the takeover of Target Corporation was tax-motivated.

Finally, there is a converse rule under IRC Section 384 that blocks a corporate acquirer from offsetting its losses with gain of a target company during the five years following the acquisition.

Other Attributes

Code Section 383 extends the Section 382 model to other attribute carryovers such as capital loss carryovers, general business credit carryovers, foreign tax credits and unused minimum tax credits. If you understand how Section 382 works, it is easy to apply the some concepts to takeovers implicating these other concepts.

Taxable Acquisition

One should not assume that the best acquisition technique is always a tax-free transaction. If the target shareholders have lost money in their investment in the target's stock, they are likely to be better off selling their stock and claiming a capital loss. Alternatively, the target might sell its assets at a loss and liquidate. That allows two losses: once for the corporation when it sells its assets and once for target corporation shareholders, because they are entitled to treat the loss on the liquidation of the corporation as a loss on the sale of their stock. The best part of the deal is that the corporation may be able to claim loss carrybacks and get tax refunds as a result of liquidating at a loss. The other way to get a taxable disposition of the target or its assets is to have it go through a taxable reorganization.

Taxable Asset Acquisition

A taxable sale of assets by a corporation normally results in the recognition of gain or loss to the corporation. The acquiring corporation takes a cost basis for the target's assets, that is, generally equal in the aggregate to the amount of cash and the fair market value of any property it paid with. The shareholders of the selling corporation recognize gain or loss only if the target distributes all or part of the sale proceeds in liquidation of the distributing corporation.

The selling corporation in a nonliquidating sale recognizes gain or loss equal to the difference between the amount realized—that is, the cash and the value of any property received—and its basis with respect to each asset. Recognized gain or loss is ordinary income or loss, long-term capital gain or loss, or short-term capital gain or loss depending on the nature and holding period of the transferred property. For example, if the selling corporation recognizes a net gain from depreciable assets that were used in its trade or business and held for the capital gain period required, which is generally more than one year, then the gain may be taxed as long-term capital gain pursuant to IRC Section 1231. Ordinary income and net short-term capital gain are generally taxed to corporations at a maximum rate of 35 percent. A corporation's net capital gain, which is the excess of net long-term gain over net short-term loss, is subject to the same tax rate; there is no special benefit for earning a capital gain unless there are unused capital loss carryovers, but capital losses are big trouble because they expire after five years.

The acquiring corporation takes a cost basis in the target assets. If it buys appreciated assets, the basis of the assets reflect the acquiring corporation's cost regardless of whether the selling corporation is taxed on the appreciation in the value of those assets. Likewise, if the assets have lost value, their basis is "stepped down" in the hands of the acquiring corporation. The acquiring corporation will not succeed to the tax history, such as carryovers, of the selling corporation.

The value of a step-up depends, in part, on the nature of the target corporation's assets. Because land is not depreciable, the benefit of stepping up its basis is generally realized only by reducing taxable gain on a later sale of the property. On the other hand, if the basis of a depreciable asset is stepped up, the acquiring corporation can claim larger depreciation deductions than would have been allowed to the selling corporation. Likewise, a step-up in the basis of inventory will eventually be reflected in the acquiring corporation's cost of goods sold.

Shareholders of a selling corporation are not taxed when the corporation sells its assets unless the corporation has made the S election that causes it to be taxed more or less like a partnership, which means it pays no taxes and flows its income and losses directly to its owners. However, if the selling corporation distributes the sale proceeds in a complete liquidation, then each of the corporation's shareholders recognizes gain or loss, generally capital in nature, equal to the difference between the value of the liquidating distributions and the basis of the stock. If the distribution is "current"—meaning not in liquidation of the corporation—then it is generally taxed as a dividend.

In contrast, if the target liquidates into its new parent company, there is no tax to the parent or the liquidating subsidiary, and the parent gets the "tax attributes" of the subsidiary, such as the tax basis of the subsidiary's assets. Corporate acquisitions are often followed by a liquidation of the newly-acquired target.

There is a complicated set of rules under IRC Section 1060 pursuant to which the buyer and seller must agree on the values of the assets that made up the transferred business. A purchase of the assets of a business is treated for tax purposes as a separate purchase and sale of each and every asset of the business, including its intangible assets. This rule applies both to a sale of all a corporation's assets and to a sale of any part, including the sale of a division that constitutes a separate line of business. Thus, both the buyer and the seller of a business must cooperatively assign part of the purchase price to each and every asset in the business in order to compare that part to the asset's basis and to separately compute gain and loss, asset by asset. The burden of apportioning the sales proceeds can be daunting if the business is substantial. The buyer and seller must generally use Form 8594, which they prepare jointly, to report the part of the sales price attributable to each asset. If there is no written allocation agreement, the parties are still obligated to use the residual method (see the following paragraph) of apportioning the purchase price to assets.

The basis of the acquired assets must be determined under the "residual method" the effect of which is to assign consideration sequentially, first to the most easily valued assets, such as cash and certain bank deposits, and last to the intangibles that are the most difficult to value, namely going concern value and goodwill, as a residual class. Goodwill and going concern value are amortizable over the same 15-year period along with numerous other intangibles described in IRC Section 197.

Ten-percent owners of businesses must report to the IRS on contracts that are related to the acquisition. This commonly forces disclosure of covenants not to compete, employment agreements, and other transactions. One major factor is that while the recipient of income under a covenant not to compete is taxed as the income is earned, the payor can only write off the expenses over 15 years.

Taxable Stock Acquisition

If the acquiring corporation buys stock from the target's shareholders, each shareholder will report a taxable gain or loss. Gain on stock sales is generally taxed at favorable capital gain rates.

Again, people benefit from capital gains and corporations do not. Thus, the target reports no gain or loss, and the basis of its assets and its tax history are unaffected. However, the acquiring corporation takes a cost basis in the purchased stock. The acquiring corporation is free to liquidate the target later or merge the target into itself.

It is common for the acquiring corporation to tender for all of the target's outstanding stock and, after purchasing a significant block, to cause a newly formed subsidiary to merge into the target corporation under applicable state law. This is the notorious "squeeze out" merger in which the target's remaining shareholders typically receive cash or installment debt for their shares or nonvoting stock of the parent company. All they can do is complain that the merger was unfair and seek to get a higher cash price in a state court action.

The purchase of a corporation's stock does not attract taxes to the corporation whose stock is sold. As a result, the basis of the target's assets is unchanged as are other attributes, such as the "earnings and profits," which are used to measure the corporation's capacity to pay taxable dividends. The big deal is the Section 382 limitation that cuts off NOLs.

The Code lets an acquiring corporation treat the target as if it was a target liquidation known as a "Section 338 election." This used to be a popular device, but changes in the tax laws have eliminated its luster. There is still one case where it works, namely where the target has losses that it can use to offset gains on the imaginary liquidation.

> **To illustrate**: Target Corporation has operating losses of $.9 million and has assets with a value of $1 million and a basis of $0. Acquiring Corporation buys 80 percent of the stock of Target Corporation and elects under Section 338 to treat Target Corporation as if it actually liquidated. The result is that Target Corporation will have a $1 million "gain" that it can offset with the $.9 million loss, leaving a taxable gain of $100,000 on which Target Corporation must pay tax. The benefit is that the tax basis Target Corporation's assets have been stepped up from $0 to $1 million, opening the door to claims of increased depreciation deductions. The move is a good one, because the Section 382 limitation (see the section titled "Obstacle Two: Objective Limits under Sections 382-384") would have cut Target Corporation's annual NOL carryforwards to very small numbers, such as $60,000 per year.

Although the acquiring corporation does not succeed to the tax history of the target, it can benefit indirectly from attributes such as carry over of NOLs (to the extent not devoured by Section 382) if the target and acquiring corporation file a consolidated return for federal income tax purpose. If the target is later liquidated into the acquiring corporation, as often happens, the target's tax history will carry over to the acquiring corporation unless the principal purpose of the transaction was tax avoidance. This can be very useful if the target has tax attributes that the acquiring corporation does not want to disturb:

> **To illustrate**: Target made a bad decision a few years back when it bought land (its only asset) for $2 million. The land is now worth only $600,000. If Acquiring Corporation, which owns many properties that have risen in value, buys the stock of Target, it can liquidate Target later on a tax-free basis under IRC Section 332. As a result, Acquiring Corporation gets a $2 million basis for the land setting the stage for a loss some years later, which it can use to offset the gains it expects to report when it sells some of its appreciated assets. Note that IRC Section 384 would require a five-year wait before taking advantage of this strategy.

Generally, if, after the acquisition, the target is included in an affiliated group of corporations that files a consolidated return, the other corporations in the affiliated group can deduct their postacquisition losses against the target's postacquisition income. Conversely, losses realized by the target after the acquisition—other than certain built-in losses described below—will offset postacquisition income generated by other members of the affiliated group. There are further complications that are beyond the scope of this book, including variations on the theme of IRC Section 382 that you saw above.

Election to Treat Sale of Stock as Sale of Assets

IRC Section 338(h)(10) offers a way for a parent corporation to sell a consolidated subsidiary's stock but treats the transaction as if the subsidiary had sold its assets to the acquiring corporation's subsidiary. The result is a major efficiency for the parties because there is no need to spend money on conveyances of specific assets and liabilities. The first step is that the Acquirer's purchase of stock must have been a qualified stock purchase. The next is the joint election under IRC Section 338(h)(10) to treat the stock sale by the parent as if it were an asset sale by the target subsidiary.

The selling parent corporation will report a gain or loss on the imaginary sale of assets to the acquirer, but it will report no gain or loss on the sale of the stock of the target subsidiary it formerly owned. An associated outcome is that the target company's tax attributes, such as earnings and profits, net operating losses, and so forth remain with the selling parent.

IRS Section 336(e) is the country cousin of IRC Section 338(h)(10). It is intended to produce the same tax result as under Section 338(h)(10) and simply extends it to situations where 80 percent of the subsidiary was owned by the seller corporation but a consolidated return was not filed. A key difference from IRC Section 338(h)(10) is that the seller can elect to use IRC Section 336(e) unilaterally. This means that the seller can control the buyer's tax treatment even after the sale is completed.

Pre-acquisition Redemption and Dividend

Imagine you owned a profitable corporation that you want to sell and you have an eager buyer, but the buyer cannot raise quite enough money to complete the purchase. One way to solve the problem would be for you to sell some of your stock back to your company, that is, redeem the stock, in exchange for cash or a note. Is this a dividend—generally bad news—or sale of the stock to the buyer? The IRS has long ago conceded that it is part of the stock sale and can qualify for capital gain treatment.[32]

Alternatively, imagine you are the president of Parent Corporation, which has a subsidiary called Subsidiary Corporation. Assume Parent Corporation wants to sell Subsidiary Corporation. You ask your tax lawyers if perhaps Subsidiary Corporation could pay a dividend to Parent Corporation so as to let Parent Corporation claim a 100 percent dividends-received deduction. Can it be done? The answer is "yes" and it is an excellent device for trimming down the size of Subsidiary to make it easier to sell.[33]

Golden Parachute

Fearing that large compensation packages in the 1980s were being used as bribes to facilitate corporate takeovers, Congress enacted IRC Section 280G as part of the Tax Reform Act of 1984. The reform imposes significant tax consequences on unusually large payments, called "parachute payments," resulting from a change in corporate ownership, which are made to individuals generally in a position both to influence a decision on and to benefit significantly from the change of ownership. If a change in the ownership or control of a corporation takes place, there are two major tax consequences of compensation paid to particular individuals as a result of the change:

- Parachute payments paid over a certain base amount, called "excess parachute payments," cannot be deducted by the paying corporation.
- Excess parachute payments are subject to an excise tax of 20 percent payable by the individual who receives the payment. The recipient cannot deduct the tax.

The more important concept is the "excess parachute payment." The rule applies if the aggregate present value of payments made to a particular individual as a result of the change is at least three times a base amount. If not, they are not parachute payments, and the payment is not subject to the tax burdens imposed on golden parachutes. On the other hand, if the value of the payments is at least three times the base amount, then all of the payments in excess of the base amount are "excess parachute payments" and are not deductible by the corporation *and* subject the recipient to a 20 percent tax.

The excess parachute payment is reduced by any amount that can be established by clear and convincing evidence as reasonable compensation for personal services actually rendered prior to the change in ownership or control.

Determining whether compensation is reasonable depends on the facts. This includes considerations such as nature of services, historic amount of compensation paid for performing services, and amount of compensation paid to individuals performing comparable services in situations where the compensation is not contingent on a change in ownership or control. Severance payments are not treated as reasonable compensation for services rendered either before or after the change in ownership or control. There are plenty of further details that are beyond the scope of this book and the patience of most readers.

Greenmail Payment

If someone receives "greenmail," then a 50 percent tax is imposed on any gain or other income of such person by reason of receiving the greenmail. The tax is levied on the amount of gain realized in the transaction even if it is otherwise nontaxable. The Code defines greenmail as any consideration paid directly or indirectly by a corporation or any person acting in concert with a corporation directly or indirectly to acquire stock of the corporation from any shareholder, if:

- the shareholder held such stock for less than two years before entering into the agreement to make the repurchase;
- at some time during the two-year period ending on the acquisition date the shareholder, any person acting in concert with such shareholder, any person related to the shareholder, or any person acting in concert with such shareholder made, or threatened to make, a public tender offer with respect to the stock of the corporation;
- acquisition is pursuant to an offer that was not made on the same terms to all shareholders.

The term "acting in concert" is not defined in the tax code. Because the excise tax is directed to a transaction governed by the securities laws, it is expected that the definitions under federal securities laws will apply.

Payments made in connection with, or in transactions related to, acquisitions are treated as paid in such acquisition. This suggests the attempt to avoid the greenmail tax by characterizing payments for stock as other types of payments will be unsuccessful, such as payments for a standstill agreement, as such payments will be treated as paid for the acquisition of stock.

The greenmail tax applies whether the tender offer is hostile or friendly, but not every expenditure related to redemption is necessarily nondeductible. For example, one court has held that fees connected with a loan, the proceeds of which were used to redeem stock, were deductible. The court was willing to split the transaction into its two component parts—the loan and the redemption. Congress adopted this holding in a "clarification" to the tax law in the Small Business Job Protection Act of 1996. Other fees may also be deductible under such an approach.

The greenmail tax attracts reporting requirements, too. Anyone liable for the greenmail tax must file Form 8725 on or before the nineteenth day following the receipt of greenmail.

Poison Pill

As noted in Chapter 1, one of the most popular antitakeover devices is the "poison pill." A poison pill is typically a right to receive extra shares at a bargain price or a special, contingent dividend by the target that vests in the event of a hostile takeover attempt of such corporation by another corporation. They raise the question of whether a poison pill should be treated as "boot" in reorganization or a dividend. The IRS indicated in a published ruling that it is willing to draw reasonable limits on the principle that special rights incorporated into the terms of the stock certificate may be treated as boot. In the ruling the IRS found the issuance of a "poison pill" is not a "taxable event," because such rights are inseparable from the stock to which they relate. As a result, poison pill rights should not be treated as boot.

That is not exactly the end of the story. The IRS kept silent in the ruling as to the consequences to the shareholders when the poison pill rights become exercisable. Thus, the IRS could assert that the vesting of such rights is a taxable dividend.

Tax-free Divestiture

The topic here is the tax-free distribution of a subsidiary's stock. A classic example was the break-up of AT&T in which the "Baby Bells" were spun off to shareholders of AT&T as settlement of a long-running antitrust suit brought by the Department of Justice (DOJ). The shareholders of AT&T wound up owning subsidiaries of AT&T with no tax to AT&T, the subsidiaries or the shareholders. But for the special rule of IRC Section 355, the deal would presumably have been a taxable dividend to the shareholders just as if they had received cash instead of the subsidiary stock.

Sometimes a divestiture can be nontaxable even though it does not satisfy the requirements of IRC Section 355. That would occur, for example, if the parent company had no accumulated profits and the stock that was distributed to the shareholders was worth less than what they paid in the past for the parent company stock. Cases like these are rare. In the usual case, the parent company is healthy and its profits will result in tagging the shareholders with a taxable dividend.

It used to be that one could perform a tax-free divestiture and then have the company that made the distribution reorganize into another company tax-free. Under the new reforms that is no longer possible in the sense that a later sale of either the distributing or distributed corporation results in a potentially large tax on the distributing corporation, as is discussed further below. One can do the tax-free reorganization as in the old days, but the divestiture is now generally taxable as if the distributing company sold the subsidiary stock and then distributed the cash proceeds.

Types of Divestitures

Tax-free divestitures fall into three patterns:

- Spin-off: this is a distribution by one corporation of the stock of its subsidiary corporation to the parent's shareholders, much like a stock dividend. The subsidiary may already be in existence or may be newly formed to accommodate the transaction.
- Split-off: this is the same as the spin-off, except that the shareholders of the parent corporation give up some of their stock in the parent corporation in exchange for stock of the subsidiary, much like a stock redemption or partial liquidation of the parent.
- Split-up: here the parent corporation distributes the stock of two or more of its subsidiaries, whether newly formed or preexisting, in complete liquidation of the parent corporation.

These three forms of divestitures are summarized in Table 6.4.

These stock distributions are usually done on a pro rata basis, but they can be specially targeted so that only one group of shareholders winds up with the stock of a particular corporation. The split-up is the clear example of a non–pro rata distribution, but it is also possible to have non–pro rata spin-offs of multiple subsidiaries and non–pro rata split-ups of multiple subsidiaries.

Technically speaking, there are two categories of tax-free corporate separations:

- Corporate divisions involving a spin-off, split-off or split-up of preexisting subsidiaries
- Divisive reorganizations involving two steps under IRC Section 368(a)(1)(D), namely the formation or transfer of assets to one or more subsidiaries, followed by the distribution of that stock as in the pure corporate divisions

The two-step division is formally a type D reorganization. The point is that there is a specially-tailored Code Section designed to accommodate forming a new subsidiary or subsidiaries that will then be distributed to shareholders. The

Table 6.4 Tax-free Divestitures

Type	Action	Liquidation
Spin-off	Parent distributes shares of subsidiary to parent's shareholders	None
Split-off	Parent's shareholders give up some of their stock in parent and receive shares of subsidiary	None
Split-up	Parent distributes shares of subsidiary to parents shareholders	Parent liquidates

differences between corporate divisions under IRC Section 355 and divisive reorganizations under IRC Section 368(a)(1)(D) are only technical.

Requirements for Nontaxable Divestitures

The divestiture rules are like the reorganization rules in several respects. First, transactions are not really tax-free. They are tax-deferred because the shareholders that get the divested stock will report a gain or loss later when they sell the stock. Second, the transaction producing the tax-deferred distribution has to be tested under demanding rules if it is to pass muster for tax-deferral. The divestiture rules are tougher than the reorganization rules. Space does not allow a deep treatment of this subject. The Treasury Regulations that interpret the rules are seemingly endless and there is a large body of case law on the subject. Nevertheless, one can offer an outline of the basic requirements.

Control
The distributing corporation must have 80 percent control of the corporation whose stock or securities are being distributed.

Minimum Distribution
The distributing corporation must distribute all of its stock and securities in the controlled corporation or at least enough stock to constitute 80 percent control. In the latter case, the distributing corporation must convince the Treasury Department that the retention of stock or securities of the controlled corporation did not occur for reasons having to do with tax avoidance. For example, it might claim that the retention will be used to satisfy obligations arising under an executive stock option plan.

Business Purpose
There must be a business purpose for the distribution at the corporate level. In AT&T's case there was an overwhelming legal duty to dispose of the subsidiary shares. The difficulty in this realm is that, with closely held corporations, it is often difficult to differentiate the interests of the corporation from those of its shareholders.

Not Device to Bail Out Profits
The biggest Congressional fear about tax-deferred divestitures is that they will be used as end-runs around dividends. Here is an example:

> **To illustrate:** The Rafferty Corporation has a long history of profitably manufacturing various fabricated items in nondescript factory buildings in Connecticut and Massachusetts. Many of the factory buildings are on land whose values are rising and could be torn down with the land sold at a great profit. If the Rafferty Corporation

were to incorporate one of the buildings by contributing it to Newco and spinning Newco off to its shareholders, the new shareholders might decide to sell the Newco stock to a developer. They could claim a long-term capital gain measured by the difference between their basis in Newco stock and what they later sold it for. By contrast, if the Rafferty Corporation sold the land and distributed the cash, there would be a dividend to the shareholders taxable (in that year) as ordinary income. The distribution of the Newco stock looks like a device to move some of Rafferty's profits to its shareholders by a restructuring whose real purpose is to let shareholders avoid income taxes.

The Code insists that the corporate division must not be a device primarily for distribution of profits of the distributing corporation, the controlled corporation, or of both combined. It casts a cold eye on prearranged sales of stock of the distributing or controlling corporation following the division.[34] The regulations identify various other evidences of a device to bail out earnings and profits on a tax-favored basis:

- Pro rata distribution of subsidiary stock
- Divestiture where either the controlled or distributing corporation winds up particularly rich with liquid assets that can easily be sold off

There are positive factors, too:

- The corporation is publicly traded and no one owns over 5 percent of its stock.
- Distributees are all corporations that can claim the benefits of the dividends-received deduction.
- Distributing and controlled corporations lack earnings and profits and are low on appreciated assets.

Active Business Requirement
The parent distributing corporation and the subsidiary must each be engaged in the active conduct of a business immediately after the distribution. Also, the parent or subsidiary must not have acquired the active business in a taxable transaction during the past five years.

Assuming all these tests are met and the shareholder gets stock of a subsidiary, she has to figure out her basis in the new stock. She computes her basis by reference to the relative value of the old and new stock. The system is logical.

To illustrate: Assume the Rafferty Corporation undertook a divestiture of Subco that qualified as a nontaxable spin-off and Ellen Rafferty held one share of Rafferty stock with a basis of $1,000 and a value of $10,000 before the distribution (worth $6,000 after the distribution) and that she also got Subco stock worth $4,000 in the divestiture. She will claim basis in the Subco equal to 40 percent of the $10,000 basis in the Rafferty stock. When the smoke clears, she owns Rafferty stock with a basis of $600 and Newco stock with a basis of $400. Her holding period for the Newco stock will be the same as her holding period for the Rafferty stock.

What follows is a description of how a business is divided.

Vertical Division

A single active business can be divided in half, or theoretically even into smaller groupings, as long as each half is a freestanding business. For example, imagine a construction business held by two feuding owners. As a result of the corporate division, each owner walks away tax-free with a separate, freestanding construction business consisting of several ongoing projects. The original business had been active in the construction industry for over five years. The Court held that the five-year active business test was met, in effect adding the five-year history of the original business to each of the parts.[35]

Horizontal Division

Successful businesses can expand geographically and expanding their product lines. Sometimes they decide to spin off a recently-opened store or to incorporate a new product line into a separate company and distribute it to its shareholders.

These ideas raise the question of whether a new location or product line is a new business or whether it is instead merely an expansion of an existing business, which can be divided up so that each part inherits the maturity of the original business. A leading example involved a corporation that sold portable potato-sorting machines in various potato-producing states in the West.[36] It later expanded its product line. In 1954 it set up a branch in Maine, which it incorporated and spun off to its shareholders in 1956. The IRS claimed the spin-off was taxable because it was a new business.

The Court was faced with the question of whether to apply a "geographical test" or a "functional test" to determine the existence and duration of a business. The functional test was accepted. Under the functional test the company was viewed as having carried on a farm equipment sales business since the late 1940s and the business in Maine was just an extension of that same business. As a result the five-year test was met, and the spin-off was treated as the nontaxable division of a single business.

The Regulations treat even the taxable acquisition of a new branch as an expansion of a preexisting business unless the acquisition so changes the character of the business that it constitutes the acquisition of a new or different business.

Divestiture of Unwanted Assets Followed by Tax-free Acquisition

An acquiring corporation might refuse to accept certain assets of the target and might insist that the target dispose of them before the tax-free acquisition. The target's shareholders may be forced to retain the unwanted assets, and the question becomes how to do so at the smallest tax cost. Basically there are two choices:

- Spin off the unwanted assets and then combine the remaining (original) corporation with the acquiring company
- Spin off the wanted assets into a new corporation and combine the new corporation with the acquiring corporation

The business and economic effects of these two choices are identical, but the tax results are vastly different.

The IRS position is that if you do it the first way, the later acquisition is generally nontaxable, but if you do it the second way, the acquisition is generally taxable.[37] Also, the divestiture regulations kindly say that a spin-off followed by a sale indicates a device, but a spin-off followed by a reorganization does not—a major concession that opens the door to combining nontaxable acquisitions with nontaxable acquisitions.

Just recently, however, Congress threw a spanner into the works. Here is the problem. It used to be that the distribution of the subsidiary with the unwanted assets was not taxable to the distributing corporation, even though either the distributing corporation or the distributed corporation was taken over by an outside group. Under the new rules, the distributing corporation is taxed *as if it sold the stock of the distributed corporation* if within two years one or more persons get a 50 percent or greater interest—measured by vote or value of stock—in the controlled corporation or the distributing corporation within two years before or after the distribution.

Why this new "reform"? If either corporation is disposed of, then the real purpose of the stock distribution was presumably to facilitate a disposition to an outside party as opposed to merely restructuring the corporation. A disposition implies something similar to a sale as opposed to a restructuring. Notice that there is not necessarily always tax trouble, because the stock being distributed might have a value equal to its basis; as a result there would be a taxable transaction, but there would be no tax bill to the distributing corporation.

Should American corporations start forming and spinning off new entities now so that businesses are easier to dispose of on a tax-free basis? Perhaps so. It is certainly worth considering.

A final comment. We know that the tax law generally permits combining tax-free divestitures with tax-free reorganizations, though it is harder to do than ever. That is not true where the second step is a taxable *sale* of either the distributing or spun off company's stock. First, the taxable transaction is evidence of a "device" to bail out profits under the divestiture regulations.[38] Second, the divestiture may be taxable because there may be a lack of continuity of proprietary interest on the part of the shareholders of whichever entity is sold. This violates the requirement of the historic shareholders of the original corporation to continue to have a major equity stake in both companies after the corporate division.

Advance Ruling and Legal Opinion

Corporate acquisitions are big-ticket events with major tax implications for the acquiring corporation, the target and the target's shareholders. Prudence dictates being confident about the results. That, in turn, requires either getting an opinion of a reputable, competent law firm or a ruling from the IRS on the key tax aspects of the deal, such as whether it is a tax-free reorganization, what kind of reorganization it is, whether certain property might constitute taxable "boot" and so forth.

Getting a private letter ruling from the IRS has the advantage of an assurance. As long as the facts described in the request for a ruling were truthful, IRS agents who later audit the taxpayer will feel obligated to respect the ruling, assuming it is favorable.

The IRS understands the need for rulings in connection with corporate acquisitions and divestitures. As a matter of practice, it is willing to accelerate the ruling process in order to help the business deal along. To get on the right side of the IRS, one needs to prepare the ruling in a highly professional manner and be familiar with how one deals with personnel at the National Office of the IRS. Because the ruling staff consists of highly specialized lawyers, it is best to use a law firm for "cultural" reasons, but accounting firms often perform the same role.

The blueprint for the ruling appears in so-called Revenue Procedures. In January of each year the IRS issues its first Revenue Procedure, such as Revenue Procedure 2000-1 for the year 2000, which provides detailed instructions as to how to go about the ruling process. It needs to be adhered to with military precision if one is to stay on a fast track. Once the IRS has received the ruling request, it will normally give an informal statement as to whether it agrees with the taxpayer's positions. If the ruling is well formed, one should expect a positive preliminary answer and a formal ruling some months later. If the confidence level is high enough, the parties can push the deal ahead although perhaps contingent on receiving a favorable ruling by a given date.

The ruling request calls for a fee to the IRS of $5,000, which will gradually rise with time. It is a bargain because of the level of confidence the private ruling produces. The process has another advantage. The very act of seeking a ruling forces the parties' tax advisors assigned to the job to carefully think through each and every important aspect of the deal—a useful discipline.

7

Process

In this chapter, I describe the negotiation process and issues that are likely to arise.

Negotiations

Mergers, acquisitions and divestitures begin, end and are ultimately based on negotiations. This means explanation and exhortation. The parties must consider both aspects.

First, be able to explain your needs and concerns. Rather than saying no, for instance, describe why you are saying no. It is possible that the other side might agree with your position if you explain the background. Second, be prepared to persuade the other side to accept your position. While explanations tend to be objective, this is where you become subjective. Muster the arguments in your favor, and lay them before the other side in the most effective way you can.

While some negotiators prefer a demanding tone, from my experience the best deals are those that are based on discussions rather than arguments. By best deals, I mean deals that stand the test of time and where the parties continue to work through issues over time. If you are selling and never expect to do business with buyer or anyone else on the other side again, a belligerent tone might work. When forming a joint venture it will not. The success of a long-term relationship is based on mutual trust and support—not domination.

Many books have been written on the negotiation process. Two of the better ones are Herb Cohen's *You Can Negotiate Anything*[1] and Roger Fisher and William Ury's *Getting to Yes*[2]. They are well worth the time and could be the difference between closing a deal and not.

For the balance of this chapter, I will apply some of these principles to the following typical negotiation process:

- First, the negotiation and execution of a confidentiality agreement under which the parties agree not to disclose their negotiations to others

- Second, the negotiation and execution of a term sheet covering the basic deal points
- Third, the conduct of due diligence, particularly by buyer who wishes to investigate seller's business and assets
- Fourth, the negotiation and execution of detailed agreements covering the purchase or merger
- Fifth, obtaining approvals from directors (usually conducted behind closed doors without public disclosure)
- Sixth, obtaining approvals from shareholders (inevitably publicly)
- Seventh, obtaining third parties approvals (can be from banks, suppliers, customers and government agencies)
- Eighth, the closing where the assets are transferred and money received

In the following sections, we will consider each stage.

Confidentiality Agreement

Both buyer and seller will be discussing privileged information during the course of your negotiations. Both parties will want to be certain that the information will not be disclosed. Therefore, before entering into substantive discussions, they must be certain that any confidential information disclosed will not be made public.

The best protection is to rely on a confidentiality agreement, also known as a nondisclosure agreement. An example of a unilateral nondisclosure agreement, called Sample NDA, can be found at http://www.RobertLBrown.info. Any party disclosing information should request the recipient to sign a similar agreement. If both parties expect to disclose information, each could request the other to sign the agreement; with a few changes, it could be turned into a bilateral agreement.

Let us review some of the major components of confidentiality agreements, which are summarized in Table 7.1. The paragraph numbers refer to those in Sample NDA.

One of the first paragraphs of most confidentiality agreements will be a fairly detailed description of confidential information. If a party can foresee any type of information that may be revealed, include it in this paragraph. Although a phrase such as "and other subject matter pertaining to the business of Disclosing Party" should pick up anything discussed, it is safer to include other forms of specific information in the definition. The information is then defined as "Confidential Information."

Section 1 typically contains the obligation to keep the information confidential. It is the heart and soul of the agreement.

Section 2 will usually describe the purpose of the disclosure. In Sample NDA the description is left blank, so do not forget to describe the purpose when using

Table 7.1 Major Provisions of Confidentiality Agreement

Section	Description
2nd par.	Description of confidential information
Sec. 1	Obligation to keep information confidential
Sec. 2	Purpose of disclosure
Sec. 3	Prohibition of disclosure
	Discloser own confidential information
	No license granted to recipient
Sec. 4	Receiver authorized to disclose to designated parties
Sec. 5	Receiver required to protect information
Sec. 6	Public and known information not covered
Sec. 7	Damages for disclosure
Sec. 8	Obligation to return information
Sec. 9	Obligations binding on successors and assigns
Sec. 10, 11	General terms and conditions

Sample NDA. Keep the definition as narrow as possible when disclosing and as broad as possible when receiving information and wanting to use it for a variety of purposes. A discloser will want to insist on retaining the last sentence so that it is not obligated to provide information unless it wishes to do so.

Section 3 will usually be the negative version of Section 1. It prohibits the recipient from disclosing it to any other person. It includes a specific statement that the Disclosing Party owns the information and is not granting a license to the Receiving Party.

Section 4 will generally authorize Receiving Party to disclose Confidential Information to its officers, agents and similar parties. The section should also contain limits on such disclosures. Future recipients must need the information and have agreed in writing to keep it confidential. The section should also impose a further obligation on Receiving Party to advise such recipients that they cannot use, reproduce, publish or disclose such information.

Section 5 will typically create a further burden on Receiving Party. It must take all necessary action to protect the confidentiality and Disclosing Party's ownership of the information.

Section 6 will likely contain the exclusions from Confidential Information. It will exclude information that the Disclosing Party cannot reasonably claim is its information or information that is confidential. Such information includes information publicly known at the time of disclosure or subsequently becoming known other than through recipient's actions, is required by a court order to be disclosed, or becomes known to recipient from an authorized source.

In many cases, the disclosure of information might cause damage that monetary awards cannot adequately compensate. If so, a section, such as Section 7, should be included to address this problem by giving Disclosing Party another remedy. It can seek an injunction to prevent the recipient from disclosing the information.

What happens to information provided to the recipient at the end of the agreement? Under Section 8 of Sample NDA, the recipient must return it to the disclosing party.

The agreement should also state that recipient's obligations are binding on its successors and assigns. In Sample NDA, this appears as Section 9. Similarly, the Disclosing Party's successors and assigns can enforce the agreement against the recipient.

The concluding sections, such as Sections 10 and 11 of Sample NDA, will contain general legal provisions—such as, entire agreement, no amendment except in writing, governing law, and recovery of attorneys' fees by the prevailing party in a dispute.

This completes the discussion of confidentiality agreements. With it in hand the parties can begin to disclose information while negotiating the letter of intent.

Letter of Intent/Term Sheet

The letter of intent, or term sheet, summarizes the deal. It has three purposes:

- Describes the key issues and makes certain the parties have agreed on them. Once they have reached a consensus on the big-ticket items, detailed agreements will cover the issues in more detail.
- Points out the issues that have not been agreed upon and need further negotiation. This is important to remember. The letter of intent does not need to resolve all issues. While the key issues should be addressed and resolved to ease the ensuing negotiations, even this is not necessary.
- Sets the timetable and assigns responsibilities in the next stage. This may be limited to describing when government approvals will be obtained and how due diligence will be conducted, but it is important to cover them.

Contents

A sample term sheet for a typical acquisition, called Sample Term Sheet, can be found at http://www.RobertLBrown.info. Let us review the key elements, which are summarized in Table 7.2. The section numbers refer to those in Sample Term Sheet.

Section 1, such as in Sample Term Sheet, is the key section. It describes the contemplated transaction—seller will sell its business and assets, and buyer will buy. Sample Term Sheet is for an asset purchase. In the case of stock purchase or merger, necessary changes must be made to the letter. This section describes the assets being purchased by referring to seller's balance sheet, but excludes assets it needs to sell in the ordinary course of business. Assets being sold include cash,

Table 7.2 Major Provisions of Term Sheet for Asset Purchase

Section	Description
Sec. 1	Description of proposed transaction—assets being acquired
Sec. 2	Price and payment
Sec. 3	Liabilities being assumed by buyer
Sec. 4	Agreement not to compete
Sec. 5	Binding nature of term sheet
Sec. 6	Closing deadline
Sec. 7	Expenses paid by each party
Sec. 8	Buyer to be given access to seller's records
Sec. 9	Right of seller to seek other buyers
Sec. 10	Confidentiality agreement remains binding

notes receivable, raw materials, work-in-process, finished goods, machinery, real property, as well as seller's intellectual property.

In Sample Term Sheet, Section 2 covers what it is going to cost buyer and when it must pay seller. This section allows some cash at closing, with the balance covered by a promissory note.

Section 3 of Sample Term Sheet describes the liabilities of seller that buyer will assume. It is the counterpart of Section 1 describing what assets it gets. For both parties' sake, it is important to describe carefully the liabilities being assumed. The section also provides that all other liabilities remain with seller. It is important to consider this section carefully. A little time spent on this section will greatly shorten negotiations later over the detailed agreement.

After the assets are purchased, buyer does not want seller turning around and starting up another operation that will compete with the business that buyer has acquired. Section 4 of Sample Term Sheet prohibits seller and its key officers and shareholders from doing so. This section must be carefully reviewed in light of local rules. States vary greatly on how much they are willing to enforce such non-competes. There are differing rules on:

- duration, the range being from about six months to two years in many cases;
- geographical area (local, state or national);
- business.

California, for instance, allows the seller of a business's goodwill and any shareholder of a corporation selling of all its shares to agree with the buyer to refrain from carrying on a similar business within specified counties or cities.[2] To enforce an agreement, the courts in California require that all shares and substantially all of the business have been sold.[3] The courts may be even more willing to accept a covenant not to compete that is related to a sale of stock.[4]

It is important, therefore, to check the prevailing rules and draft a provision that the courts will enforce. Provisions that violate allowable state limits may be stricken completely or narrowed to fit the acceptable limits.

We will discuss Section 5 of Sample Term Sheet section titled "Binding Nature."

Section 6 of Sample Term Sheet sets the deadline for a closing, which is the date when assets will be transferred and payment made. Be certain that the deadline is far enough in the future to obtain financing and government approvals, such as under the Hart-Scott-Rodino Antitrust Improvements Act (HSR). Alternatively, the section can be redrafted to state that the closing will be held on the earlier of a certain date or ten days, for instance, after receiving HSR approval.

Section 7 of Sample Term Sheet requires the parties to pay their own expenses. An exception appears for HSR filing fees, which are to be split equally. Often buyers will demand that sellers pay such fees.

In the next section I will discuss the due diligence that buyer will be conducting to ensure that the assets are worth what is being paid. In Sample Term Sheet, Section 8 requires seller to give buyer access to records and information it needs to value the business.

Section 9 of Sample Term Sheet will be discussed in the section titled, "Lock-up."

Section 10 of Sample Term Sheet states that the previously discussed confidentiality agreement remains binding. This is intended to eliminate any argument that the letter of intent cancels or supercedes any separate confidentiality obligations. In some cases, the letter of intent will contain confidentiality provisions, and thus a separate confidentiality agreement will not be executed.

Binding Nature

In Sample Term Sheet, the agreement is couched as a nonbinding letter. For instance, it is called a letter of intent and refers to a "Contemplated Transaction". In Section 5, the letter explicitly states that the legal obligations of the parties will be covered by a "Definitive Agreement."

Following Section 10 of Sample Term Sheet is a paragraph that states that the purpose of the letter is to memorialize the parties' expression of interest and to outline the basic terms and conditions. It also provides that the letter is only based on information through the date of the letter. It goes on to provide that, other than in a few stated exceptions, the parties' legal obligations will only be contained in the Definitive Agreement.

The net effect of these provisions is to create a road map without obligating the parties to take the road.

A party is not prohibited in subsequent negotiations from trying to change the terms reflected in the term sheet or letter of intent. Unless there has been a change of circumstances, however, such a position will antagonize the other side and might cause it to walk away from the deal.

Lock-up

If the parties want to take the road mapped out for them in the letter, they can take a more aggressive approach. They can, for instance, make the letter binding. Sample Term Sheet, for instance, specifically provides that Sections 7 (expenses), 8 (access to information for due diligence), and 10 (confidentiality) are binding.

Additionally, a buyer who wants a unique asset owned by seller may be particularly interested in tying the hands of seller—particularly in a rising market. On the other hand, if seller believes the market has peaked or will drop, it might want to force buyer to take the asset if certain conditions are met.

Section 9 of Sample Term Sheet addresses this issue by prohibiting seller from shopping the deal to others. Specifically, it cannot:

- solicit or accept other offers;
- negotiate or discuss other agreements;
- disclose the existence of the letter or the negotiations to others.

In Sample Term Sheet, there is a 90-day limitation from execution of the letter on the first two items. There is no time limit on the last.

Many states dislike no-shop or no-talk clauses. They feel that they violate the director's duty of care by preventing directors from making an informed decision. In response, some letters of intent contain a fiduciary-out clause that allows the board to deal with a third party if the board determines the third party's proposal is superior.

Remedies

What happens if the other side violates a binding obligation, such as the no-shop or no-talk limitation? There are three possible approaches—breach, tortious interference and break-up fees.

The most likely argument is that seller has breached its contractual obligations and is liable to buyer. The problem is that courts have been reluctant to find meaningful damages in such cases.[5]

Another argument used by buyers is to sue the successful bidder that has beaten it. The legal theory is tortuous interference with a contract.[6] Again, the problem is that most buyers have been dissatisfied with the damages awarded to them.

A more successful approach has been to agree in advance on what the damages are. Some agreements take an even more aggressive approach by requiring seller to pay a break-up fee to buyer if it does shop the deal or talk to others.[7] The courts have applied different standards in evaluating the acceptability of such fees. Some states have applied a liquidated damage test rather than a business judgment rule. Under the liquidated damages test, the fee must be reasonable and the damages uncertain or difficult to determine. The courts have not been willing to accept exorbitant or punitive fees. Fees of 1–3 percent, may be up to 5 percent with other compensation such as lock-up options, of the value of the deal are likely to be accepted by the courts.

Disclosure Effect

For securities law purposes, if a letter of intent is signed it probably means that negotiations have progressed to a point that an announcement may be necessary by publicly traded companies. Such an announcement has several disadvantages.

First and most important, the announcement lets others know about a pending deal before it is closed. For buyer, the announcement might encourage other bidders to come forward. For seller, it might cause a momentary or permanent drop in sales. Customers might wait for the deal to close before placing long-term orders or might go elsewhere if they begin to fear that a key supplier may be lost.

Second, if the transaction is not finalized after such an announcement, it can cause embarrassment to the two companies and could affect their stock prices. For seller, it could mean that other buyers will be less willing to negotiate with it, and the price it can get in the future may be reduced.

For these reasons, many companies prefer not to enter into a letter of intent but to move directly to the main agreement. Such a solution might not be sufficient. The U.S. Supreme Court has held that preliminary negotiations even before the execution of a letter of intent may be sufficient to require a public announcement.[8]

Due Diligence

Due diligence refers to the preclosing period during which buyer and seller evaluate each other.

Purpose

The main purpose of due diligence is to give buyer a chance to look for the bad news. Buyer is usually given thirty to sixty days to review seller's records, access senior managers, and ask questions. During this period, it has a chance to confirm that the price it is paying is appropriate. If the news is better than expected, buyer will be pleased and anxious to close. There is no renegotiation of the price. If the news is as expected, again the price stays the same and closing proceeds. If the news is not as good as expected, buyer is likely first to try to renegotiate the price unless the news is so materially adverse as to negate the true value of the deal. Failing a price reduction, buyer will withdraw.

Due diligence, however, can serve other purposes:

- Allow seller to understand buyer and ensure that buyer will be able to pay the purchase price and perform its obligations
- Permit seller to confirm buyer is an appropriate person to take over the business, a more likely concern when seller is a closely held business and the owners want to make certain buyer will continue or grow the business
- Help buyer to understand seller's business and what its obligations are likely to be
- Lay the foundation for integrating buyer and seller's operations
- Identify warranties, representations and covenants that buyer will want from seller in the main agreement
- Identify third party consents that must be obtained
- Identify agreements that will be required
- Prepare a timetable for consents and closing

If you are seller, keep a copy of all written information disclosed and notes about oral information conveyed to buyer during this phase. In case of a dispute as to what was disclosed such evidence could be your best evidence.

Timing

With all the work that must be done during due diligence, it is important to have a plan of what you are looking for. The plan should assign responsibilities and state who will be doing what and when the work must be accomplished. Tasks will usually be split up among outsiders and insiders. Outsiders will include lawyers, accountants and investment bankers. Insiders will include individuals from many departments in the two companies. For instance, buyer's information systems (IS) people will discuss issues with seller's IS people. Similar matching will occur for human resources, accounting, credit, research, purchasing, production, marketing and distribution.

The issue is when to get different departments involved. For integration purposes, sooner is better. There are several reasons, however, why this is neither possible nor advisable. The principal ones concern confidentiality and antitrust.

From a confidentiality standpoint, seller will not want to turn over trade secrets until closing. Even with a nonconfidentiality agreement, such information should not be released. The more people with access, the more chance it will be released.

From an antitrust standpoint, certain types of information cannot be disclosed before closing. If buyer and seller are in the same business, such disclosures may be treated as a sharing of information between competitors—an activity that is a per se violation of the antitrust rules.[9] To reduce the risk of disclosures during the due diligence period violating the antitrust laws, there are several rules or policies that should be followed by buyer and seller. The more their businesses overlap and compete, the more important these rules become.

- Remain competitors during the premerger phase. Regardless of how good the negotiations are proceeding, something might happen to prevent a closing—including the government deciding that the deal is not advisable. Anticipate the worst and that the deal will not close. Do not give government and competitors the chance to argue that during the due diligence period the two parties coordinated their businesses. This might enable them to argue that lessons learned during this period permitted the two parties to coordinate their activities and that the entire proposed acquisition was just a sham to allow them to exchange information. Even if the deal closes, a competitor who loses market share during the due diligence period might argue that the loss was the result of illegal coordination during that period.
- Exchange only what is necessary. While some information is important to evaluating the other party, the risks and the liabilities being transferred, draw the line at what is essential to that purpose.
- Exchange only when necessary. Defer disclosing information until as late as possible, with closing being the ideal time.
- Limit who gets information. Only those individuals who need the information should be given access to it. It should not be available to anyone involved in day-to-day operations. Most importantly, it should not be turned over to anyone setting prices for competing products or services.
- Avoid joint meetings with customers.

To make certain these rules are met, it is safest to have antitrust counsel present when information is being exchanged and to have documents passed through them.

Checklist

An example of a due diligence checklist, called Sample Checklist, can be found at http://www.RobertLBrown.info. It covers most of the topics and issues that are likely to arise in an asset acquisition and the types of information that you are likely to want or have to disclose. The form is drafted as a certificate to be signed by an officer of seller. This encourages seller to take seriously what is being disclosed.

It also provides buyer with a misrepresentation argument if the information is not accurate. Such a representation will be eliminated in the main agreement, which will contain a statement that it is the entire agreement with all of seller's representations and all other agreements and representations replaced by it. If the main agreement is not executed, however, the representation in the checklist remains effective and can be the grounds for buyer recovering costs.

In the following discussion, I will describe the disclosures from the standpoint of buyer, as summarized in Table 7.3. The section numbers refer to those in Sample Checklist.

Starting with the basics, as reflected in Section 1 of Sample Checklist, you want copies of their corporate records. This allows you to confirm the number of shares outstanding and who owns them. You will also want to review board minutes to make certain they are in order, proper actions have been taken and prior securities and agreements have been approved, and to determine what needs to be done for approval of your transaction.

In this area, you will look for evidence of securities law violations, including registration and periodic filings, shareholder meetings and reports, insider trading, self-dealing, and fraud.

You will also be concerned with whether buyer is qualified in the states where it is doing business. This will be addressed at closing by good standing certificates from each state where it does business. These are issued by the secretary of state. Be careful of the fatal four (Arkansas,[10] Alabama,[11] Mississippi[12] and Vermont[13])

Table 7.3 Major Provisions of Due Diligence Checklist

Section	Description
Sec. 1	Corporate records
Sec. 2	References
Sec. 3	Financial statements
Sec. 4	Accounting procedures
Sec. 5	Products
Sec. 6	Services
Sec. 7	Market and market share
Sec. 8	Customers
Sec. 9	Competitors
Sec. 10	Property, plant and equipment
Sec. 11	Material contracts and agreements
Sec. 12	Distribution agreements
Sec. 13	Inventory
Sec. 14	Warranties
Sec. 15	Officers
Sec. 16	Employees
Sec. 17	Intellectual property
Sec. 18	Litigation
Sec. 19	Insurance
Sec. 20	Regulatory compliance
Sec. 21	Financing arrangements
Sec. 22	Taxes
Sec. 23	Bank accounts
Sec. 24	Other information
Last par.	Representation and signature by seller

where transactions prior to qualification are invalid and cannot be cured by subsequent registration.

Section 2 of Sample Checklist addresses references. If you are in the same business, this is less important. If seller is publicly traded or has a well-established market, references might similarly not be important. It can be very important, however, if seller is closely held and is an emerging company. Personally, I am not a big fan of references. Most people can produce a few people willing to vouch for their wisdom. With employment rules becoming stricter, what former employers are able to disclose is becoming narrow. Nevertheless, it is amazing what one can sometimes learn.

Section 3 of Sample Checklist covers seller's financial statements. These may be the most important disclosures since they are the most objective reflection of seller's business. Be clear what you need in terms of financials, make certain you get all you need and review them carefully. The financial team must be well qualified and able to understand someone else's financials. For this reason, someone from buyer's credit or accounting department may be particularly helpful as an internal team member.

In Sample Checklist, Section 4 addresses seller's accounting procedures. Consider how seller recognizes revenue and its accounting policies. Make certain they are consistently applied.

Sections 5 and 6 of Sample Checklist ask for information on seller's existing products and services and those in development. If buyer is in the same business, it is probably already aware of the existing products and services. From an antitrust standpoint, buyer probably cannot ask for those in development.

Having information on seller's products and services, the next issue is what the market is. Related to that is seller's market share. Buyer will be interested in the market, seller's share at present, and how it is changing. These issues are covered by Section 7 of Sample Checklist.

In Section 8 of Sample Checklist, the emphasis is on seller's customers. How does seller market and sell? Related questions are, Whom is it selling to?; Who are the important customers?; and What new customers are there?

Section 9 of Sample Checklist looks at seller's competitors—who they are, how they compete, and how strong they are.

In Section 10 of Sample Checklist, we look more carefully at seller's property, plant and equipment. Critical areas are a description of the property it owns and leases and liens on them. For owned real property, buyer will want copies of the title reports. For owned personal property, buyer will need copies of tax and UCC (Uniform Commercial Code) state and local filings to see what liens have been recorded.

Sections 11 and 12 of Sample Checklist focus on contracts that are important to seller. Under this category, buyer will also be interested in seller's material agreements. It should review the documents that are keys to seller's business. There are some things to look for in particular:

- Agreements requiring consents to the purchase. Seller, on the other hand, will be concerned with its postclosing obligations and liabilities once the contracts are assigned.
- For purchase obligations, look to see how secure important sources are.
- On the sale side, look to see how firm major customer contracts are. Also check for type and severity of warranties.
- Most loan agreements contain negative covenants prohibiting share and asset sales without lenders' written consent. If the asset being transferred has been pledged or a lender has a security interest, lender's approval must be obtained.
- Leases traditionally require consents to asset and stock sales, so pay particular attention to these. Also look for extensions and options.
- Be certain key employees are under contract to seller. Even if they are, look for change-of-control provisions that allow them to leave with golden parachutes containing options and bonuses. Any such benefits exceeding three times the employee's average compensation over the prior five-year period are nondeductible by seller.

Section 12 of Sample Checklist considers distribution agreements—agency, distributor and reseller.

In Sample Checklist, Section 13 considers seller's inventory. What is there? How long has it been there? How many of them are returned goods? Are any obsolete? What is seller's inventory accounting practices?

In Section 14 of Sample Checklist, the issue is warranties given to customers. What are the reps and warranties, and how expensive have they been to seller in the past as measured by damages paid?

The next two sections look to the people inside seller. Section 15 of Sample Checklist asks questions about its officers. Who are they, how much are they paid, what are their employment agreements, and how reputable are they?

In Section 16 of Sample Checklist, buyer asks for information on seller's employees, starting with an organizational table and job descriptions. In this section when buyer asks for a list of fired employees, it is really looking for leads. Disgruntled employees are more likely to give bad news about seller. Similarly, buyer wants to know how good seller's relations are with employees and unions and if there have been any problems, such as lawsuits or strikes in the past. In this area buyer will also be asking for information on pension benefits and the adequacy of their funding.

Section 17 of Sample Checklist turns to seller's intellectual property (IP). This checklist is more focussed on a hi-tech company with limited manufacturing. The questions on seller's IP are, therefore, extensive. The questions address seller's software, hardware and Internet presence.

If, on the other hand, manufacturing is a critical function for seller, questions on its manufacturing operations need to be added. They should focus on life and expectancy of equipment, expansion capabilities, quality control, inventory control, and just-in-time supplier relations.

In Sample Checklist, Section 18 asks about seller's litigation experiences. Is it presently involved in any cases or arbitrations? Has it been? Are any threatened?

In Section 19 of Sample Checklist, seller is asked to provide information about its insurance policies. This includes the policies, the risks covered, the maximum amounts covered, deductibles, and pending claims.

Section 20 of Sample Checklist covers sellers' regulatory compliance. Seller should have business licenses issued by government agencies for the business it conducts. Unfortunately, many licenses may not be transferable. For these, buyer will have to seek new ones once the transaction closes. Seller is also asked about noncompliance with governmental rules and any government reports it has had to file. Such reports will likely give buyer great insight into seller's business. Environmental compliance is very important. Under the Comprehensive Environmental Response, Compensation and Liability Act (CERCLA or Superfund Act),[14] owners and operators of facilities, including lessees, are strictly liable for remedial costs if hazardous wastes or materials are discovered. Therefore, it is important to review all existing and prior uses of property. An indemnity in the main agreement may not be sufficient if seller ceases to exist after the transaction closes.

Section 21 of Sample Checklist looks at seller's financing arrangements. It requests copies of all its financing agreements, including loans, mortgages, liens and capitalized leases. Information on defaults, collateral and guarantees is also requested.

Section 22 of Sample Checklist considers seller's tax structure. It requests copies of its national, federal and state filings for the past three years. To evaluate future risks for past activities, it asks for information on current tax audits. In this area, buyer should consider if any taxes are likely to arise on assets being transferred to it.

In Section 23 of Sample Checklist, seller is asked to provide information on its bank accounts. Buyer will be looking for financial controls and location of accounts.

Finally, Section 24 of Sample Checklist is a catchall covering any other relevant information, such as management or consultant reports on seller. They can be a gold mine of information.

Main Agreement

The type of transaction will determine the core documents required.

In stock purchases, seller must sign a document transferring the stocks it owns. This will usually be a stock power.

In mergers, the controlling document is the merger plan filed with the appropriate state agency. All assets and liabilities are transferred, the disappearing entity is dissolved, and shares are converted without further action.

Assets purchases are more difficult. Each asset must be transferred. While there will be one master agreement covering, summarizing and acting as a blueprint for the entire transaction, there will be individual transfer agreements covering different types of assets and the filing required to implement them. For example:

- Patents and trademarks will be covered by one or more assignments filed with the U.S. Patent and Trademark Office.
- Real property will be covered by separate conveyances filed with the county clerk's office where the property is located.
- Personal property will be covered by a bill of sale that may be filed with a local county clerk's office.
- Leases will be covered by separate assignments with a copy provided to each lessor.
- Vehicles may be covered by separate bills of sale filed with the state department of motor vehicles.

For a major company, identifying each asset to be transferred and preparing the appropriate form is a tremendous task. Because of the complexity of documenting an asset purchase and the preference for them, in the remainder of this chapter I will focus on asset transactions. Most of the comments, however, are equally applicable to stock purchases and mergers.

My comments will follow the form of the Asset Purchase Agreement, an example of which can be found at http://www.RobertLBrown.info and in this chapter is called Sample Purchase Agreement. It is keyed to the acquisition of a hi-tech business (Internet and e-commerce), thus making it more relevant to present acquisition trends. The key issues are summarized in Table 7.4. The section numbers refer to those in Sample Purchase Agreement.

Deal Provisions

The first part of the agreement will contain the main points of the deal. In Sample Purchase Agreement, they appear as first paragraph, recitals, Section 2, as well as the definitions in Section 1. The most important issues are parties, transaction, price and payment method.

Parties and Transaction

The transaction must be described in detail. The parties are covered in the first paragraph. The next question is what is being acquired—stock or assets? If the

Table 7.4 Major Provisions of Asset Purchase Agreement

Section	Description
1st par.	Names of parties
Sec. 1	Key definitions
Sec. 2	Description of proposed transaction—assets being acquired
Sec. 3	Closing
Sec. 4	Representations and warranties of seller
Sec. 5	Representations and warranties of buyer
Sec. 6	Covenants of seller prior to closing
Sec. 7	Covenants of buyer prior to closing
Sec. 8	Covenants of parties at closing and postclosing
Sec. 9	Conditions that must be satisfied before buyer must close
Sec. 10	Conditions that must be satisfied before seller must close
Sec. 11	Termination of agreement
Sec. 12	Actions at closing
Sec. 13	Indemnification
Sec. 14	General terms and conditions
Exhibits	Various

latter, will any liabilities be acquired? In Sample Purchase Agreement, these issues are covered in Section 2.

Price and Payment

The price can be fixed or depend on future events. Fixed prices can be measured in cash, stock or other asset. For instance, the price may be one million dollars, one million shares of buyer's common stock, or one parcel of land. In Section 2.7 of Sample Purchase Agreement, the price is paid in common stock of buyer.

In some cases, the price can be a combination of fixed and dependent. Fixed assets may be transferred at a fixed price and current assets at the price current at closing. In such cases, a mechanism should be established to allow an adjustment in the price for changes in current asset values.

There are two types of changes that can be made to price. First, the price may be adjusted for business changes between signing and closing. These are usually adjustments based on a multiple of earnings or changes to working capital, book value or price of asset being used as consideration.

Problems often arise if the calculation of earnings, working capital or book value is made on a closing day that does not coincide with the end of a financial period for seller. An example is a closing in the middle of a month rather than at the end of a fiscal month. In this case, interim adjustments must be made with difficult decisions based on interim allocations and accruals. For instance, should year-end bonuses or other once-a-year expenses be accrued or charged as an expense when expended?

These calculation difficulties arise whether income statements, such as adjustments for earnings, or balance sheets, such as adjustments for book value, are used. Adjustments might require shifting income, expense or asset. For instance, if seller reports an annual charge, such as property tax, when the bill is received rather than for the period covered, a large increase in the current period's bill may not be reflected in the interim income statement. The same problem can exist if an asset has been purchased but not yet delivered and thus not included on seller's balance sheet.

Second, the price may be adjusted for performance. The performance could be between signing and closing or even after closing. This second type of price change is called an **earn-out** and ties the price to how well the assets or acquired company does in the future. The better the performance, the higher the price paid. In some cases, the price can be a combination of fixed and earn-out. A certain amount is paid at closing with seller being entitled to an additional amount or bonus depending on future performance.

Earn-outs raise two issues. First, seller should establish in detail what buyer can and cannot do with the assets acquired. Buyer, on the other hand, will want great autonomy in its handling of the acquired asset, such as being able to act in its best judgment without any fiduciary duty to seller. Second, instruments reflecting an earn-out obligation are not a security that must be registered under the Securities Act of 1933—as long as the deferred payment rights are granted to seller "not as an investment, but as an integral part of the consideration for the sale."[15]

If the purchase price is not fixed but adjusted at closing or some date after closing, a mechanism for handling adjustment disputes should be established. A common approach is to have seller's accountants prepare the calculations, buyer's accountants review them, and a mutually agreed upon third set of accountants resolve any differences between the first two.

Payment is the fourth key part of the deal. Will the price be paid at closing or in installments? If in installments, is there interest? Will tax authorities impute an interest factor? How will payment occur—presumably by wire transfer rather than bank cashier's check, but it is best to be clear on the point.

If payment is delayed, as with an earn-out, seller will have to conduct its own due diligence on buyer's ability to make future payments. It will also want to strengthen buyer's representations regarding its financial condition and any events likely to affect its ability to pay in the future.

Seller should also address the question of what happens if buyer is unable to make a future payment. Unwinding a merged asset is usually quite difficult, and as a result, few mergers are unwound.[16] Seller might want to insist on some security, such as in the assets transferred or a pledge of the stock that buyer is acquiring. Another approach is a letter of credit or guarantee from buyer's stockholders, affiliates or banks.

Representations and Warranties

Each party to the transaction must make certain representations about its business and the transaction. They serve three purposes:

- Establish base line for what the parties believe and are relying on
- Enable either party not to close if any representation (rep) or warranty is not true at closing
- Enable either party to recover under the indemnity provision for a breach

The most important reps and warranties are contained in Sections 4 and 5 of Sample Purchase Agreement. They cover due incorporation, qualification to do business, approval of the transaction by necessary parties, receipt of regulatory approvals and third party consents, compliance with generally accepted accounting principles, accuracy of financial statements, and the absence of material adverse change in its business.

The financial statements receive great attention in the representations. There are some issues that are likely to be addressed:

- Accuracy of financial statements as a whole
- Accuracy of information on particular assets
- Collectibility of accounts receivable. If this provision exists, an allowance for bad debts should be included.
- Value and obsolescence of inventory
- Usability and value of assets, including prepaid items
- Lack of undisclosed liabilities
- Product warranty liability and customer claims: the parties should discuss how to handle postclosing claims. Seller will want to resist such claims and argue they are expenses of the business acquired. Seller will also argue that buyer has no incentive to resist such claims if it can treat them as adjustments to the purchase price or reduce its earn-out payment.
- Tax liabilities, including those arising on the transaction. The parties should establish a mechanism on how to handle postclosing tax claims. There is likely to be different perspectives as with claims. Seller will want to resist all claims, while buyer will be more inclined to concede and charge back the amount to seller.
- Compliance with laws: this provision is usually a blanket statement that seller is in compliance with all laws, regardless of how unlikely the statement is. My favorite example is an executive who received a parking ticket while at a closing, and arguable caused the company to be in breach of the provision. A limitation to material violations of material laws should logically be included, but is difficult to obtain.
- Description of pending, threatened and unasserted claims.

It is important to describe carefully what representations each party is liable for. Oral statements by a lower level employee should probably not constitute a representation. For this reason, most agreements specify what representations a party is liable for. This will usually be written statements. Often it will only be those by designated individuals or contained in specific documents provided in due diligence. Representations in other agreements, however, are often included and not allowed to be superseded by the main agreement.

Another question that should be addressed is whether the representation is based on actual condition or knowledge? Is the representation an absolute statement that must be true, or can it be based on the maker's knowledge? If knowledge-based, whose knowledge is relevant? As with statements, knowledge of lower-level employees should not be the trigger. It is more common to designate the individuals or class of officers whose knowledge is important.

What happens if one party, buyer for instance, knows a representation is false at time of signing? Can it later sue on grounds of misrepresentation? This is called **sandbagging** and is permitted unless the agreement provides otherwise. It is wise, therefore, to include an **antisandbagging** provision that no liability applies to a statement that buyer knew or had reason to know was false at time of signing.

Seller

In an asset sale, the selling company makes seller's representations. In a stock sale, they are made by the individual shareholders selling their shares. In Sample Purchase Agreement they appear in Section 4.

As due diligence progresses, the types of representations by seller will become more fleshed out and specific. When buyer identifies an issue that it feels uncomfortable about, it will try to insert a representation from seller about it. In Sample Purchase Agreement, Sections 4.9 and 4.12 reflect issues that arose during due diligence. For this reason, it is important that the team conducting the due diligence be the same as, or works closely with, those drafting the main agreement.

On the other hand, if the purchase price represents a significant discount, seller may be able to insist on minimal representations.

Since seller is taking buyer's stock as payment in Sample Purchase Agreement, securities representations appear in Section 4.15. They state that seller is acquiring the payment securities for its own account. These representations mean buyer is less likely to have to register its common stock because of such payment and is more likely to be covered by one of the exemptions described in Chapter 3.

Buyer

In Sample Purchase Agreement, buyer's representations appear in Section 5. Since buyer was paying the purchase price by issuing its common stock, Section 5.2 of Sample Purchase Agreement was added to make certain the stock was valid and to confirm the percentage of ownership that it represents.

Future

Representations are a snapshot picture of the present. Seller or buyer describes what the condition is at present. This raises two problems. First, if closing occurs after the agreement is signed, new representations should be made as of the closing date. This is called a **bring-down certificate**.

Covenants

Second, one party might want to rely on the other's actions in the future. In other words, it might want to change the snapshot picture into a motion picture. This is achieved by covenants, which can regulate the other party's actions between signing and closing or even after closing. Covenants control actions during the entire period, whereas representations only describe conditions at fixed times— such as signing or closing.

There are usually two types of covenants. First is "conduct of business," which regulates how the parties will operate their business. They are usually limited to the interim period between signing and closing and require seller to conduct its business in the ordinary course. Seller cannot, for instance, sell off assets other than as it normally does. In Sample Purchase Agreement, these appear as Section 6—especially Section 6.2 for seller—and Section 7 for buyer.

Covenants can also apply during the postclosing period. In Sample Purchase Agreement, they appear as Section 8. On seller's side, such covenants can limit for a fixed period seller's ability to reenter the business being sold, compete with buyer, solicit buyer's employees, or contact buyer's customers. This is found in Section 8.8 of Sample Purchase Agreement. On buyer's side, they can be important, for instance, when an earn-out payment provision applies. Buyer could be obligated to conduct the acquired business diligently in order to achieve the earn-out levels. In Sample Purchase Agreement, since buyer is paying the purchase price in its common stock, Section 8.6 was added to limit its ability to dilute the value of that stock by issuing additional shares.

The second type of covenant is to "facilitate closing" in which the parties may be obligated to take certain actions to make certain the closing occurs. They can include filing government reports, seeking third parties consents, and obtaining director and shareholder approvals. In Section 6.1 of Sample Purchase Agreement, seller must give buyer access to information it needs for due diligence, and in Sections 6.5 and 7.1 both parties must use their best efforts to close. The agreement could also include limitations on seller's ability to market the assets or stock to other potential buyers and on how it can respond to such inquiries between signing and closing (Section 6.4 of Sample Purchase Agreement).

Conditions

Conditions set the ground rules for when the parties must close the transaction. Extensive lists are prepared for both parties on what must happen before they are obligated to complete the deal. In Sample Purchase Agreement, they appear as Section 9 for buyer's obligation to close and as Section 10 for seller's obligation. The most important conditions are:

- Accuracy of representations
- Obtaining tax ruling
- Expiration of any premerger notice period
- Compliance with securities law requirements
- Approval by boards of directors and shareholders
- Execution of related agreements, such as employment agreements and agreements not to compete
- Absence of any pending, threatened or unasserted claim

A deadline for the closing is usually established and is subject to extension by mutual agreement. In Sample Purchase Agreement, the issue is covered by closing in Section 3 and termination provisions in Section 11.

In some agreements, a separate description of what actions must be taken at the closing is also included. It lists what each party must bring and deliver at the closing and can be a handy checklist. Sample Purchase Agreement contains such a provision. Section 12.1 lists what seller must provide with Section 12.2 listing what buyer must deliver.

Indemnification

Indemnification is important in two cases:

- If the deal does not close because of one party's actions, such as failure to obtain necessary consent or refusal to close
- If the deal closes, but one party does not get what it bargained for because of the other's actions, such as misrepresentation or breach of covenant

In either case, the damaged party will want reimbursement for its out-of-pocket expenses and losses. In the first case, break-up fees are an example. Damages are an example of the second case.

Seller will usually want to limit its liability in three ways—notice, time and amount. Seller should require notice of claims and the right to handle third-party claims rather than allowing buyer to settle them. It should also request a deadline by which indemnity claims must be made and possibly a separate deadline by which the basis of the claims must arise. Seller should also exclude claims that only shift liabilities during postclosing periods and request a maximum liability or cap. The cap could be tied to the purchase price—for instance, no more than 50 percent or 100 percent of the purchase price. Seller might also want minimum levels and aggregation, such as no liability until claims reach $100,000 with buyer aggregating claims until they reach that amount.

In Sample Purchase Agreement, the indemnification provision appears in Section 13. Section 13.1 describes seller's indemnity and Section 13.5 covers buyer's indemnity.

Miscellaneous

These provisions are usually called the boilerplate, since the concepts reappear repeatedly in agreements. Most business people begin to skim the agreement when they get to this point. Nevertheless, some of these provisions are dependent on the transaction. It is important to recognize them, review their terms and tailor them to the circumstances.

Choice of Law

When buyer and seller are in the same state, the laws of that state will usually be selected as governing law. When they are from different states, the choice is a bit more difficult. If one party is dominant, its local law will most likely be chosen. If the two are of equivalent negotiating position, a neutral state such as Delaware may be chosen.

As Sgt. Phil Esterhaus, the desk sergeant played by Michael Conrad in the 1981–1987 NBC television show *Hill Street Blues*, used to say, "Let's be careful out there."[17] Be selective when agreeing to a particular state's governing law. Check to be certain that the actions you are undertaking or the way you are conducting business does not violate its laws. Also look to see what you may be liable for in case of a breach. Does local law allow consequential damages? What about punitive damages?

Dispute Settlement and Consent to Jurisdiction

A related issue is how and where disputes will be handled.

Regarding how disputes will be handled, it can be subject to mediation, arbitration, litigation or a combination. A recent preference is to mandate nonbinding mediation, which becomes arbitration if unsuccessful. Many parties have not been completely satisfied with their institutional arbitration experiences, particularly what they perceive as the tendency of arbitrators to split the parties' differences. As a result, in some agreements, parties appoint their own arbitrators.

As to where disputes will be handled, it does not have to be the same location as the place of the governing law. The parties could have Delaware as governing law but agree to have the dispute handled in another jurisdiction. Whatever the choice, if the parties are relying on arbitration, they should be certain that there are adequate and trained arbitrators in the location.

Even in the twenty-first century, bias for local companies can be strong. This is something to consider when agreeing upon a dispute-resolution place.

Regardless of the location chosen, each party should make sure that it has jurisdiction over the other party. This is best accomplished by having both parties specifically agree that they will submit any dispute to a specific arbitration tribunal or court and that they will be subject to its jurisdiction. Particularly when the dispute is handled by arbitrators, take it one step further and have them agree on which courts can enforce any decision.

Fees

Agreements usually include two provisions on fees. First, each party agrees to pay its own expenses and fees and possibly share premerger filing fees.

Second, there will be a representation by each party as to whether it used any brokers including investment bankers, and if so who was used. In Sample Purchase Agreement, these appear as Sections 4.13 and 5.6. If any brokers were used, the agreement then provides who pays their fees. In case of a breach of the representation, the party breaching will be liable for any other broker fees.

Exhibits and Schedules

Many issues requiring a great deal of space, as well as lists, will be turned into separate exhibits and schedules. One advantage is that materials from other sources can be attached without inputting them into the main agreement. Additionally, revisions in those external-source documents can be made easily by substituting pages, even until closing, without having to go back and change the main agreement.

Approval—Directors, Stockholders, Government and Third Parties

As noted in Chapter 2, many approvals will be required before the transaction can be finalized. The four main categories are boards of directors, stockholders, government and third parties.

Boards of Directors

Whether board approval is required, as noted in Chapter 2, depends on the type of transaction.

- Stock purchases: seller's board must approve if the transaction is material to it. Buyer's board must approve if it is a party to the acquisition.
- Asset purchases: seller's board must usually approve sale of substantially all of its assets and sales not in the ordinary course of business. Buyer's board must approve if the acquisition is material to it.
- Mergers: seller's and buyer's boards must approve. In forward and reverse subsidiary mergers, board approval of the parent will also be required if it is a party to the transaction or issues securities.
- Share exchanges: seller's and buyer's boards must approve.

The standards that board members must adhere to when voting to approve or reject is covered in Chapter 2. Examples are:

- **Duty of care:**[18] directors have a duty to inform themselves of all material information reasonably available to them prior to making a business decision. Having informed themselves, they must act with requisite care. In some states, this is close to the ordinary prudent person.
- **Duty of loyalty:**[19] directors have an affirmative duty to protect the interests of the company and an obligation to refrain from conduct that would injure the company or deprive it of a profit or advantage. This usually means directors must be independent and disinterested. Therefore, only outside directors should vote on acquisitions.
- **Business judgment rule:**[20] directors are presumed to have acted on an informed basis, in good faith and in the honest belief the action was taken in the best interest of the company. This is the reverse of the duty of care and places the burden of proof on the plaintiff.
- **Enhanced business judgment rule:**[21] a variation of the previous rule, this one places the burden of proof on the board in hostile tender offers.
- **Fair auction test:**[22] if seller decides to conduct an auction sale of its assets, directors cannot favor one bidder. The auction must be conducted fairly and is subject to the business judgment rule.
- **Intrinsic fairness test:**[23] directors are not required to conduct an auction, but if they do it must be fair.

An example of a resolution by a seller's board of directors approving a sale or merger can be found as Sample Board Resolution at http://www.Robert LBrown.info. It contains extensive recitations on the actions taken by the board in an attempt to confirm that the directors have met their legal obligations.

Stockholders

As noted in Chapter 2, the need for a stockholder approval depends on the type of transaction.

For stock purchases, no approval by seller's stockholders is required since buyer is purchasing directly from seller's stockholders, and they indicate their approval by selling their shares. However, some states have adopted **control share acquisition statutes**[24] that prohibit buyers from voting acquired shares over a certain percentage unless the acquisition has been approved by a majority of the disinterested stockholders.

Asset purchases require approval of seller's stockholders if substantially all assets are sold. Such approval is generally not required for less than substantially all assets.

The majority of buyers' and sellers' shareholders must approve in the case of mergers. In some states, two-thirds approval is required. As noted in Chapter 2, exceptions might apply to companies with supermajority requirements.

In share exchanges, approval of seller's stockholders is generally required.

Many stock exchanges have rules that might modify the above requirements. The NYSE and NASDAQ, for instance, adopted rules requiring approval of stock option plans except those issued in connection with a merger or acquisition.[25]

An example of a shareholder's consent signed by one or more shareholders holding a majority of seller's shares can be found at http://www.Robert LBrown.info. Following its execution, notice is given to other shareholders with the signed mailing receipt confirming such notice.

Government

As discussed in Chapter 3, governmental approval of stock and asset purchases and mergers is often required. The most important government approvals are for regulated industries, antitrust and securities.

Regulated Industries
If seller or buyer is in a regulated industry, some governmental approvals may be necessary, as discussed in Chapter 3. Examples are companies involved with alcohol, aviation, banking, communications, insurance, transportation and public utilities.

Antitrust
Under the Hart-Scott-Rodino Antitrust Improvements Act of 1976 (HSR), mergers and acquisitions in excess of a certain size must be reported to the Department of Justice (DOJ) and Federal Trade Commission (FTC). More information on this act appears in Chapter 3. After the filing, buyer and seller must wait for thirty days—fifteen days in a stock purchase by a cash tender offer.[26] The waiting period can be extended by either agency if it requests additional information in a Second Request.[27]

Securities

As discussed in Chapter 3, reports might have to be filed with the Securities and Exchange Commission (SEC) or with state securities agencies. No closing can occur until the filings are made and the applicable waiting period is over.

The most common securities filings are:

- Register securities under the Securities Act of 1933
- Qualify an indenture under the Trust Indenture Act of 1939
- File a proxy or consent statement in connection with obtaining shareholder approval (**proxy solicitations** in a **tender offer**) under the Securities Exchange Act of 1934
- Shareholder approval of merger under state law.

In some states, the timing is reversed with the agreement signed first and then submitted to shareholders for their approval. It can take several weeks to compile the necessary information and another thirty to sixty days to complete SEC review process. A typical example of the time involved is found in Table 7.5.

As indicated in the table, the total time involved can easily be four months.

Third Party

The approval of many other persons may be required in case of change of control, mergers and sales of substantial assets. Examples are:

- Unions: collective bargaining agreements might require approval of the union.

Table 7.5 Time Schedule for Securities Offering

Day	Activity
1	All Hands Meeting to Organize Offering
25	Review Officers and Directors Questionnaires
40	Distribute First Draft of Registration Statement
45	All Hands Meeting to Revise Registration Statement
50	Distribute Revised Draft of Registration Statement
55	All Hands Meeting to Revise Registration Statement for SEC Filing
60	File Registration Statement with SEC
61	Mail Red Herrings to Proposed Underwriters
65	Road Show Begins
100	Receive SEC Comment Letter
114	All Hands Meeting to Revise Registration Statement to Reflect SEC Comments
115	Effective Date
120	Closing

- ESOP Trustees: if buyer insists on purchasing a minimum percent of seller's shares, and some of its shares are held under an employee stock ownership plan, then the approval of the trustees of the plan may be required to meet the minimum.
- Creditors: most bank loans require approval of the lender or lessor.
- Lessors: most lessors require their consent to assignment of their leases. In some cases, they will require the assignee to execute a new lease. If so, the original lessee should require that it be released. An example of such a release can be found at http://www.RobertLBrown.info.

Investment Banker Fees

Two basic payments will be made at the closing. Buyer will pay the agreed upon purchase price. Seller, on the other hand, will usually pay broker fees to investment bankers. The usual broker fee will be set in the agreement between seller and its investment banker. It is usually a range of 5 percent to 1 percent based on the value of the transaction. The full 5 percent will be paid on the first million, 4 percent on the second, and so on, with 1 percent on $5 million and over. A modified version starts at 6 percent and works its way down to 1 percent.

At times more than one investment banker may be involved. Seller and buyer might each have retained bankers. Seller might have sought an advisor to help it sell an asset or its business. Buyer might have retained an advisor to help it identify acquisition targets. In such cases, each party will be liable for its own banker with the fees negotiated in advance at the time the banker is retained.

Payments are usually made by wire transfer or bank cashier's check.

Closing

The closing depends on two issues—timing and documents produced.

Timing

In its simplest form, the closing is when the main agreement is signed, stock or assets are transferred, and the money is paid. This is usually called a **simultaneous closing**. There are many variations, however.

The parties might sign the main agreement, and while the stock or assets are transferred at closing, not all consideration is paid. Instead, some part of the purchase price is delayed. Such deferral could be a mandatory payment, such as a note covering a future, required payment. It could also be conditional, such as an earn-out dependent on the acquired business achieving certain sales levels.

In some cases, the parties might sign the main agreement but postpone closing until certain events occur. Once those events occur, the stock or assets are
transferred, and the money is paid. This is usually called a **deferred closing**.

The most obvious examples of factors deferring closings are arranging financing, obtaining board and shareholder approval, and obtaining government
approvals. The larger the transaction, the more government approvals likely to
be required. In the previous section, we discussed regulated industry, antitrust
premerger notice, and securities compliance, which are some of the more important
ones. In addition, a closing might depend on obtaining a favorable tax ruling.

In a deferred closing, representations and warranties should be updated or
restated. A new certificate delivered at the deferred closing can accomplish this
by confirming the reps and warranties are still true.

Deliveries at Closing

In addition to the main agreement, many other agreements will be signed and
exchanged at closing.

Transfer Documents

As noted earlier, in an asset purchase, many documents will be needed to transfer title to the various assets:

- Deeds for real property, which are filed with the county clerk's office where
  the property is located
- Assignments of leases, which must be given to and, depending on the lease
  terms, approved by the appropriate lessor
- Assignments for patents and trademarks, which are filed with the U.S.
  Patent and Trademark Office
- Bills of sale for personal property, which are filed with the local county
  clerk's office
- Bills of sale, which are filed with the state department of motor vehicles

Payment

Possibly the most important payment is the purchase price. The payment can be
money, stock or other consideration. The closing will usually be confirmed and
documents released only when payment is received.

Payment will usually be by wire transfer to a bank account designated by seller
for large transactions. Lesser amounts may be by bank cashier's check.

In the case of stock, properly endorsed certificates will be delivered. If there
are many sellers, a guarantee of signatures may be required.

Certificates

Seller and buyer will also exchange a number of certificates. Examples are:

- Good standing and tax clearance certificates: issued by secretary of state and state taxing authorities certifying that the company is in good standing (meaning it continues to exist as a company and has paid its annual filing fee) and has filed its state tax return.
- Articles of incorporation and bylaw certificates: signed by corporate secretary attaching and certifying copies of current articles of incorporation and bylaws.
- Secretary certificates: signed by corporate secretary of each party certifying that the necessary board of directors (and, where appropriate, shareholder) approval has been obtained.
- Bring-down certificates: signed by officer confirming that the representations and warranties in the main agreement, which related to the date it was signed, are still true on the closing date.
- Update certificates: used in deferred closings, signed by officer that update disclosure schedules, representations and warranties to reflect changes between execution of main agreement and closing.

Legal Opinion
Each party's law firm will be asked to issue certain opinions:

- Its client is duly organized, validly existing and in good standing. This opinion means the party was properly formed, adopted its bylaws, appointed its officers, has not dissolved or ceased to exist, and has paid its taxes and annual state filing fees.
- Its client is qualified in all jurisdictions where the failure to be qualified would have a material adverse effect on its business. While getting good standing certificates is easy, the hard part is ensuring that the company has qualified in each state where its business requires.
- Its client has the requisite power to own its properties and conduct its business. Before giving this opinion, counsel will review the client's organizational documents to make certain the company is not limited in the type of business it can conduct.
- Its client has the requisite corporate power to enter into the closing agreements.
- Closing agreements have been duly authorized by all necessary board and shareholder approvals, and have been duly executed and delivered. In granting the opinion, counsel might rely on corporate secretary certificates.
- Closing agreements are valid, binding and enforceable in accordance with their terms, except as limited by equity and bankruptcy. This opinion means that the client has the legal capacity and power to enter into the agreements; the agreements have been duly authorized, executed and delivered; the agreements are binding and are not invalid under any specific statute or contrary to public policy; and remedies are available to the other party for breach.

- Property being transferred is as described. In some cases, title insurance rather than the opinion might cover this.

When stock is being issued as part of the transaction, counsel may also be asked to opine on:

- the amount of authorized and outstanding shares;
- new shares are duly authorized and validly issued;
- new shares were issued for proper and sufficient consideration and are fully paid and nonassessable.

Typical opinions contain the following provisions:

- Date
- Person to whom opinion is issued, with an attempted disclaimer that only that specific person is allowed to rely on the opinion
- Description of transaction
- Relationship of attorney to transaction
- Client's scope of engagement of counsel
- Statutory and contractual requirements of the opinion
- Key definitions
- Scope of counsel's review including records inspected, persons interviewed, and certificates relied on
- Assumptions such as conformity of copies to originals, facts stated in representations and certificates, legal capacity to execute documents, and due execution of documents if not observed by counsel
- Qualifications such as materiality, limitation to particular state laws plus federal law, and enforceability exceptions for bankruptcy, equity, usury, choice of law, penalties and public policy.

Standard forms of opinions have begun to evolve over the past decade, beginning with the 1989 Silverado conference sponsored by the American Bar Association's Business Law Section.[28] Nevertheless, opinions are still influenced by the parties' bargaining positions, including whether opinions are required at all, and their needs, such as requirements of law that they be provided and address certain issues.

Attorneys can be liable if their opinions are not accurate.[29] In specialized areas such as tax, they will be held to a higher standard of prudent expert. As a result, their opinions only address legal issues and documents reviewed by them. Frequently, the issues and documents are listed in the opinion. For these reasons, the opinions might incorporate by reference opinions issued by other law firms on local law issues or factual backup statements signed by officers of the client.

Accountant Opinion

In two cases seller's accountants may be asked to provide an opinion in addition to any auditor's report. First, if seller does not have audited financial statements, its accountants may be asked to give a comfort letter confirming seller's financial statements appear to be accurate. Second, if the transaction requires a proxy statement with the SEC or involves a registration statement under the Securities Act of 1933, a comfort letter may be requested to show due diligence.

Investment Banker Opinion

Many boards require that investment bankers involved in a transaction issue **fairness opinions**. The opinions state that the price being received is fair to seller and are designed to reduce the potential liability of seller's board members for failure to meet their obligations.

Other Documents

At the closing, a number of related documents may be executed that do not involve the transfer of assets or stock. Examples are covenants not to compete, releases, employment agreements, consulting agreements and leases.

Press Release

Although not exchanged between buyer and seller, a press release agreed upon by the parties and their attorneys who review it for securities law compliance will usually be released summarizing the transaction.

8

Divestiture

In this chapter, I describe the last M.A.D. element–divestiture. At its simplest level, divestiture refers to the reverse of what we have discussed. The acquirer of the target sells off what it acquired, meaning that the buyer becomes the seller.

In such a simple scenario, what I described in the previous chapters could be reversed and applied. Instead, I will cover divestitures that differ significantly from the usual sale of an acquired business. There are two such basic transactions:

- Workout: this refers to debt restructuring negotiations with lenders outside of bankruptcy. They might include principal reduction, repayment postponement, and interest rate reduction. In exchange, the borrower might offer cash or new securities.
- Reorganization: this refers to the same negotiations taking place in proceedings under Chapter 11 of the Bankruptcy Code. That chapter allows companies to continue to operate by renegotiating with their lenders and security holders. I only briefly cover Chapter 7 liquidations in this chapter, since they involve the closing down of a business rather than its sale.

But, first, let's consider why workouts and reorganizations have become important.

Trends

To finance their acquisitions during the 1980s and 1990s, many buyers loaded up on debt. This allowed them to avoid diluting capital and to maintain high equity returns. It also meant they ended up with a lot of debt.

In light of this trend, financial analysts lowered the debt coverage they were willing to accept. At the beginning of the 1980s, companies were expected to have debt coverage of 2:1, meaning projected earnings had to be twice interest obligations. By the mid-1980s, the ratio dropped to 1:1. At the end of the 1980s, the ratio was eliminated. Debt instruments were not required to pay interest currently or in cash. For many deals in the 1990s, acquirers were allowed to defer paying interest for several years by issuing:

*   original issue discount;
*   zero coupon;
*   deferred coupon;
*   pay-in-kind (PIK) security, which was discussed in Chapter 3.

Table 8.1 highlights this increasing use of debt, particularly by large companies, beginning in the 1980s and reflecting the greater use of debt for mergers and acquisitions. In the chart, we see that the debt burden at large companies rose nearly 6.5 times, while it rose 5.5 times in small companies.

Buyers, however, were forced to rely on the willingness of lenders to keep deferring principal and interest. When junk bonds no longer became available, and interest rates rose in the late 1980s, many borrowers were forced to renegotiate with their lenders or go into bankruptcy.

In Table 8.2, we can see the effect of these relaxed lending practices and increasing interest rates on bankruptcy filings. As lending became easier so did bankruptcy. The chart also shows the variations by regions with the most dramatic changes in Atlantic coast states where many of the largest mergers and acquisitions took place.

In Table 8.3 we see that public companies entering bankruptcy tended to be in the energy, telecommunications and technology sectors, which was where mergers and acquisitions were concentrated during the 1980s and 1990s.

Workout

In this section I describe the stages of a workout negotiation, the methods usually agreed upon, and the application of the securities laws.

Table 8.1 Ratio of Debt to Net Worth in Percent[1]

Year	Nonfarm Nonfinancial Corporate Business (Large Companies)	Nonfarm Noncorporate Business (Small Companies)
1980	27	27
1983	48	50
1986	60	75
1989	90	100
1992	100	100
1995	95	95
1998	125	100
2001	175	150

Table 8.2 Percent Change in Bankruptcy Filings by Time Period and Geographical Region[2]

Census Division & States	1987–1992	1992–1994	1994–1998
New England	382.9%	-16.5%	70.4%
CT, MA, ME, NH, RI, VT			
Mid-Atlantic	162.2%	-10.8%	87.6%
NJ, NY, PA			
East North Central	50.3%	-17.6%	79.2%
IL, IN, MI, OH			
West North Central	52.8%	-17.2%	68.8%
IA, KS, MN, MO, ND, NE, SD			
South Atlantic	115.5%	-13.8%	83.2%
DC, DE, FL, GA, MD, NC, SC, VA, WV			
East South Central	56.9%	-13.7%	54.8%
AL, KY, MS, TN			
West South Central	19.7%	-15.4%	80.8%
AR, LA, OK, TX			
Mountain	33.6%	-19.5%	80.3%
AZ, CO, ID, MT, NM, NV, UT, WY			
Pacific	59.4%	-10.9%	54.8%
AK, CA, HI, OR, WA	69.0%	-14.3%	73.2%
National Average			

Table 8.3 Public Company Bankruptcy Filings in 2001[3]

Sector	Percent
Energy related	33
Telecommunications and technology related	12
Insurance related	6
Finance related	5
Automotive	4
All other	40

Stages

A frequent solution for debtors experiencing financial difficulty is to bring in new investors. While they offer new money, the new investors will want control in exchange. They might want a senior equity position that gives them priority over distributions and in liquidation. They will certainly want priority over unsecured debt. Outside of a bankruptcy court, they are unlikely to get priority over secured creditors. Many of them might also seek indemnification or guarantees from principal shareholders.

The next alternative is usually for a company to look for assets and either borrow against them if they are not already pledged or sell them if the company does not need them. The cash raised can be used to pay down debt or, more likely, fund operations.

After these choices have been explored, the company must next meet with debtors and investors to work out its debt and equity situation more aggressively. The company's central argument is that its assets are worth more as an operating business than if liquidated.

Initially, lenders will prefer to grant interim relief—just enough to see if the borrower's condition improves. This usually means deferrals and extensions rather than debt reductions. Unsecured lenders, particularly junk bond lenders, are more at risk and will be more willing to cooperate in this way. Secured lenders will be reluctant to cooperate at this point and will grant minimal relief while threatening foreclosure.

In response, the company's ultimate bargaining chip is the threat of filing a bankruptcy petition. This threat applies to unsecured creditors who might lose everything in a liquidation as well as to secured creditors who might have their secured asset tied up in bankruptcy court for years and pay legal fees during the entire period.

The give and take between the positions usually depends on three points:

- Terms of loan agreements, including rate, maturity, optional and mandatory redemption, sinking fund requirements, conversion rights, prepayment rights and penalties, and negative and positive covenants
- Statutory limitations, such as the Trust Indenture Act[4] that requires unanimous consent of holders of public debt indentures before principal, interest and maturity can be changed
- Lenders' perception of borrower's future prospects. The better the outlook, the more likely creditors and investors are to accept a voluntary workout.

Consider the typical scenario for these types of negotiations. Debtor has debt that is traded at a significant discount from its face value if at all. Let's say $.10 on the dollar. Debtor offers to buy back its debt at a premium over the prevailing market rate, let's say $.40 on the dollar if 75 percent of outstanding principal amount is tendered or turned in or if new debt issued in replacement will have simplified covenants.

Debt holders have a tremendous incentive to take the $.40 over the market rate of $.10. Granted it is less than the face value, but in economic terms the face value is a sunk cost and is no longer relevant.

Methods

Once agreed upon, the borrower will use one or both of two approaches to work out its debt:

- Tender offer of cash, securities or new debt in exchange for existing debt. The exchange will be at a discount that reduces the outstanding debt, extends average maturity and lowers interest payments. Debt holders have the option of accepting the tender offer, but it is usually negotiated with the largest holders who have committed to accept the offer.
- Consent of debt holders to amend the terms of their debt. Since unanimous consent is required under the Trust Indenture Act[5] to amend the principal terms, a consent solicitation is required. First, consent is obtained to remove covenants preventing debtor from changing the key terms. Usually a majority or supermajority of holders must give their consent to such a change. Second, with the power to change the key terms, debtor does so. Since this approach is usually used in conjunction with a tender offer and the holders granting consent usually tender their debt, this strategy is called **exit consent**.

Securities Rules

For the most part, debt workouts are not subject to the securities laws. There are five instances, however, when the securities laws might apply.

The first instance is Section 14(e) of the Securities Exchange Act of 1934[6] and rules issued under it regulate tender offers, including tender offers in a debt restructuring. The rules require notice and a waiting period for tender offers. The Securities and Exchange Commission (SEC), however, has been willing to waive the twenty-day time limits under Rule 14e-1 if the offer:

- is available to all holders;
- gives holders a reasonable time to tender;
- includes details about the terms;
- is not in response to another tender offer.

Second, solicitations asking debt holders to waive covenants under their trust indentures may be subject to Section 14(a) of the Securities Exchange Act[7]. That section regulates solicitation of proxies and written consents for any security registered under Section 12 of the Act, whether security, debt or equity. If the debt security is not registered, the proxy rules do not apply.

Third, the general antifraud provisions of Section 10(b) and 14(e) of the Securities Exchange Act[8] apply. These sections necessitate disclosure of material information in any solicitation.

Fourth, if the debtor has registered securities and is making annual and quarterly reports to the SEC, it must consider what to disclose in each report. Most companies are reluctant to make any disclosures until the last moment necessary. At times they hope conditions improve. At other times, they simply do not want to scare suppliers, customers, investors and lenders by issuing bad news until needed. Since interim reports between annual or quarterly reports using Form 8-K[9] are required only for bankruptcy or receivership, most managers rely on this provision to wait until the next scheduled report.

Fifth, if the self-tender offer is an exchange offer, any new instrument must be registered under the Securities Act of 1933. Exemptions under Section 3(a)(9), however, exist for:

- security being offered and tendered by the same issuer;
- offerings only to existing security holders;
- holders only being asked to tender existing securities;
- cases when no compensation being paid to those soliciting the tender offer.[10]

Reorganization

Reorganizations under the Bankruptcy Code[11] are intended to answer three questions:

1. Can the company be revived?
2. What will it take to accomplish the revival?
3. Will investors and lenders accept what it takes?

Ironically, while the questions are financial, they are resolved in a legal context and attempt to achieve a business success.

If a "yes" cannot be given to all three questions, then the business will be liquidated under Chapter 7 of the Bankruptcy Code.[12] Liquidation is usually the least favored solution, since the value of goodwill, tax losses, executory contracts, and employees will be lost. As a result, creditors receive less. If it is necessary to liquidate under Chapter 7, it should be done slowly and orderly to achieve the greatest return. This is usually not possible.

Stages

Reorganizations usually begin with a debtor filing a Chapter 11 petition. The petition creates an automatic stay, as discussed below, while the company continues to do business in the "ordinary course." The presumption is that existing management, called debtor in possession or DIP, should remain in place. If creditors object to the way the DIP is running the business, the court will appoint an examiner to investigate and monitor the debtor's business. In extreme cases, the court can replace the DIP with a trustee in bankruptcy (TIB).[13]

With the breathing space given by the automatic stay, the DIP or TIB is able to sell losing divisions, reduce staff, cut expenses and take other steps to make debtor profitable. Once it has better control of the situation, the DIP or TIB begins to negotiate a restructuring plan with its major creditors. A creditors' committee representing the principal creditors is appointed to negotiate the plan with the DIP or TIB.[14]

The plan will describe how much the debtor proposes to pay each creditor class. This is usually expressed as a percentage of their claims over a fixed period of time. Along with a detailed explanation, the plan will be distributed to all creditors who have filed claims. Dissenting creditors must receive at least as much as they would have received if the company were liquidated under Chapter 7 of the Bankruptcy Code.[15]

The plan must be approved by a simple majority of creditors by number and two-thirds by amount of debt of those voting. It must also be approved by two-thirds of the equity holders. If these conditions are met, the bankruptcy court will confirm the plan.[16]

Even if the required number of votes of a class—secured, unsecured or equity—approving the plan is not obtained, the court can confirm the plan. Before doing so, it must find that the nonconsenting class will not be "impaired" by the plan, or that the plan is "fair and equitable" to each of the secured, unsecured and equity classes. In reaching its determination, the bankruptcy court will apply the absolute priority rule under which:

- liens of secured creditors must be preserved;
- secured creditors must be paid present value of their claims;
- unsecured creditors and preferred stockholders must be paid in full, or parties junior to them must not be entitled to anything under the plan.[17]

An exception exists for **new capital**, which allows a creditor contributing new money to receive a distribution or retain an interest, even though senior classes are not paid in full. The new capital contribution must be reasonably equivalent in value to the interest retained or distribution received.[18]

Since common stockholders often get little value out of reorganization, the court must typically force the plan over their nonconsent. To do so, the court will usually find fairness and equity but no impairment, since the common stock has little value. This process is called **confirmation by cram-down**.

Once the court has confirmed the plan, the debtor is discharged from its prepetition debts except as shown in the plan.

Waiting in the wings of these negotiations with creditors is the threat of Chapter 7. The Chapter 11 proceeding can become liquidation under Chapter 7 in three cases:

- Debtor can convert
- Creditors can apply to the court to convert
- When creditors do not approve the plan of reorganization, the proceedings are converted[19]

These possibilities will be in the minds of all parties to reorganization negotiations.

Methods

To increase the chance of a successful reorganization, the DIP, TIB and bankruptcy court are given significant powers to increase the likelihood of a successful reorganization:

- Automatic stay restraining secured creditors, tax authorities, landlords and others from seizing property or canceling contracts[20]
- Interest on unsecured debt accruing during automatic stay accumulates but does not have to be paid during the stay. Debtor can use the unpaid but accumulated money to pay down debt or meet its other obligations.[21]
- Debtor allowed to obtain unsecured credit in ordinary course of business without court approval. Creditors, such as trade creditors or suppliers, are usually willing to provide such credit, since they will have priority in bankruptcy as administrative expenses, which rank above prepetition claims.[22]
- If unsecured credit is not available, on debtor's request and after notice and hearing, bankruptcy court might authorize borrowing with super priority even above administrative expenses.[23]
- In extraordinary circumstances, the bankruptcy court can allow the debtor to borrow money on a secured basis by granting a lien senior or equal to existing liens. In such case, existing holders must be given adequate protection.[24]
- Permit debtor to propose in the plan various recapitalization plans, such as extensions, postponements, compositions and exchange of debt for equity.[25]
- Unlike workouts that require approval of all creditors, debtor can force dissenting creditors to accept reorganization plans accepted by a majority of creditors.[26]

Securities Rules

In Chapter 11 proceedings, creditors and equity holders are often asked to exchange their claims and interests for new securities under the reorganization plan. For the most part, such securities are not subject to the securities laws.

There are several reasons for this non-application of the securities laws. First, the Bankruptcy Code provides that such securities do not have to be registered under the Securities Act of 1933.[27] Second, recipients of such securities have fewer restrictions imposed on them during the resale of the securities.[28] Third, the disclosure provisions of the Securities Act of 1933 do not apply to the preparation and distribution of the disclosure statement, which accompanies the plan.[29] Fourth, parties seeking approval of reorganization plans do not have to comply with the proxy solicitation regulations under the Securities Exchange Act of 1934.[30] Fifth, the determination of whether the disclosure statement contains adequate information is a question of fact to be made exclusively by the bankruptcy court and not the SEC.[31]

Disadvantages

Bankruptcy reorganization is not an easy road to travel. It is fraught with many risks:

- Management may be forced out and replaced by TIB.
- Expenses can eat into cash reserves, with the debtor having to pay several sets of lawyers, appraisers, financial advisors and accountants. Manville Corp. incurred legal fees of about $100 million in its bankruptcy.
- Operations are subject to supervision and scrutiny by court and creditors.
- Court approval is required of many actions.
- Managers have fiduciary duties, and must manage the company for the benefit of its creditors. This exposes them to liability and potential lawsuits by lenders and might require them to institute lawsuits against former shareholders and creditors.

Notes

Chapter 1

1. R. Charles Moyer, James R. McGuigan and William J. Kretlow, *Contemporary Financial Management* (New York: Thomson South-Western, 2006), 767.
2. "Tech Merger Meter 2006," *The Wall Street Journal Online*. http://www.wsj.com. May 12, 2007
3. "Banner Year for Private Equity," *The Wall Street Journal Online*.
4. Thomson Financial, quoted in ibid.
5. Ibid.
6. Harry S. Dent, Jr., *The Great Boom Ahead* (New York: Hyperion, 1993).
7. Dent, Jr. *The Roaring 2000s: Building the Wealth and Lifestyle You Desire in the Greatest Boom in History* (New York: Simon & Schuster, 1998).
8. Alan S. Gutterman, Robert Brown and James Stanislaw, *Professional Guide to Doing Business on the Internet* (San Diego: Harcourt Professional Publishing, 2000), 225–26.
9. "National Statistics Omnibus Survey," http://www.statistics.gov.uk/ STATBASE/ DatasetType.asp.
10. Paul Healy, "Does Corporate Performance Improve after Mergers?" *Journal of Financial Economics* 31 (1992): 135–76.
11. Healy, Krishna Palepu and Richard Ruback, "Which Takeovers Are Profitable? Strategic or Financial?" *Sloan Management Review* 38 (Summer 1997): 45–57.
12. David Birch, cited in Robert F. Bruner, "Does M&A Pay? A Survey of Evidence for the Decision-Maker" (Darden Graduate School of Business, University of Virginia, 2001).
13. Mitchell Madison and Kenneth Smith, cited in Bruner, "Does M&A Pay?"
14. Michael Bradley, Anand Desai, and E. Han Kim, "Synergistic Gains from Corporate Acquisitions and Their Division Between the Stockholders of Target and Acquiring Firms," *Journal of Financial Economics* 21 (May 1988): 3–40.
15. Malcolm Salter and Wolf Weinhold, *Diversification through Acquisition: Strategies for Maximizing Economic Value* (New York: Free Press, 1979).
16. McKinsey and Company, cited in Bruner, "Does M&A Pay?"
17. D. Ravescraft and F. M. Scherer, *Mergers, Sell-Offs, and Economic Efficiency* (Washington, DC: The Brookings Institute, 1987).
18. PA Consulting of London, cited in Bruner, "Does M&A Pay?"
19. Mark Sirower, *The Synergy Trap: How Companies Lose the Acquisition Game* (New York: Free Press, 1997).
20. Mercer Management Consulting and Business Week, cited in Bruner, "Does M&A Pay?"

21. David Mitchell, *Making Acquisitions Work: Learning from Companies' Successes and Failures* (London: Economist Intelligence Unit, 1996).

22. Mercer Management Consulting and Business Week, cited in Bruner, "Does M&A Pay?"

23. Tim Loughran and Anand Vijh, "Do Long-Term Shareholders Benefit From Corporate Acquisitions?" *Journal of Finance* 52 (December 1997): 1765–90.

Chapter 2

1. Model Business Corporation Act, American Bar Association, Section of Business Law, Committee on Corporate Laws, Model Business Corporation Act Annotated, Third Edition (Chicago: American Bar Foundation, 1983).

2. Revised Model Business Corporation Act, American Bar Association, Section of Business Law, Committee on Corporate Laws, Model Business Corporation Act Annotated, Third Edition (Chicago: American Bar Foundation, 2002).

3. 1 Corporations §1107(b), California Corporations Code.

4. 1 Corporations §1107(c), California Corporations Code.

5. 15 Fletcher, Cyclopedia of Corporations §7122 (rev. ed. 1999).

6. Arness, Sutin and Plotkin, Preventing Successor Liability for Defective Products: Safeguards for Acquiring Corporations, Wash. U.L.Q. 67 (1989): 353, 363.

7. *Ray v. Alad Corp.*, 560 P.2d 3, 7 (Cal. 1977).

8. *Marks v. Minnesota Mining & Mfg Co.*, 232 Cal. Rptr. 594, 598 (Cal. Ct. App. 1986).

9. *Bud Antle, Inc.* 758 F.2d 1456 (11th Cir. 1985).

10. *Dayton v. Peck, Stow & Wilcox Co.*, 739 F.2d 690, 693 (1984).

11. *DeLapp v. Xtraman, Inc.*, 417 N.W.2d 219, 221 (Iowa 1987).

12. *Ray v. Alad Corp.*, 560 P.2d 3, 9 (Cal. 1977).

13. Ibid.

14. Restatement (Third) of Torts: Product Liability, §10 (New York: American Law Institute, 1998).

15. Comprehensive Environmental Response, Compensation and Liability Act, 42 U.S.C. 9601, 94 Stat. 2767.

16. Fort, et. al., Avoiding Liability for Hazardous Waste: RCRA, CERCLA, and Related Corporate Law Issues, 57-2nd C.P.S. (BNA), §X, Real Estate Transfers.

17. *Weeler v. Snyder Buick, Inc.*, 794 F2d 1228 (CA7 1986).

18. National Labor Relations Board v. Burns International Security Services, Inc., 406 U.S. 272, 32 L Ed 2d 61, 92 S Ct 1571, distg John Wiley & Sons, Inc. v. Livingston, 376 U.S. 543, 550, 11 L Ed 2d 898, 84 S Ct 909.

19. *Carter v. CMTA-Molders & Allied Workers Health & Welfare Trust*, 563 F Supp 244 (ND Cal 1983) (applying California law).

20. *National Labor Relations Board v. Burns International Security Services, Inc.*, 406 U.S. 272, 32 L Ed 2d 61, 92 S Ct 1571, distg *John Wiley & Sons, Inc. v. Livingston*, 376 U.S. 543, 550, 11 L Ed 2d 898, 84 S Ct 909.

21. *United Paperworkers International Union v. Penntech Papers, Inc.*, 439 F Supp 610 (D Me), distg 417 U.S. 249, 41 L Ed 2d 46, 94 S Ct 2236.

22. 19 Del. Code Ann. §1109.

23. Cal. Lab. Code §227.3.

24. Worker Adjustment and Retraining Notification Act, 29 U.S.C. 2101, PL 100–379, 102 Stat. 890.

25. Worker Adjustment and Retraining Notification Act, 29 U.S.C. 2104, PL 100–379, 102 Stat. 890.

26. Ibid.

27. Employee Retirement Income Security Act of 1974, 29 U.S.C. 1001, et. seq., 29 CFR 2509.

28. Internal Revenue Code, Sections 401(a) or 403(a).

29. Employee Retirement Income Security Act of 1974, 29 U.S.C. 4068(d)(1).

30. Employee Retirement Income Security Act of 1974, 29 U.S.C. 4003(e)(1).

31. Employee Retirement Income Security Act of 1974, 29 U.S.C. 3037(A)(I).

32. Employee Retirement Income Security Act of 1974, 29 U.S.C. 4069.

33. E.g., Cal Unemp. Ins. Code §1731.

34. Metropolitan Life Insurance Company and Jefferson-Pilot Life Insurance company v. RJR Nabisco, Inc. and F. Ross Johnson, 716 F. Supp. 1504, 1989 U.S. Dist. LEXIS 6253.

35. Roberta Romano, "Comment: What Is the Value of Other Constituency Statutes to Shareholders?" *University of Toronto Law Journal.* 43 (Summer, 1993): 533–42

36. Richard A. Booth, "Capital Requirements in United States Corporation Law," University of Maryland Legal Studies Research Paper No. 2005064 (November 2005).

37. Model Business Corporation Act.

38. Uniform Fraudulent Conveyance Act, 7A U.L.A. 6 (1999).

39. Uniform Fraudulent Transfer Act, 7A U.L.A. 274 (1999).

40. Bankruptcy Code, 11 U.S.C. 548.

41. Uniform Fraudulent Transfer Act, 7A U.L.A. 301–2, 330 (1999).

42. Uniform Commercial Code, Article 6, 3B U.L.A. (1999).

43. T. Quinn, Uniform Commercial Code Commentary and Law Digest, §6–106 (2d ed. 1991).

44. 6 Del. Code Ann. §6–101.

45. E.g., Indiana Control Share Acquisitions Act, 23 Indiana Code 1023-1-42-1-et. seq.

46. *Pomierski v. W.R. Grace & Co.*, 282 F Supp 385.

47. E.g., Indiana Control Share Acquisitions Act, 23 Indiana Code 1023-1-42-1-et. seq.

48. E.g., Md. Gen. Corp. Law §§3–601 et. seq.

49. E.g., Connecticut General Statutes §361–701a.

50. New York Stock Exchange, Listed Company Manual, Section 312.

51. American Stock Exchange, Company Guide, Section 712.

52. NASD Rule 4460(i).

53. Revised Model Business Corporation Act.

54. E.g., 8 Del Code Ann. §262(b)(1)(i).

55. 8 Del. Code Ann. §262.

56. Model Business Corporation Act.

57. *Shell Petroleum, Inc. v. Smith,* 606 A2d 112 (Del 1992).

58. *Weinberger v. UOP, Inc.*, 457 A.2d 701 (Del. 1983); *Lewis v. Clark*, 911 F2d 1558 (CA11 1990).

59. *Insuranshares Corp. v. Northern Fiscal Corp.*, 35 F. Supp. 22 (E.D. Pa 1940).

60. *Perlman v. Feldman*, 219 F.2d 173 (2d Cir.), cert. denied 349 U.S. 952 (1955),

61. Howing Co. Nationwide Corp., 927 F.2d 263 (CA6 1991).

62. Ruder, "Duty of Loyalty—Law Professor's Status Report," 40 Bus. Law. 1383 (1985).

63. *Essex Universal Corp. v. Yates*, 305 F.2d 572 (2d Cir. 1962).

64. *Umstead v. Durham Hosiery Mills, Inc.*, 578 F Supp 342 (MD NC 1984).
65. Victor Brudney and Marvin A. Chirelstein, "Fair Shares in Corporate Mergers and Takeovers," Harvard L.R. 88 (December 1974): 297.
66. *Aronson v. Lewis*, 473 A.2d 805 (Del. 1984).
67. *Guth v. Loft*, 5 A.2d 503 (Del. Ch. 1939).
68. *Aronson v. Lewis*, 473 A.2d 805 (Del. 1984).
69. *Johnson v. Trueblood*, 629 F2d 287 (3d Cir. 1980).
70. *McMullin v. Beram*, 765 A.2d 910 (Del. 2000).
71. *Smith v. Van Gorkom*, 488 A.2d 858 (Del. 1985).
72. *Unocal Corp. v. Mesa Petroleum Co.*, 493 A.2d 946 (Del. 1985).
73. *Revlon, Inc. v. MacAndrews & Forbes Holdings, Inc.*, 506 A.2d 173 (Del. 1986).
74. *Mills Acquisition Co. v. Macmillan, Inc.*, 559 A.2d 1261 (Del. 1989).
75. *Roberts v. General Instrument Corp.*, [1990 Transfer Binder] CCH Fed. Sec. L. Rep. §95,465.
76. *Paramount Communications Inc. v. QVC Network Inc.*, 637 A.2d 34 (1993).
77. *Kahn v. Tremont Corp.*, 694 A.2d 422 (Del. 1997).
78. Peter Drucker, "The Bored Board," *Towards the Next Economics and Other Essays* (London: Heinemann, 1981).
79. Sarbanes-Oxley Act, 15 U.S.C. 7201, PL 107–204, 116 Stat. 745.
80. *In re Walt Disney Co. Derivative Litigation*, 906 A.2d 27 (Del. Supr. 2006).
81. *Texaco, Inc. v. Pennzoil, Co.*, No. 84-05905 (Dist. Harris County, Tex. Dec. 10, 1985, aff'd in part 729 S.W.2d 768 (Tex. App. 1987), cert. dismissed 485 U.S. 994 (1988), appeal dismissed on agreement of the parties 748 S.W.2d 631 (Tex. App. 1988).
82. *H. Rosenblum, Inc. v. Adler*, 461 A2d 138 (N.J. 1983).
83. Pension Protection Act of 2006, H.R. 4.
84. Model Business Corporation Act.

Chapter 3

1. Securities Act, Section 5, 15 U.S.C. 77a–77z, 77aa, 48 Stat. 74.
2. Securities Exchange Act, 15 U.S.C. 17b, 48 Stat. 881.
3. SEC Rule 145, Securities Act, 15 U.S.C. 77a–77z, 77aa, 48 Stat. 74.
4. Securities Act, Section 4(6), 15 U.S.C. 77a–77z, 77aa, 48 Stat. 74.
5. SEC Regulation D (SEC Rules 501–508), Securities Act, 15 U.S.C. 77a–77z, 77aa, 48 Stat. 74.
6. SEC Regulation A (SEC Rules 251–263), Securities Act, 15 U.S.C. 77a–77z, 77aa, 48 Stat. 74.
7. Securities Act, Section 4(2), 15 U.S.C. 77a–77z, 77aa, 48 Stat. 74.
8. Securities Act, Section 3(a)(10), 15 U.S.C. 77a–77z, 77aa, 48 Stat. 74.
9. Securities Act, Section 3(a)(11), 15 U.S.C. 77a–77z, 77aa, 48 Stat. 74; SEC Rule 147.
10. SEC Rule 144, Securities Act, 15 U.S.C. 77a–77z, 77aa, 48 Stat. 74.
11. SEC Rule 145, Securities Act, 15 U.S.C. 77a–77z, 77aa, 48 Stat. 74.
12. Securities Act, Section 4(1), 15 U.S.C. 77a–77z, 77aa, 48 Stat. 74; SEC Rule 147.
13. Securities Act, Section 4(1) and 4(2), 15 U.S.C. 77a–77z, 77aa, 48 Stat. 74; SEC Rule 147
14. SEC Rule 10b-5, Securities Exchange Act, 15 U.S.C. 17b, 48 Stat. 881.
15. C.F.R. §249.308.
16. Regulation M-A, SEC Rel. Nos. 33-7760; 34-422055; IC-24107 (Oct. 22, 1999).

17. Regulation FD, Securities Exchange Act, 15 U.S.C. 17b, 48 Stat. 881.
18. Regulation 14A, Securities Exchange Act, 15 U.S.C. 17b, 48 Stat. 881.
19. Securities Exchange Act, Section 16 (b), 15 U.S.C. 17b, 48 Stat. 881.
20. Investment Company Act, 15 U.S.C. 80a, 54 Stat. 789.
21. Uniform Securities Act, 7C, 56 and 02 Act 5.
22. Uniform Securities Act, §§401(b)(3)-(5).
23. Uniform Securities Act, §§401(a)(7).
24. Uniform Securities Act, §§402(10), 402(b)(9), and 402(14).
25. Uniform Securities Act, §303.
26. Uniform Securities Act, §302.
27. Ibid.
28. Williams Act, PL 90-439, 82 Stat. 454.
29. Securities Exchange Act, Section 13(e); SEC Rule 13e-4.
30. Securities Exchange Act, Section 14(d); SEC Regulation 14D.
31. SEC Regulation M-A
32. Securities Exchange Act, Section 13(e); SEC Rule 13e-4.
33. Tektronix, SEC No-Action Letter, 1987 SEC No. Act. LEXIS 2162 (June 19, 1987).
34. Securities Exchange Act, Section 14(d); SEC Regulation 14D.
35. Securities Exchange Act, Section 14(d)(1); SEC Regulation 14D.
36. Securities Exchange Act, Section 14(d)-4(b); SEC Regulation 14D.
37. SEC Rule 14d-4(d)(2)(i)-(ii).
38. SEC Rule 14d-8.
39. SEC Rule 14d-10(a)(1)
40. Securities Exchange Act, Section 14(e).
41. SEC Rule 14e-1.
42. SEC Rule 14e-3.
43. Schedule TO, Items 1–11.
44. Schedule 14D-9.
45. Regulation U, 12 C.F.R. §§221.1 et. seq.
46. Regulation T, 12 C.F.R. §§220.1 et. seq.
47. Regulation X, 12 C.F.R. §§224.1 et. seq.
48. Edgar v. Mite Corp., 457 U.S. 624 (1982)
49. E.g., Indiana Control Share Acquisitions Act, 23 Indiana Code 1023-1-42-1-et. seq.
50. Eric S. Rosengren, "State Restrictions on Hostile Takeovers," *Publius: The Journal of Federalism* 18 (Summer 1988): 67.
51. Indiana Control Share Acquisitions Act, 23 Indiana Code 1023-1-42-1-et. seq.
52. Rosengren, "State Restrictions.".
53. Ibid.
54. Roberta Romano, "The Genius of American Corporate Law," *The American Journal of Comparative Law* 42 (Summer 1994): 655–70.
55. Clayton Act, 15 U.S.C. 12, 1914, 38 Stat. 730.
56. "1992 Horizontal Merger Guidelines," http://www.ftc.gov/bc/docs/horizmer.htm. May 12, 2007.
57. "FTC, DOJ Issue Joint Commentary on the Horizontal Merger Guidelines," http://www.ftc.gove/opa/2006/03/mergercom.htm.
58. "1992 Horizontal Merger Guidelines," Section 1.51, http://www.ftc.gov/bc/docs/horizmer.htm.
59. "1992 Horizontal Merger Guidelines," Sections 2–5, http://www.ftc.gov/bc/docs/horizmer.htm.

60. Hart-Scott-Rodino Antitrust Improvements Act, 15 U.S.C. §18(a).
61. Department of Justice, Antitrust Division, "Merger Process Review Initiative," http://www.usdoj.gov/atr.
62. Hart-Scott-Rodino Antitrust Improvements Act, 15 U.S.C. §18(a)(g)(1).
63. Federal Trade Commission, Revised Jurisdictional Thresholds for Section 7A of the Clayton Act.
64. Hart-Scott-Rodino Antitrust Improvements Act, 15 U.S.C. §18(c); 16 C.F.R. §802.50–51.
65. Law Relating to Prohibition of Private Monopoly and Methods of Preserving Fair Trade.
66. European Commission, Guidelines on the Assessment of Horizontal Mergers.
67. Gramm-Leach-Bliley Act, P.L. 106–102.
68. Glass-Steagall Act, 12 U.S.C. §24.
69. Banking Act of 1933, 12 U.S.C. §24, 48 Stat. 162.
70. International Investment and Trade in Services Survey Act, 22 U.S.C. §§3101–3108.
71. 15 C.F.R. §806.15(j)(3).
72. 15 C.F.R. §806.15(j)(4).
73. 15 C.F.R. §806.15(h).
74. 15 C.F.R. §806.15(i).
75. 15 C.F.R. §806.15(g).
76. 15 C.F.R. §806.15(j)(2).
77. Exon-Florio Amendments, Sec. 721 of Defense Production Act 1950, 50 U.S.C. App. 2158 et. seq., 102 Stat. 1425.
78. 31 C.F.R. §§800.401 et. seq.
79. Byrd Amendment, Section 837(a) of the National Defense Authorization Act for Fiscal Year 1993, Pub. L. 102–484, 106 Stat. 2315, 2463, amending Section 721 of the Defense Production Act (Exon-Florio Amendments).

Chapter 4

1. Robert Brown and Alan S. Gutterman, *Financing Start-Ups: How to Raise Money for Emerging Companies* (New York: Aspen, 2002), 6–8.
2. Brown and Gutterman, *Emerging Companies Guide: A Resource for Professionals and Entrepreneurs* (Chicago: American Bar Association, 2005), 89.
3. Brown and Gutterman, *Financing Start-Ups*, 15–16.
4. Ibid., 17–23.
5. Brown and Gutterman, *Emerging Companies Guide*, 219–32.
6. Brown and Gutterman, *Financing Start-Ups*, 23–25.
7. Ibid., 25–28.
8. Ibid., 28–30.
9. Ibid., 42–46.
10. Paul Asquith, David W. Mullins, Jr., and Eric D. Wolff, "Original Issue High-Yield Bonds: Aging Analyses of Defaults, Exchanges, and Calls," *The Journal of Finance* 44 (September 1989): 923–52.
11. "Update: U.S. high-grade, junk issuance break records," Reuters (December 29, 2006, 3:08pm ET).

12. Richard Peterson, senior researcher at Thomson Financial, in Newark, New Jersey, quoted in "Update: U.S. high-grade, junk issuance break records," Reuters (December 29, 2006, 3:08pm ET).

13. "Henry Ford," http://www.abelard.org/ford/ford2-business.php#dodge_bros.

14. *Dodge v. Ford Motor Co.* 204 Mich. 459, 170 N.W. 668 (1919).

15. "Dodge v. Ford Motor Co." http://www.everything2.com/index.pl?node_id= 1768159.

16. "Henry Ford," http://www.willamette.edu/~fthompso/MgmtCon/Henry_Ford .html.

17. Bryan Burrough and John Helyar, *Barbarians at the Gate* (New York: HarperCollins, 1990).

18. "Biggest buyout ever ends, falls short for KKR," Corporate Growth Report Weekly, March 27, 1995.

19. R. Charles Moyer, James R. McGuigan, and William J. Kretlow, *Contemporary Financial Management* (New York: Thomson South-Western, 2006), 261.

20. John S. Lueken and John R. Cummins, "Estate Planning," in Brown and Gutterman, *Emerging Companies Guide*, 538–40.

21. Moyer, McGuigan, and Kretlow, *Contemporary Financial Management*, 775.

22. Ibid.

23. Ibid., 776.

Chapter 5

1. Financial Accounting Standards Board, "Business Combinations," *Statement of Financial Accounting Standards No. 141* (New York: Financial Accounting Standards Board, 2001).

2. Staff Accounting Bulletin, No. 54, "Application of 'Pushdown' Basis of Accounting in Financial Statements of Subsidiaries Acquired by Purchase," (SAB 54).

3. Securities and Exchange Commission, "Push Down Accounting Where Public Debt Is Not Significant," *Speeches by the Staff of the Office of the Chief Accountant* (Washington, DC: Securities and Exchange Commission, 1999).

4. Securities and Exchange Commission, "Leveraged Recapitalization of a Division," *Speeches by the Staff of the Office of the Chief Accountant* (Washington, DC: Securities and Exchange Commission, 1998).

5. Emerging Issues Task Force, "Basis in Leveraged Buyout Transactions," *EITF Issue No. 88-16* (New York: Financial Accounting Standards Board, 1988).

6. Financial Accounting Standards Board, "Accounting for the Impairment of Long-Lived Assets and for Long-Lived Assets to Be Disposed of," *Statement of Financial Accounting Standards No. 121* (New York: Financial Accounting Standards Board, 1995); Financial Accounting Standards Board, "Goodwill and Other Intangible Assets," *Statement of Financial Accounting Standards No. 142* (New York: Financial Accounting Standards Board, 2001); and Financial Accounting Standards Board, "Accounting for the Impairment or Disposal of Long-Lived Assets," *Statement of Financial Accounting Standards No. 144* (New York: Financial Accounting Standards Board, 2001).

7. Accounting Principles Board, "Opinion No. 16: Business Combinations," *Opinions of the Accounting Principles Board* (New York: American Institute of Certified Public Accountants, Inc., 1970).

8. Financial Accounting Standards Board, "Accounting for Income Taxes," *Statement of Financial Accounting Standards No. 96* (New York: Financial Accounting Standards Board, 1987); and Financial Accounting Standards Board, "Accounting for Income Taxes," *Statement of Financial Accounting Standards No. 109* (New York: Financial Accounting Standards Board, 1992).

9. Accounting Principles Board, "Opinion No. 16."

10. Securities and Exchange Commission, "Effect of Treasury Stock Transactions on Account for Business Combinations," *Accounting Series Release Nos. 146* (Washington, DC: Securities and Exchange Commission, 1973); and Securities and Exchange Commission, "Statement of Policy and Interpretations in Regard to ASR No. 146," *Accounting Series Release Nos. 146A* (Washington, DC: Securities and Exchange Commission, 1974).

11. Accounting Principles Board, "Opinion No. 16.".

12. Accounting Principles Board, "Opinion No. 18: The Equity Method of Accounting for Investments in Common Stock," *Opinions of the Accounting Principles Board* (New York: American Institute of Certified Public Accountants, Inc., 1971).

13. Investment Company Act, 1940, 15 U.S.C. §1, et. seq.

14. Financial Accounting Standards Board, "Consolidation of All Majority-owned Subsidiaries," *Statement of Financial Accounting Standards No. 94* (New York: Financial Accounting Standards Board, 1987).

15. Accounting Principles Board, "Opinion No. 18."

16. D. Douglas Alkema, "Remarks at the 2003 Thirty-First AICPA National Conference on Current SEC Developments," *Speech by SEC Staff* (Washington, DC: Securities and Exchange Commission, 2003).

17. Accounting Principles Board, "Opinion No. 18."

18. Accounting Principles Board, "Opinion No. 30: Reporting the Results of Operations—Reporting the Effects of Disposal of a Segment of a Business, and Extraordinary, Unusual and Infrequently Occurring Events and Transactions," *Opinions of the Accounting Principles Board* (New York: American Institute of Certified Public Accountants, Inc., 1973).

19. Ibid.

20. *Staff Legal Bulletin No. 4* (Washington, DC: Securities and Exchange Commission, 1997).

Chapter 6

1. Pub. L. No. 65-254, 40 Stat. 1057.

2. S. Rep. No. 617, 65th Cong., 2nd Sess. 5 (1918). 2. S. Rep. No. 617, 65

3. Section 368, Internal Revenue Code.

4. Reg. §1.368-1.

5. Section 368(a)(1)(C), Internal Revenue Code.

6. Section 361, Internal Revenue Code.

7. Section 354, Internal Revenue Code.

8. Section 302, Internal Revenue Code.

9. Section 1032, Internal Revenue Code.

10. Section 381, Internal Revenue Code.

11. Section 351, Internal Revenue Code.

12. Section 279, Internal Revenue Code.

13. Section 163(j), Internal Revenue Code.
14. Section 163(d), Internal Revenue Code.
15. Section 163(e) and (i), Internal Revenue Code.
16. Section 263, Internal Revenue Code.
17. *INDOPCO, Inc. v. Commissioner*, 503 U.S. 792 (1992).
18. Rev. Rul. 94-77, 1994-2 C.B. 19.
19. Section 269, Internal Revenue Code.
20. Section 381, Internal Revenue Code.
21. Section 269, Internal Revenue Code.
22. Sections 382–384, Internal Revenue Code.
23. Section 382(f), Internal Revenue Code.
24. Section 382(c), Internal Revenue Code.
25. Section 382(g)(2), Internal Revenue Code.
26. Section 382(k)(6)(A), Internal Revenue Code.
27. Section 382(k)(6)(B), Internal Revenue Code.
28. Section 382(l)(3)(A)(iv), Internal Revenue Code.
29. Section 382(l)(3)(A)(i), Internal Revenue Code.
30. Section 382(c), Internal Revenue Code.
31. Section 382(h)(3)(B).
32. Rev. Rul. 54-458, 1954-2 C.B. 167.
33. *Litton Industries, Inc.. v. Commissioner*, 89 T.C. 1086 (1987).
34. Section 355(a)(1)(B), Internal Revenue Code.
35. See *Coady v. Commissioner*, 33 T.C. 771 (1960).
36. Lockwood's *Estate v. Commissioner*, 350 F.2d 712 (8th Cir. 1965).
37. Reg. §1.355-2(d)(2)(iii)(E).
38. Reg. §1.355-2(d)(ii).

Chapter 7

1. Herb Cohen, *You Can Negotiate Anything* (New York: Bantam Books, 1980), 255.
2. California Business and Professions Code, §16601.
3. *Fleming v. Ray-Suzuki*, 225 Cal. App. 3d 574, 275 Cal. Rptr. 150 (1990).
4. *Monogram Industries, Inc. v. SAR Industries*, 64 Cal. App. 3d 692, 134 Cal. Rptr 714 (1976).
5. *Venture Associates Corp. v. Zenith Data Systems Corp.*, 96 F.3d 275 (7th Cir. 1996).
6. Restatement (Second) of Torts §766 (1979).
7. In re Food Management Group, LLC, •• B.R. •••, 2007 WL 458022, Bkrtcy. S.D.N.Y., February 13, 2007.
8. *Basic, Inc. v. Levinson*, 485 U.S. 224, 108 S.Ct. 978, 99 L.Ed.2d 194 (1988).
9. Sherman Antitrust Act, 15 U.S.C. §1.
10. Ark. Code Ann 4-3-27-15 A (2007).
11. Ala. Code §10-2B-15.01 (1975).
12. Miss. Code Ann. §79-4-15.01 (2007).
13. 11A V.S.A. §15.01 (2005).
14. Comprehensive Environmental Response, Compensation and Liability Act, 42 U.S.C. Chapter 103.
15. Lorimar Inc. (Nov. 4, 1985) 1985 WL 54459 (S.E.C.).

16. Albert A. Foer, "Comments Of the American Antitrust Institute on Horizontal Merger Analysis and the Role of Concentration in the Merger Guidelines," American Antitrust Institute, February 10, 2004, p. 5.
17. http://www.hillstreetblues.net/cast/cast.html.
18. *Aronson v. Lewis*, 473 A.2d 805 (Del. 1984).
19. *Revlon, Inc. v. MacAndrews & Forbes Holdings, Inc.*, 506 A.2d 173 (Del. 1986).
20. *Smith v. Van Gorkom*, 488 A. 2d 858 (Del. 1985).
21. *Unocal Corp. v. Mesa Petroleum Co., 493 A.2d 946, 955 (Del. 1985).*
22. *Mills Acquisition Co. v. Macmillan, Inc.*, 559 A.2d 1261 (Del. 1989).
23. *Weinberger v. UOP, Inc.*, 457 A.2d 701, (Del. 1983)
24. Arthur Fleischer & Alexander R. Sussman, *Takeover Defense*, 5th ed., Vol. 1 (New York: Aspen), Exhibit 14.
25. Release No. 34-48108, Self-Regulatory Organization; New York Stock Exchange, Inc. and National Association of Securities Dealers, Inc.: Order Approving NYSE and NASDAQ Proposed Rule Changes and NASDAQ Amendment No. 1 and Notice of Filing and Order Granting Accelerated Approval to NYSE Amendments No. 1 and 2 and NASDAQ Amendments No. 2 and 3 Thereto Relating to Equity Compensation Plans (June 30, 2003).
26. 15 U.S.C. §18a(b)(1); 16 C.F.R. §803.10(b).
27. 15 U.S.C. §18a(e); 16 C.F.R. §803.20.
28. American Bar Association, Business Law Section, Committee on Legal Opinions, "Third Party Legal Opinion Report including the Legal Opinion Accord," 47 Bus. Law No. 1 (November 1991).
29. *Lucas v. Hamm*, 56 Cal. 2d 583, 15 Cal. Rptr. 821, cert. denied, 368 U.S. 987 (1961).

Chapter 8

1. Federal Reserve Board, Flow of Funds (Haver Analytics).
2. Ibid.
3. BankruptcyData.com.
4. Trust Indenture Act, 15 USC 77 aaa, et. seq.
5. Section 316, Trust Indenture Act, 15 USC 77 ppp.
6. Section 14(e), Securities Exchange Act of 1934, 15 USC 17b, 48 Stat. 881.
7. Section 14(a), Securities Exchange Act of 1934, 15 USC 17b, 48 Stat. 881.
8. Sections 10(b), 14(e), Securities Exchange Act of 1934, 15 USC 17b, 48 Stat. 881.
9. Sections 13, 15(d), Securities Exchange Act of 1934, 15 USC 17b, 48 Stat. 881.
10. Section 3(a)(9), Securities Act of 1933, 15 USC 77a–77z, 77aa, 48 Stat. 74.
11. Bankruptcy Code, 11 USC 101, et. seq.
12. Bankruptcy Code, 11 USC Chapter 7.
13. Bankruptcy Code, 11 USC 1104.
14. Bankruptcy Code, 11 USC 1102.
15. Bankruptcy Code, 11 USC 1129(a)(7)(A)(ii).
16. Bankruptcy Code, 11 USC 1129.
17. Bankruptcy Code, 11 USC 1129(b)(2)(B)(ii).
18. Bankruptcy Code, 11 USC 1129.
19. Bankruptcy Code, 11 USC 1112(b).
20. Bankruptcy Code, 11 USC 362.
21. Bankruptcy Code, 11 USC 362(a).

22. Bankruptcy Code, 11 USC 363(b)(c).
23. Bankruptcy Code, 11 USC 364(a).
24. Bankruptcy Code, 11 USC 364(c).
25. Bankruptcy Code, 11 USC 364(d).
26. Bankruptcy Code, see generally, 11 USC 1123.
27. Bankruptcy Code, 11 USC 1129(b).
28. Bankruptcy Code, 11 USC 1145(a).
29. Bankruptcy Code, 11 USC 1125(d).
30. Bankruptcy Code, 11 USC 1145(e).
31. Bankruptcy Code, see generally 11 USC 1125(d); see also In re: Brandon Mill Farms, Ltd. 37 B.R. 190 (Bankr. N.D. Ga 1984).

Index

accountants, 14; opinions, 201

Accounting Principles Board, 122; opinions, 122

Accredited in Business Valuation (ABV), 109

accredited investors, 58

Accredited Senior Appraiser (ASA), 109

acquisitions, 22; asset, 22; nontaxable, 138–43 (*see also* reorganization); stock, 22; taxable, 157–61

alter ego, 31

American Institute of Certified Public Accountants (AICPA), 109

American Law Institute (ALI), 41

American Society of Appraisers (ASA), 109

American Stock Exchange (AMEX), 43

antitakeover provisions, 67

antitrust, 74–78, 195

appraisals: acts, 73; rights, 44; rights, market out, 45

auctions: Dutch, 69; modified Dutch, 69

automatic stays, 210

Banking Act, 80

bankruptcy, 26

Bankruptcy Code, 203; Chapter 7, 203; Chapter 11, 203; Section 14(e), 207

blank checks, 19

boards of directors, 18, 47, 193; business judgment rule, 49, 53, 194; duty of care, 48, 194; duty of good faith, 48; duty of loyalty, 48, 194; enhanced business judgment rule, 49, 194; fair auction test, 50, 194; general powers, 20; independent directors, 51; intrinsic fairness test, 50, 194; staggered, 18

bonds. *See* debt, bonds

bring-down certificates, 190

brokers, 12

bulk sales, 40

Bureau of Alcohol, Tobacco, and Firearms (ATF), 81

business combination acts, 43, 73

business continuity, 156

buybacks, 68; defensive, 68; debt, 68

cash-out acts. *See* appraisals: acts

Certified Business Appraiser (CBA), 109

Certified Valuation Analyst (CVA), 109

charter power, 19

Clayton Act, 74

closings, 197; deferred, 198; simultaneous, 197

Cohen, Herb, 171

collection bargaining agreements, 35; tin parachute, 35

commercial banks, 101

commercial finance companies, 101

Committee on Foreign Investment in the United States (CFIUS), 82

Comprehensive Environmental Response, Compensation, and Liability Act (CERCLA), 33

confidentiality agreements, 172

consolidations, 25

constituency statutes, 39

continuations, 31

control share acts, 42, 73

cram-down, 209